THE TREES
AROUND US

OVERLEAF *Trees in design: the "disappearing path"
at Hascombe Court, Surrey.*

THE TREES AROUND US

Peter Barber and C. E. Lucas Phillips

Drawings by Delia Delderfield

Published in collaboration with The Royal Horticultural Society

Weidenfeld and Nicolson London

To Barbara and Marina

House editor *Ann Wilson*
House art editor *Tim Higgins*
Layout by *Sheila Sherwen*
for George Weidenfeld and Nicolson Ltd
11 St John's Hill, London SW11

ISBN 0 297 76932 4

Filmset by Keyspools Limited, Golborne, Lancs
Printed by Tinling (1973) Limited,
Prescot, Merseyside
(A member of the Oxley Printing Group)

Contents

Acknowledgments

THE MANUSCRIPT OF THIS BOOK was submitted, either wholly or in part, to the scrutiny of Mr Harold Hillier, VMH, Mr Alan Mitchell, VMH (Silviculturist to the Forestry Commission), Mr William Flemer III (of Princeton, New Jersey), and Mr Roy Lancaster, who are numbered among the world's leading authorities, and we are immensely grateful to them for their numerous helpful comments. No less are we obliged to Mr C. D. Brickell, BSc, Director of the Royal Horticultural Society's Garden at Wisley, for scrutinising the proofs and for piloting us through the shoals, currents and tide-races that imperil the adventurer into botanical waters, and to Mr Douglas Harris, who has diligently read the proofs with a keen and experienced eye.

As in other fields, these highly specialised authorities do not always agree in minor botanical or horticultural detail, but we have followed what seems to us the most acceptable course, knowing that, to the practical designer or gardener, they are not of compelling importance.

A list of the chief textual authorities consulted is given in the introduction to the Register.

THE PHOTOGRAPHS are supplied by, or reproduced by kind permission of the following. Grateful acknowledgment is given to Mrs M. E. Pilkington and her gardener, Mr F. Grant, for the illustrations on pages 24 and 25, and to the Vicomte de Noailles for those on pages 34 and 35.

William Flemer III *59*
French Embassy, London 14
Interphototèque – D. F. Sodel – M. Brigaud 35
C. Lewis 72, 74, 92, *107*, 113
M. Nimmo 21, 47, 50, 66, 69, 83, 87, 89, 98, 102, 106, 117, 131, 136, 139, 142, 144, 151 above, 152 right, 154, 157, 160, 166, 168, 170, 172, 178
Leslie S. Slinger *150*
Harry Smith 22, 25, *39, 40, 43, 60, 61, 62*, 64 below, 70, *76, 77, 78*, 80, 82, *86*, 88, 94 above and below, *99, 100, 108, 109*, 110, 115, 119, 121, *123, 125, 126, 134*, 143, *147, 148, 149*, 151 below, 156 above, 162, *163, 164*
Southern Photographic (Southampton) Ltd 55, 103, 127, 128, 156 below, 165, 167
Weidenfeld and Nicolson archives 2, 12, 30, 36
Dennis Woodland 64 top, 67

The maps on pages 50–1 were drawn by Edward McAndrew Purcell.

Foreword

by Edmund de Rothschild

THERE IS VERY LITTLE that has given me so much pleasure as to have been asked to contribute the Foreword to *The Trees Around Us*, particularly as Peter Barber, one of the co-authors of this book, has been my friend since we first met in 1943 during the war. His life at Exbury as my agent has been the inspiration of his tree and plant interests. With his cousin, Peter Lucas Phillips (also a comrade-in-arms and himself a horticulturalist of high repute) he first collaborated on *The Rothschild Rhododendrons*, which described so well my father's great work at Exbury.

Once again the two Peters have collaborated with conspicuous success in a work which has been beautifully presented by the publishers. The book is surely compulsive reading for all who appreciate trees, whether for use in very small gardens or in large landscapes. The authors do well to emphasise the urgency of the environmental problems that confront many countries today. Too many public authorities, from governments downwards, have allowed construction work of all kinds to overwhelm human sensitivities. Trees are vital to man's existence both materially and aesthetically, and it comes as a shock to learn that, in Britain alone, trees are being lost at an estimated rate of two million a year; and it is not only the atmosphere, but also the scenery that is being sadly polluted.

A heavy duty must therefore be laid on all public authorities to insist upon a speeding up in the planting of trees – not only of oaks, poplars, sycamores etc., but also of the less familiar but beautiful trees whose merits are set out in this far-ranging text. Too often does one see examples of the wrong tree sited in the wrong place; only too frequently does one see them neglected or mutilated; so that the discernment which the authors display in their choices deserves to be rated as a positive public service. However, it is most encouraging to note how wide is the range of trees that can be grown for the reclamation of soils made derelict by either the ravages of man or the deficiencies of nature.

These and many other matters concerning the choices and culture of trees in the north temperate zones are set out in a forthright, pungent and engaging style; it is refreshing to read the authors' tart comments on those botanical formalists whose pedantry serves only to discourage the common man's love of plants of all sorts.

Fortunately, in the past few years many people have begun to be more conscious of trees and shrubs, and therefore I know that this fine work will help to improve their knowledge of trees tremendously. I certainly will benefit from studying this informative and unusual book.

EDMUND DE ROTHSCHILD
Inchmery, October 1974

Introduction

by David G. Leach
President of the American Horticultural Society

WHO DOES NOT HAVE warm and pleasant associations with trees? As childhood aeries, as tenders of cool and welcome shade, stark tracers of gothic arches in winter, many of them fountains of flowers in spring, writhing in resistance to a storm, they have become symbols of dignity and endurance, sometimes even of ominous happenings: William Faulkner wrote of "the clashing of the palms". Trees loom large, in history, in literature and in the prosaism of our everyday lives. Beloved by poets, extolled by essayists, trees have had but one opponent known to me – the legendary lady from Boston, born and bred a city girl, who abhorred the exodus of her friends for country weekends and invariably admonished them, "Kick a tree for me".

Interchange of trees between nations began at a very early date and the discovery of the Americas opened up an immense treasury to Europe. The robinia was introduced to the Old World by Jean Robin, herbalist of King Henry IV of France, and was established in England as early as 1601. By 1688 English gardens were growing the swamp cypress, black walnut, tulip tree, Virginia magnolia and *Acer negundo* ("box elder"). The traffic was, of course, a two-way one; emigrants from Europe brought seeds of their own native plants to the New World and later the glories of China, Japan and the Himalayas further enriched not only the gardens but also the economies of the world at large. Western civilisation could not have evolved as it did without trees. They furnished fuel for our fires, planks and masts for our ships, the substance of our houses, the material for our paper, and even, at one time, the ploughshares that tilled the soil.

Now, ironically, metals and plastics, masonry and concrete have greatly diminished their utility but the advent of these wood substitutes has, in turn, enormously enhanced the importance of trees in a totally different context – the mental, emotional and even the physical health of urban dwellers. We have all begun to realise that mankind's paleolithic genes are in lethal opposition to a lifeless, hardened cityscape; that the ancient genetic bond with the natural world is broken at heavy cost; and that squalor and monotony in our urban centres spawns squalid, listless and eventually rebellious people. We know now that we are at the point of confrontation, figuratively, between machinery and vegetation, and so it is that the trees, the most conspicuous and valuable solace for the innate yearning for the green and growing, assume a new and crucial significance.

In fact, the issue rushes from other considerations toward biological necessity. The emerald necklace may save us all from strangulation. Many scientists say that trees are vital in preserving the delicate, life-sustaining balances of gases in the atmosphere. They precipitate upon their leaf surfaces particulate pollution in the air we breathe. They muffle traffic noises that erode our psychic equanimity, and they screen the hideous industrial excesses in the landscape. They shield from the harassing wind midwestern American homesteads and seaside dwellers in Britain. A tree nursery in the United States uses the slogan "We grow clean air machines".

So it is that *The Trees Around Us* is a welcome addition to the literature of trees. In some respects it is a unique work in its sensitive perception of the role of trees in creating and preserving a civilised amenity in the environment.

But which trees to plant? Where? How? For what purpose? In town or country, in private garden or public park, on city street or in rural glade, the best trees for planting in temperate climates, well known or not are described. This is a book for the beginner and the expert. The chapter on trees in design is a classic primer for the landscape architect. Elsewhere the most basic instruction is given for the novice. Written in courtly, gracious, almost Victorian prose, with acute mental imagery, the interesting allusions, both literary and historical, add spice to the swift flow of fact.

Co-author Peter Barber knows trees. He grows 500,000 extra-heavy standards, about half of them at the renowned Exbury Estate near Southampton, and the remainder in various counties through England. The famous nurseryman, Harold Hillier, has described them as the best in England and the best in Europe. C. E. Lucas Phillips, a widely read historian and a highly experienced horticulturalist, collaborated with him also in the writing of *The Rothschild Rhododendrons*.

Most trees are international and intercontinental in their interest to those who plant them, so *The Trees Around Us* could almost as well have been written in the United States or for the temperate climate of any other land. Readers will profit by the exposure to the practicalities of growing trees as well as to their lore and legends, wherever they may live.

PART I

I
"Gross Handiworks"

OUR PURPOSE IN THIS BOOK will be to make a wide-ranging survey of the trees of the Temperate Zones and to select from among them those that can most profitably be put to use for man's delight.

We do so as our contribution to those movements, so far all too weak, that aim to bring home to men's minds the social and aesthetic consequences of the wastage and neglect of the trees around us and to stir those in authority to more effective action. The need is pressing. The effect of trees on the environment is profound; so also, however unconsciously, is their effect on our minds and moods. Whether in town or countryside, whether economically or philosophically, trees are a necessity in the ecology of man.

Man began his existence among or near to trees but ever since the end of the last ice age, some 10,000 years ago, he has been steadily destroying them. Somewhere about 1000 BC Homer declared that "the din of woodcutters in the glades of the mountains" was like that of a battle. The barren, sterile landscape of most of Greece today is the result. Before the Christian era was very far advanced the great natural forests of Europe had been almost completely ravished, and by about AD 1500 the Caledonian Forest in Scotland had gone. In the next two centuries England was busy felling great oaks for her navy and her merchant ships, while in France the nobility were sweeping away whole forests to make splendid vistas for their châteaux. In Egypt more than half the palms were lost and most of North Africa became a man-made desert, as barren as the plain of Lethe in Hades.

The massacre of trees reached its utmost extent, however, in the nineteenth century in America, where the vast natural forests were cut to pieces to provide houses, factories, roads, railways, ships, paper and fuel, or simply to clear land for agriculture. A large tract of the West became a desolation of tree stumps, riven with gullies from the inevitable soil erosion. Elwes, the sharp-tongued Englishman, wrote of America's Eastern White Pine (*Pinus strobus*) that "men grew rich by destroying it". Thoreau, the American naturalist, was angered that men were "making the earth bald before its time". By about 1920 some 200 million acres had been scalped and much of it eroded. Gene Marine, in his remarkable book *America the Raped*,

OPPOSITE *Tree scene at Hascombe Court, Surrey.*

13

ascribed all this devastation to "the engineering mentality" which exploited for private gain. Great fires added to the waste. In 1871 the Peshtigo fire in Wisconsin and Michigan destroyed nearly four million acres.

In Europe the tide began hesitantly to turn. France set an example to the world in her noble avenues, culminating later in the splendid ranks of planes and chestnuts of the Champs Elysées. In Britain the great landowners put posterity in their debt, creating beautiful park-like landscapes of well-spaced trees and splendid new woods. Successive Dukes of Argyll have planted many millions of larch since about 1620. The Duke of Montagu planted seventy-two miles of elm avenues in the eighteenth century. Lord Weymouth planted great quantities of pines in the same era. The third Earl of Bute, however deplorable as a politician, deserves our gratitude for his part in founding the Royal Botanical Gardens at Kew, the world's leading botanical institute. Added to these have been innumerable men of wealth and a few great horticultural institutes and nurseries that, scouring the farthest corners of the globe, have made Britain, and Scotland in particular, the richest and most versatile tree country in the world. Nevertheless, Britain today is still losing her trees at an estimated rate of two million a year.

The great landowners, who "thought big", with an eye to posterity, have gone and their places in Europe and America have by no means been filled by public authorities, who, for the greater part, are very much swayed by "the engineering mentality". The towns still sprawl, the factories erupt, the motor roads lacerate the land with long gashes of concrete. Airfields cut great swathes across all vegetation. The quarryman hacks out his deep wounds and the miner piles up his mountains of waste. Disease annihilates the elms. Chemicals poison the air and the soil. Splendid private estates which their former owners adorned with noble trees in parks, avenues, copses and groves become fragmented and mutilated by industry, by local authorities and by covetous builders. In Britain the farmers liquidate the field maples, the elms and the picturesque hedgerows, not caring that they have taken the first steps in creating a dust-bowl. Horizons shrink and panoramas wither.

In these circumstances, aggravated by the stresses of modern life, it becomes more and more difficult for people to enjoy "green thoughts in a green shade" and to find solace from the crowding artefacts of man. Of course, there are people who are insensitive to such things; there are even people who dislike trees, but most of us, we believe, enjoy the influence of the green textures, the billowing forms and often the sumptuous flowers with which trees serve to relieve harsh rectangular shapes or fill out an undistinguished panorama. Gardens, wrote Francis Bacon, are "the greatest refreshment to the spirit of men, without which buildings and palaces are but gross handiworks". We know today, moreover, that, besides their aesthetic pleasure and besides their more obvious benefits, trees ameliorate the climate and purify the air, particularly in towns, where they absorb carbon dioxide and give out oxygen. They baffle sounds and filter winds.

Such considerations are humanly important not only to people of mature

OPPOSITE *Plane trees in the Avenue d'Iéna, Paris.*

14

sensibilities but also to those of starved and undeveloped feelings, to deprived children in city streets and to all people whose lives are cramped, colourless and stricken by poverty, ill-health and the suffocation of mean surroundings.

For all such refreshments of man's spirit the private gardener has quite a dramatic part to play, for what you plant in your garden is seen by your neighbours and by all passers-by and can be a precious gift to the environment. To a much greater extent, however, we have to rely today upon various public authorities and upon those who inflict industrial buildings upon the country-side. People who disfigure it with such horrors as oil refineries, cement factories, mine workings, generating stations and all other "gross handiworks" of the engineering mentality should be legally obliged to plant the tallest and densest possible screens of trees. Garages and filling stations, too. Cities, suburbs and most villages should intensify their plantings in streets and open places, as much as traffic allows. The approaches to many towns cry out for boulevards or avenues. Our generation is much in need of all sorts of trees and the next generation will be even more so.

There are some public authorities and some distinguished professional planners who are well alive to these environmental and aesthetic issues. Looking beyond today, they are keenly aware of the world-wide problems of land utilisation, of conserving existing pleasaunces, or re-vitalising derelict places, of fighting pollution and of creating a free flow for traffic. The needs of the human being are at last beginning to be balanced against the demands of industry and commerce. The new town of Tapiola, in Finland (which we have not ourselves seen), sets a model in the conception of maintaining the link between man and nature.

These enlightening influences, however, have not yet by any means penetrated the darker recesses of officialdom. The politician, the town councillor and the industrial baron to a large extent still live in aesthetic gloom. "Development" is the pressing theme; "environment" is a fancy word and they know not all that it means. Even some professional planners, imbued wholly with the engineering mentality, are no better. A thick book by a leading British town-planner, with a knightly handle to his name, makes no mention whatever of trees. In nearly all projects trees are regarded as a mere afterthought, whereas they ought to be incorporated in the original plan, for they are themselves architectural features of great influence.

Municipal authorities likewise emerge far too slowly from the darkness, perhaps less slowly in North America than in most European countries. Here and there one finds shining examples, but most of them are concerned almost wholly with gross handiworks and expect nothing more from their horticultural departments (often headed by professionals of high qualifications) than playing fields, gaudy bedding displays in the parks and exotic hothouse blooms for mayoral functions. The choice of such trees as are planted (and here the professional cannot escape some criticism) is extremely limited and afterwards they are too often grossly neglected or mutilated by unskilled labour. First, one must have the right kind of tree for each situation, of the "extra-heavy standard" type, not flimsy nurslings; then they must be planted

OPPOSITE *A young Crimean linden (Tilia × euchlora) at Blackfriars Bridge, London.*

and maintained by skilled labour and secured against vandalism. It is encouraging to find that a few of the larger cities in Britain, following the initiative of Exbury Gardens, have founded their own special nurseries for providing sturdy young stock.

The Handiworks of Nature

BEFORE BEGINNING TO PONDER on the various considerations affecting our choice of trees it will be as well to order our minds by setting out the main uses to which we can put them. They are:

To supply timber for commercial purposes; with this topic we shall not here be concerned.

To ornament a landscape or townscape.

To provide shade in hot weather to man and beast and to give light cover to such shade-loving shrubs as rhododendrons and pieris.

To obscure some hideous object or at least to temper its depressing impact upon the senses.

To provide shelter from high winds and from salt spray in coastal places. The shelter belt may be to protect less hardy plants, or it may be to protect buildings, giving comfort and reducing fuel costs.

To prevent the erosion of hillsides and of sharp declivities created by man.

To give simple pleasure by the mere contemplation of the trees themselves – for us the most important purpose of all.

For all these there is a rich treasure for us to pick from – the rounded and billowing trees, the elliptical, the slim and spear-like, the langorously "weeping" and many another. We shall find them in all sizes and adaptable to most situations, and in forms that are heavily mantled with foliage or light and airy, responsive to the impulses of the wind. We shall find them also in a great variety of textures, which may be of compelling influence for our purpose. The density of the conifers contrasts delightfully with the airy delicacy of the silver birch and the glittering platinum of *Sorbus aria* 'Lutescens'. The big, bold leaves of the catalpa and magnolias find companionable opposites in the multiple leaflets of the mountain ash and the finely shredded ones of the cut-leaf beech. The gloss of the statuesque *Magnolia grandiflora* is set off by the trembling, silvered leaves of the aspen. The wealth of choice is, indeed, inexhaustible.

We shall assume at the outset that the reader has at least a basic understanding of cultural matters: the diverse characters of soils, the processes of preparing the ground, the fundamental importance, before all else, of good drainage and similar considerations. For the benefit of readers of limited experience (and perhaps some others also) we give in Part III a brief dissertation on names and terms in "The Botanical Jungle", to which is added a short glossary. It would be helpful to study this part before embarking on Part II. To readers of more mature experience we particularly point out that, as far as possible, we eschew all botanical mumbo-jumbo and all words and terms the meanings of which are not reasonably obvious to the common man. Cuneate, terete, acicular, pulvinus, petiole, rachis, umbo and such terms will find no place, though sometimes technical terms are unavoidable. As expressly permitted by the International Code on nomenclature, we prefer the term "variety" to "cultivar", though we do not wholly ban the more stilted word. To the grower who goes to the best nurseries it makes not the slightest difference. What does it matter whether the blue Atlas cedar is described as *Cedrus atlantica* 'Glauca' or *Cedrus atlantica* var. *glauca*? Botanists themselves disagree, there being three different versions in this example alone.

Likewise in the running script in Roman type we acknowledge no compulsion to write magnolia, camellia, sorbus and other generic names with a capital initial – a silly kind of formalism – but rather as though anyone would write oak, beech or elm. We have not, however, had sufficient strength of mind to challenge the orthodox custom of setting the formal names of genus and species in italic type, a quite unnecessary irritation of the page, which vexes and deters the average reader. Horticulture is far too much bedevilled by those who are anxious to make it appear an esoteric science, the effect of which is to scare away a great many people who prefer to think of it as a simple human pleasure.

Mr C. D. Brickell, Director of the Royal Horticultural Society's Garden, comments however: "It can make a considerable difference to the gardener whether a plant is a botanical "variety" or "forma" rather than a "cultivar" or "clone". In the latter case he should get a selected and definitely fixed individual, vegetatively propagated; in the former he may get a seedling which is inferior to the best in some respect, although good nurseries ensure that their stock is the best available." This is not to be denied in a great many cases, but confusion arises between a botanical variety and a garden variety, as the International Horticultural Code treats "variety" and "cultivar" as being synonymous. Other interpreters consider "cultivar" as merely an international term for the vernacular "variety" (or variété, etc.). What is apparent is that the Code itself needs simple and clear-thinking revision by someone other than Mr Dryasdust. See more fully in "The Botanical Jungle".

2
Trees and the Elements

Soil – Cold – Wind – Moisture – Sun and Shade – Sea Salt

TO ACHIEVE LASTING SATISFACTION from trees in any site, large or small, several factors have to be taken into account before making any plan or choosing any trees. We set them out in short order and on simple lines.

Soils Although we have said that we shall assume the reader to have some basic horticultural knowledge, we should emphasise at the beginning the difference between acid soils and alkaline or limy ones. An acid soil is simply one with a low lime content and an alkaline one is the opposite. They are measured by the *pH* scale, a purely arbitrary system in which *pH* 7 represents neutrality, all numbers below 7 represent varying degrees of acidity and all above it degrees of alkalinity. It is widely agreed that a slightly acid soil, *pH* 6·5, is the ideal for most plants.

Certain groups of trees and other plants languish in a limy soil, their roots not being equipped to absorb necessary iron compounds when in the presence of lime. The degree of acidity can, however, be excessive and very few trees will prosper in a *pH* of less than 4·5. On the other hand, nearly all plants accustomed to alkaline soils will prosper equally well, or nearly so, in acid soils. Unless we state otherwise in our Register, it may be assumed that all our trees will face both kinds of soil with impartiality. A list of those that specifically demand acid soils is given in Part III.

An extreme form of lime is chalk, prevalent in many parts of Europe. If near the surface of the soil, chalk presents difficulties of its own. Apart from the hard labour of digging it, it demands the incorporation of large quantities of other organic matter ("other" because chalk is itself organic) and the frequent addition of similar matter by top-dressing. For digging in (but not top-dressing) chopped up turves are excellent, not being so quickly leached out of the soil as manure, compost, leaves, peat, etc.

In the selection of trees account must also be taken of other qualities of the soil, whether light and sandy, heavy and clayey, or rich and loamy, bearing in mind that, in general terms, light soils are dry and heavy ones are retentive of moisture and sometimes too wet. Extreme conditions of either sort are inimical to most plants, though there are indeed trees that grow well in pure sand and others that thrive in swamps, among the whispering reeds and the darts of the kingfisher.

OPPOSITE *The first powdering of snow on the trunks of the Western red "cedar",* Thuja plicata.

20

Stewartia pseudocamellia.

We may also encounter derelict soils, which have been completely played out by industrial or engineer workings. The worst, no doubt, are the slag heaps from mines, the underground spoil from deep excavations and the waste land left by abandoned factories. A short list of trees for even these desperate situations is given in Part III. Soils that have been seriously poisoned by chemical works are usually hopeless. Poisoning by salts we shall discuss later in this chapter and in the chapter on planting.

Cold This is the most elemental of all the elements affecting a choice of trees. It cannot be considered alone, however, for it may be powerfully affected by other factors. On the score of cold-hardiness alone the range of trees presented here is very wide, from the sub-arctic to the sub-tropic. Some of these factors we consider in this chapter and others are mentioned in the introduction to the Register. Every tree in this book is classified for cold-hardiness by the zoning system originated by the Arnold Arboretum, which is explained in the same introduction and illustrated by the maps on pages 50–1. Even in mild zones, however, we must beware of the low-lying frost pocket, for what in summer looks like a warm and cosy dell, out of the wind, may well trap the waves of frost flowing down unseen from above.

Wind A tree may be considerably cold-hardy but yet not wind-hardy, especially in youth. The silver maple (*Acer saccharinum*) is prone to splitting down the middle in severe storms and the eucalypts, robinias and varieties of the neo-cypresses, such as Lawson's and Leyland's, may be blown clean out of the ground until their root systems, which are not very strong, have taken a very firm grip. Plenty of other trees shiver and shrivel under the desiccating breath of fierce winds and in very exposed places it becomes necessary to plant a protective shelter belt of wind-hardy trees. Plenty will be described in these pages, many decorative, some merely utilitarian, such as the Corsican pine, the yews, larches, the common ash, the hawthorns, the sycamore, some willows and some elms.

Moisture The need of all plants for some degree of rain, each according to its kind, needs no emphasis. What is less obvious is the craving that some trees have for atmospheric moisture. This is felt particularly by trees whose native habitat is near the sea coast or in a region of high rainfall and particularly by evergreen trees, whether broadleaf or conifer, such as the redwood of the California coastlands. The luxuriance of plants in such climates as those of the west coast of Britain, California, British Columbia and Ireland teaches us a useful lesson.

"Continental" or far-inland territories, such as those of the central Euro-Asian mass and the central areas of America, tend to be much drier than those of islands, coastlands and lakesides, except where mountain masses induce ample rainfall. Continental climates also experience greater extremes of heat and cold. There are, of course, plenty of trees that are drought-hardy or nearly so, and a list of them is given in Part III.

Sun and Shade Whether in small gardens or in large landscapes, one of the first things we must do is to take note of the points of the compass, observing which parts are or will be in shade and which in sun, for this vitally affects our choice of all plants. Some enjoy shade positively, others endure it and a great many are very happy in dappled shade. A list of such is given in Part III. In general, the more sun the better, although this by no means always implies very hot sun, as we shall point out in special cases. A fair share of sun is necessary to ripen bark and bud and to stimulate the manufacture of food, but what is of equal importance is *light*.

Many trees will grow well enough if "crowded into a shade" by dense planting, as they often are in natural woodland and in the forester's serried ranks, but the full splendour of each tree is lost. Therefore the gardener and the landscape designer, when not concerned with erecting screens or hedges, should give each tree ample room to stretch its limbs, choosing an open situation with plenty of all-round light, remembering that in a crowded plantation each tree casts its shade upon another.

It is heart-rending to see a beautiful cherry, maple or silver birch mutilated by pruning because it is jostling other trees or has spread across a road or path or is too close to buildings. A rough rule of thumb for round-headed trees is to allow a width equal to two-thirds of their expected ultimate height, but a good many, particularly some oaks, will grow broader than high. Columnar and pinnacle trees obviously have limited lateral growth and can be planted quite close together, though their roots spread far.

A terrain planted with saplings at proper spacing will look pretty naked, but can appear reasonably well clothed if, at some expense, it is planted with the "extra heavy standards" or "semi-mature trees" which we discuss in the next chapter. The blanks between saplings can be filled with quick-growing shrubs or other plants, or the slower, long-lived trees can be interplanted with quick "filler" trees, which should be removed later, a requirement too often neglected.

Though unavoidable shade creates problems, we frequently need to create shade positively, especially in the warmer climates, either as a relief from an over-mighty sun or to create a canopy beneath which we may "weave the garments of repose".

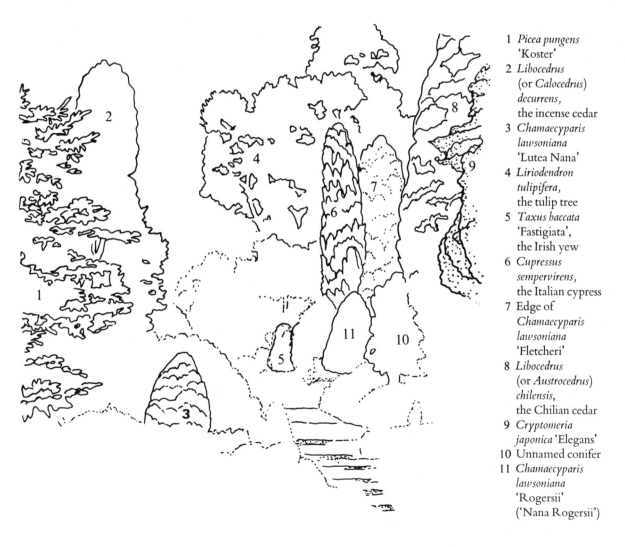

OPPOSITE *A walk between mixed trees at Grayswood Hill, Surrey. See key drawing, right, for identification.*

1 *Picea pungens* 'Koster'
2 *Libocedrus* (or *Calocedrus*) *decurrens*, the incense cedar
3 *Chamaecyparis lawsoniana* 'Lutea Nana'
4 *Liriodendron tulipifera*, the tulip tree
5 *Taxus baccata* 'Fastigiata', the Irish yew
6 *Cupressus sempervirens*, the Italian cypress
7 Edge of *Chamaecyparis lawsoniana* 'Fletcheri'
8 *Libocedrus* (or *Austrocedrus*) *chilensis*, the Chilian cedar
9 *Cryptomeria japonica* 'Elegans'
10 Unnamed conifer
11 *Chamaecyparis lawsoniana* 'Rogersii' ('Nana Rogersii')

These are much demanded in the private garden, in streets and in the wide landscape.

Besides their usefulness, tree shadows add immensely to the beauty of the garden picture, whether small or large, creating monochrome reflections in dark pools and, as evening approaches, stealing across lawns and meadows, duplicating the forms of long avenues and breaking the hard outlines of town buildings and industrial artefacts. Though the oaks, lindens, chestnuts, maples, beeches and the deodar create the densest and most "slumbrous" umbrage, there is also a particular charm in the long, slim, pencil shadows of the cypresses, the incense cedar, the beautiful fastigiate oak and the Dawyck beech as they lengthen and slide across grass and shrubs and walls.

Sea Salt This is extremely damaging to nearly all plants, especially as it is so often hurled in upon them by the wrath of furious gales, together with stinging particles of sand which abrade the barks of trees and persecute their leaves. Salt also taints the soil. When conjoined, salt, wind and sand bar us from many pleasures in coastal gardens and the first task is to create a shelter belt of those trees and shrubs which do, in fact, defy the elements of the ocean.

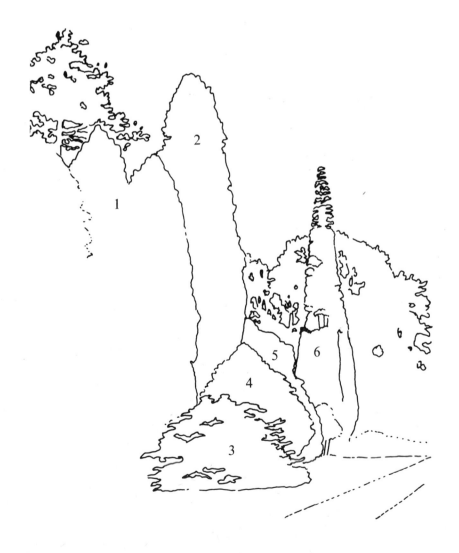

1 *Chamaecyparis lawsoniana* 'Lutea'
2 *Cupressus macrocarpa* 'Aurea'
3 *Juniperus chinensis* 'Pfitzeriana'
4 *Acer palmatum* 'Heptalobum Elegans Purpurea'
5 *Picrasma quassioides*
6 *Libocedrus* (or *Calocedrus*) *decurrens*

OPPOSITE *A group of conifers in the Westonbirt Arboretum, Gloucestershire. See key drawing, left, for identification.*

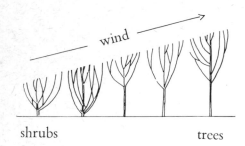

shrubs   trees

A coastal shelter belt.

Badly exposed positions call for a deep shelter belt. The aim should be not to build a solid wall which the wind will swoosh over and descend in swirling turbulence on the inner side, but rather a filter, which will abate the force of the elements. On the seaward side of the belt go small, tough shrubs, such as tamarisk, sea-buckthorn, gorse, daisy bush (*Olearia*), elder and (in all but very cold districts) griselinia.

Within this low shock-absorber you erect a screen of such big trees as the holm oak, sycamore, Monterey cypress, Swedish whitebeam, Bishop pine, Cornish elm and *Pinus thunbergii* to a depth of 30 feet if you can. The finest all-rounder of all is the Corsican pine, which will grow bravely right down to the high-water mark. That maid-of-all-work, the tree of heaven, even allows the sea to wash her toes. The effect of such a "defence in depth", with small infantry covering the big guns, will be to carry the salt-laden gales high up, where the salt, though it has to come down again, will be widely dispersed. A list of other maritime trees is given in Part III.

Shifting sand can be stabilised by various maritime grasses and by *Pinus pinaster*; shingle by such plants as the deep-rooting sea-kale (*Crambe maritima*), sea-campion (*Silene maritima*) and sea-beet (*Beta maritima*).

3
Trees in Design

THE MAN WHO DESIGNS any kind of scene whatever – whether an open landscape, a tiny town garden, a roadside planting, a renaissance of degenerate soils or a screening of factories – must obviously first have some knowledge of plants. He must also, however, have taste, judgement and imagination. These are qualities by no means possessed by all landscape architects. Good design calls for an eye for decorative beauty, a sensitive appreciation of textures, shapes and colours, a feeling for contrasts of light and shade and for the association of trees with buildings and with other plants. But what matters most of all, we should say, is imagination. A great many of the world's most sumptuous gardens have been the imaginative creations of amateurs.

For three hundred years or more the great exponents have emphasised, in one way or another, that the prime object is "to paint a picture". Alexander Pope declared more emphatically still that "all gardening is landscape painting". Vanbrugh, when asked to advise on the grounds of Blenheim Palace, replied "send for a landscape painter". In all, and expressly so in the words of the nature poet Shenstone, was the idea of "stimulating the imagination" and by such means were we freed from the cramps of the horticultural geometrician.

Maxims of Design

OBVIOUSLY THIS CONCEPTION means attention to the tenets of proportion, perspective, balance and unity. The siting of trees in particular is very far from what Wordsworth called "a mere mechanic exercise", for trees are the dominant feature in nearly all settings. Does the prospect call for a slim, Italianate cypress, for a big, full-bosomed sycamore, for the airy grace of a silver birch or for a flower-spangled magnolia, cherry or laburnum? Is the canvas suitable for the "rich, harmonious masses" of William Chambers or for the strict discipline of isolated specimens of perfect form? No less critical, especially to a private gardener, will be the juxtaposition of trees and buildings. Indeed, we must always think of trees in architectural terms of line, form and texture.

29

Trees in design: the "disappearing path" at Winterthur, Delaware, the garden created by the late F. du Pont.

A lesson to be learned very early from the painters, writers and the best landscape practitioners is "to keep the centre open". Do not litter up the middle ground. Particularly, do not fragment it by running a path down the centre. Usually the open centre will be of grass, but in special situations it may be an expanse of water or in a tiny town garden it may be of stone paving or even of gravel. Build your main strong-points beyond the middle distance and on the flanks. Take advantage of any interesting object that there may fortunately be in the far distance, such as a church or the sea, and lead the eye up to it by a break in the tree plantings or perhaps by an avenue. If there is a hill crest within the property and nothing else is visible beyond, leave a part of the hill crest unplanted, so as to give the illusion that beyond it is the world's end, as was so skilfully done by Major Lawrence Johnson, an American who came to England and created that lovely garden at Hidcote Manor.

This trick is an adaptation of the designer's (and the soldier's) maxim of "surprise".

Let not each beauty everywhere be spied,
Where half the skill is decently to hide.

So Alexander Pope in a famous passage. Even in quite small gardens this can often be accomplished, though not easily with trees. But in any place large enough, a disappearing path through woodland or even round a bank of shrubs, will entice you on, to discover some surprise beyond the bend.

"Mass" is a military maxim of very special import to designers of gardens or the countryside. If you have only three silver birches or only three eucalypts, plant them all together. If you have them by the hundred or the thousand, divide them if you will but still muster them in compact companies or squadrons. Only occasionally is dispersion effective, as, for example, where a mass of round forms calls for the contrast of a narrow, columnar one, or where the splendour of the blue Atlas cedar serves to complement a plantation of mountain ashes, whitebeams, gold-washed cypresses, dark visaged bays or fluttering aspens.

Really large and very broad trees, such as your oaks and sycamores, do not readily answer to the precept of mass, except insofar as each itself becomes a mass in time. They are really park trees, to be planted at very wide intervals, or, where appropriate, as an avenue of roadside trees or set in some chosen, very prominent spot in town or besides a village green. The big conifers can be used in much the same way, though very few are happy in large towns.

Movement is an attribute very much to be desired in any kind of setting and here we have some fine flying squadrons at our service. The weeping willow's golden tresses stream out before the wind and there are the excited rufflings and flutterings, as of many small birds, of lindens, whitebeams, poplars and all those trees that coat the reverse side of their leaves with a soft, white down. Such movement makes a panorama live.

Tree Styles

IN APPLYING THESE MAXIMS, the designer on any scale can begin the exciting task of brooding on what particular trees he will select. His treasury is well stocked. He will often be confounded with an embarrassment of riches. He can then begin to exercise his imagination as well as his judgement. He may perhaps begin to see on his mental canvas a picture of high woods tossing their banners against a stormy sky or arraying themselves in "the slumbrous foliage of high midsummer's wealth"; or in other settings he may see a noble avenue of chestnuts, or Kipling's "gnarled and writhen thorn" on wind-bitten headlands, or a plantation of sycamore or Monterey

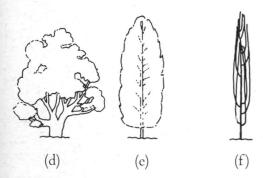

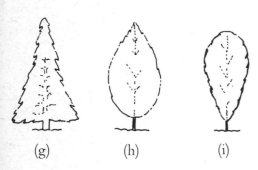

Tree profiles:
(a) *feathered (very young);*
(b) *standard, round-headed;*
(c) *standard, elliptical;*
(d) *low-forking;*
(e) *columnar;* (f) *fastigiate (vertical branches pressed close together);*
(g) *pyramidal or conical;*
(h) *ovate;* (i) *obovate.*

pine to break the assaults of ocean gales, or merely a severe rank of poplars planted to hide a factory.

One of the great delights of trees is their infinite variety of styles, textures and colours. We have said a little about their shapes and textures at the end of Chapter I and the designer must exercise his taste and imagination in composing a picture of stylish contrasts, not too abrupt and startling but agreeable one with another. In small places, however, he must also exercise self-discipline, not making a heterogenous collection of many plants in ones and twos; it is better to restrict the number of species to a few that grow harmoniously together, and to have several of each. If there is room, let us say, for twelve trees, it is far better to have three each of four species, rather than one each of twelve species.

Besides diversity of form and texture there is also an astonishing range of colours in the leaves of trees. In addition to the many shades of greens, we can choose from the red or purple leaves of the maple 'Crimson King', the copper beech and several crabs and cherries, the pink of the sycamore 'Brilliantissimum', the golden tints in the gleditsia and many conifers, the blue of the eucalypts and spruce, and the gilt or silvery variations of a great number of trees. But autumn, of course, is the romantic time for leaf colour, when, more especially in acid soils, the nyssas, liquidambars, maples, the red oak and the stewartia set the countryside on fire with "the exquisite chromatics of decay".

To crown all is the glory of flower with which so many trees ornament their robes in due season, from such large, imperial trees as the chestnuts and the tuliptree, through those of moderate size in the catalpa, the sophoras and the magnolias, down to the smaller graces that so appropriately enliven private as well as public gardens, particularly the cherries, the laburnums and the dogwoods. To flower we may also add fruit, as in the strawberry tree (*Arbutus*), rowans, crab-apples and persimmons.

The designer must think also of branch structure, consorting the bold, strong limbs of, let us say, the catalpa, the arbutus and the Amur cork-tree with the more delicate ones of the silver birch, the true acacia and the smaller mountain ashes. The brilliant bark colours of the snake-bark maples and *Prunus serrula* are also telling in the garden picture. In winter branches of all sorts, bold and delicate, embroider the sky with delightful patterns, as we may see in a long file of elms marching along the horizon, all the more beautiful when powdered with frost.

Towns

ALL THE FACTORS that we have been discussing apply in greater or less degree almost everywhere, but special considerations come into force in towns, whether public places or private gardens. The choice of round-headed tree forms to contrast with the rectilinear shapes of buildings assumes importance, but in the average town street and on the peripheries of car parks there is an obvious need for narrower, upright trees, which must also not drop too much litter. In broader streets and in ample boulevards the choice widens dramatically and in community centres and village greens we look especially for the luxury of blossom, from the big horse chestnuts to the smaller gean and the still smaller flowering cherries, hawthorns and crabs, remembering also, where the climate allows, the fluffy blossoms of the true acacias and the pretty hoheria. For courtyards and small squares there are the beautiful and strangely neglected sophoras, ideal town trees, as well as the catalpa, the koelreuteria, the Judas tree (which we prefer to call the Judaea tree, as the French do) and a great many others. For larger squares there are the traditional London plane, the tree of heaven, the ginkgo, the lindens and many others to relieve the monotony of buildings and to give shade in the noonday heat. In towns or cities that suffer from pollution of the atmosphere and the soil we have to take particular care to make the right choices and we discuss this problem in the next chapter.

Even in little town gardens trees have a high purpose to fill, but the choice is obviously limited. The most frequent mistake by those of no great experience is a failure to appreciate that "Great oaks from little acorns grow". How endearing is the silhouette of a young weeping willow, how elegant the bearing of a little blue Atlas cedar when seen in the nursery or the garden centre! Yet how disastrous are the consequences when they are planted too near to a house or path! The error is very noticeable in the small gardens of new houses in America, which many "landscape" contractors grossly overload with trees.

Still, there is a pretty wide choice. The slim, fastigiate flowering cherry 'Amano-gawa' will delightfully fill any corner not heavily shaded, growing quite tall but occupying no more than a square yard of ground. So will the rare fastigiate form of the koelreuteria. The warm pink cherry 'Okame', of more formal tree shape, is almost tailor-made for small gardens, taking several years to spread its arms wider than 12 feet. Several crab apples are rather smaller still, such as the beautiful pink *Malus halliana* 'Parkmanii' and the stunning white *Malus sargentii* (both too small to include in our Register). The hawthorns or mays also quickly answer the prayer of the small gardener with both their blossom and their fruits, such as Lavalle's Thorn, the handsome coloured forms of the English hawthorn (*Crataegus oxyacantha*) and the exceptional columnar variety of the Washington thorn. For a golden touch we have the richness of the laburnums, with due regard to what is said in the Register. To these little flowering trees striking contrasts of form and texture are provided by some of the elegant small conifers and they are indeed almost essential for painting a garden picture, though few of them care for town life.

Large Landscapes

THESE, WHETHER PUBLIC OR PRIVATE, call for some skill, experience and what soldiers and huntsmen call "an eye for country". First there must be a professional survey, clearly defining the contours. The next care must be to devise a planting plan in sympathy with the land form, not in contradiction of it. Hard rectangles, most of all black rectangles of conifers, severely mar any landscape. Plantations should follow the lie of the land, accentuating its natural modelling and giving rhythm to it. Where the landscape is not a flat one some contrast between the high ground and the low can be delightful, as by planting the spurs or ribs with conifers and the re-entrants with broadleaves. At all costs shun hard, straight lines, a mutilation that conifers are prone to inflict. Unless you are a forester or unless the panorama is mountainous, use conifers with caution, but they can often be very meaningful as a contrast in colour and texture and they do marry in singular happiness with the silver birch, the rowan, the eucalyptus and similar broadleaves of light and airy texture.

On the very large scale, tree planting tends to become a matter of forestry, well away from towns, and then the vital landscape consideration becomes one of integrating the woodland acres with the agriculture of the place, with open spaces and with the haunts of man. The temptation to over-plant must be resisted.

The sensitive designer of these and similar scenes is too often confounded by the lay-out of roads. Modern engineers seldom have any artistic sense and the roads that they build are rarely in sympathy with land forms and leave grievous scars across the landscape. No doubt the engineer very often has little choice and he can point to the fact that the Romans did just the same! In such plights the landscape lover will himself have no choice but to accept the formal matrix confronting him and to soften its severity by means of an avenue. What sort of avenue will depend on the breadth of the verge, the lines of sight of the motorist and other factors, but any opportunity that there may be of planting a copse or glade or some such

OPPOSITE *The world's most famous avenue in a city of avenues – the Champs Elysées, with the Arc de Triomphe, Paris. London planes run the full length of the avenue, with a plantation of* Sophora japonica *surrounding the Arc and horse chestnuts in the distance. See key drawing, right, for identification.*

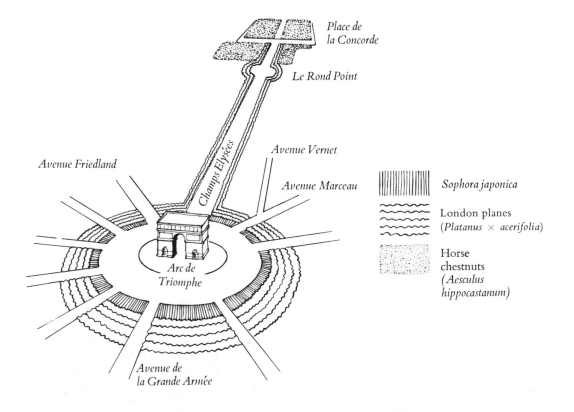

Place de la Concorde

Le Rond Point

Avenue Friedland

Avenue Vernet

Avenue Marceau

Champs Elysées

Arc de Triomphe

Avenue de la Grande Armée

Sophora japonica

London planes (Platanus × acerifolia)

Horse chestnuts (Aesculus hippocastanum)

aggregation of trees should be seized with both hands. A further hazard to be faced is that roadside soils are liable to have been degraded by the engineer or severely compacted by his earth-moving machinery. Given the right conditions, a vast choice of avenue trees is at hand, whether the formality of the slim Lombardy poplar or the rounded forms of oaks, lindens or maples or the floral gaiety of the cherries and crabs.

OPPOSITE *A woodland glade at Abbotswood, Gloucestershire.*

Woodland

TO ANY MAN WHO HAS SPACE we strongly commend the creation of a woodland garden. At a little distance from the house, and after only a few years of culture, it gives great delight as a private world, in which you may walk with a mind free from care, or sit at ease in some leafy bower of your own contriving, far removed from "the fever of the world". You will have trees of your own choosing and beneath them you will have a choice of flowering shrubs of all colours, lilies, daffodils, primroses, violets and a thousand small treasures. In this private woodland you will design a grassy glade – maybe more than one – giving you a sunlit vista to some chosen object or gently curving and enticing you onwards. Happy the man who has measureless acres for such a garden of repose, but you can contrive it in even half an acre.

Patience

WE HAVE TO RECOGNISE, however, that most trees are slow starters and take some time to attain an effective size. There will be a temptation to choose those that grow fast, but the temptation must be avoided if they are not otherwise absolutely right choices for the position, unless they are regarded as merely temporary. A good many trees, however, can be transplanted from the nursery when in an advanced state of growth, at a price.

We can also bring to our aid what are called "extra-heavy standards" or "semi-mature trees". These are fairly new developments, in which young trees are grown on by nurseries for some years in controlled conditions. The extra heavies are an outstanding speciality of Exbury, near Southampton, and the semi-matures are mainly the product of America, where the Princeton Nurseries has probably the largest tree production of any in the world. These trees, which are all of high quality, not only help to create an "instant garden", but furthermore they are far less subject to the vandalism that kills so many trees in streets and other public places, being much tougher and having well developed heads. We have seen ordinary, very young standards with their flimsy and vulnerable heads completely broken off by vandals. Strong winds can do the same.

Trees of still larger sizes, but limited in kind, can sometimes be got from specialist nurseries at still higher cost and require special equipment for their transporting and planting.

4
Planting

HAVING CONSIDERED these basic factors, we can go forward to plant our selected trees.

First, make sure that the drainage is satisfactory. Only swamp trees, such as the taxodiums, the alders, *Larix laricina* and the river birch, care to have their feet in standing water, though there are others, headed by the pin oak, that like things very damp. Prepare the soil conscientiously, cultivating at least 20in. deep, incorporating plenty of organic matter (especially well-rotted cow or horse manure if you can get it). If more than one tree is to be planted, cultivate over the whole area, by hand or mechanically. Carefully plot the site for each tree, having regard to its spread and its physical needs.

Three kinds of roots are to be found, in the main. The commonest are fibrous roots, consisting of thread-like growths, maybe very dense, maybe rather loose, open and perhaps coarse. These are easy to plant, needing only to be well spread out and if too long for convenience can be cut back. A second kind is fleshy and brittle, as in the magnolia and the tulip-tree. These are easily injured and need gentle handling and must on no account be stamped on after planting. A third kind is the tap-root, which extends itself deep into the soil in the manner of a carrot, parsnip or lupin. These also, though fairly tough, must be planted with some care, making sure that the hole is deep enough for their full length, without any twisting or curling; hickories, walnuts and some oaks are examples. These and the fleshy-rooted sorts are as a rule both best planted in the spring. Variations in soils may change the character of a root, so that one which begins fibrous may develop a tap.

Dig the hole for each tree somewhat wider and deeper than the root area. On sloping ground make the site level. For solo trees in a lawn or elsewhere make the hole a good 4ft square, though for convenience in mowing an oval bed (not round) is better. Line the hole with an inch or so of peat, to give the roots an easy start in their new home. "Offer up" the sapling in the hole to see if it fits comfortably, being particularly careful that it is not planted deeper than the soil mark on the trunk, which shows the depth at which it stood in the nursery. Prune the sapling if necessary (see next chapter).

OPPOSITE *"Extra heavy standards" of the purple sycamore,* Acer pseudoplatanus *'Atropurpureum'* *("Spaethii" of nurseries) in the nursery rows at Exbury.*

38

PLANTING

Plant a stake of size conformable to the tree and tie the two together temporarily with a twist or two of string. Some trees have to be planted when very small, such as hickory, eucalyptus, arbutus and the Judaea tree, but they will still need staking.

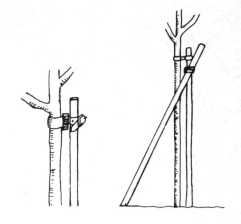

Then fill the hole with good, crumbly soil or with a prepared planting mixture which includes a mild, non-caustic fertiliser (such as bonemeal) and a good proportion of organic matter if it is sandy. Broken-up turf is of very good, lasting value in sandy soils. If the tree has come with bare roots make sure that all the interstices of the roots are filled with fine particles of soil, peat or compost. When the hole is half-filled give it a *light* firming. If the roots have been "balled" in the nursery with a material of loose weave, the material need not be wholly removed if there is a fear of the ball-soil falling away, but it should be opened out and the top part cut away. Plastic wrappings of any sort must be wholly removed.

Before finally filling up spread a light layer of manure or other good organic matter over the hole. Fresh manure or "hot" fertiliser must never come in close contact with roots. At soil level, shape a shallow saucer to hold water and then give the tree a thorough sousing. Finish by tying stake and tree together firmly, but not so as to cause chafing of the bark. Trees that are not wind-firm, such as the neo-cypresses, robinias and eucalypts, need special care. Trees of standard size in a very exposed spot may need two or even three stakes cross-braced.

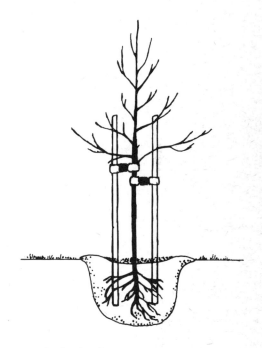

Do *not* at this stage give the soil a very hard pounding with the feet to firm it, or else it will be compacted. Water itself is an excellent firmer, as engineers will tell you. A firming with the feet may follow after twenty-four hours or so, when the water has got right through. Be extra careful of trees with fleshy, brittle roots that grow close to the surface, as in magnolias and the tulip-tree.

A few trees, as will be seen in the Register, do their best in lean, stony soils and for them manure and fertiliser should be withheld. Indeed, if the natural soil is a rich one, they will benefit from a liberal basket-full of stones or broken bricks.

Methods of staking.

Thereafter your chief care must be to see that the young plants never lack water. Give special attention to young evergreens, whether broadleaf or conifer, for they transpire water vapour continuously, even in winter. Whenever the heavens fail you for more than a few days, syringe the foliage generously and often, as well as supplying water to the roots, but in heavy clay soil watering of the roots once a week is enough. These attentions you must be sure to keep up for all evergreens for the whole of the first year at least.

After any passage of rough weather and after every thaw see that the young plant and its stake have not been loosened. In regions of severe winters provide some form of protective wrapping according to the practice of that region, whether it be mounds of bracken, straw, pine needles or wrappings of coarse material. When spring promises to come round again remove the protection as soon as possible, but the organic substances may be spread out as a mulch if desired.

We have mentioned earlier the "extra-heavy standards" and the "semi-mature" trees grown with great skill at Exbury and in some of the top American nurseries

OPPOSITE *The cedar of Lebanon,* Cedrus libani, *at Exbury House.*

and in smaller numbers and usually with less skill by the large municipalities. These naturally need particular care in planting but do not always get it. Their staking must be very firm and they must be protected by iron tree guards against damage by the passing multitudes or the mower as, of course, must all newly planted trees.

When to Plant

THE BASIC PRECEPT is to plant in autumn, while the soil is still warm and when there is the virtual certainty of some rain, with maybe snow to follow. October is usually the very best time of all in most regions, but any time up to next April is acceptable, provided that the soil is not sodden or frozen. Much is gained if the young plants can get a good toe-hold early and begin to feel their way at the first stirring of spring. Some plants, however, prefer to move in spring, such as catalpas, the Judaea tree, the hickories, magnolias, tulip tree and walnuts; many people, indeed, advise spring for nearly all trees, especially conifers and other evergreens. A great deal depends on the climate of the zone, but we would say that in the milder zones (certainly in zones 7–10) and in any site with a southerly exposure autumn is the time, in the absence of any good reason to the contrary. Likewise a Zone 5 tree is safely planted in autumn in Zone 6. A temporising policy would be to plant in early April when in doubt, but the peril of spring planting is spring drought.

Planting in Towns

IN THE STREETS and shopping "concourses" of towns and cities we face special difficulties. The worst of them is pollution of the atmosphere and the soil, but even when this is not present we are likely to encounter degenerate soil, compaction, reflected heat from pavings and buildings, vandalism and lack of water. We will look first at **pollution**.

This takes two forms – poisoning of the atmosphere by chemicals and poisoning of the soil, chiefly by the de-icing salts spread by municipal authorities in and near towns, a trouble which is far more prevalent in the United States and Canada than elsewhere. Vast and, indeed, quite excessive quantities of salts (chiefly sodium and calcium chloride) are strewn in the streets and are then splashed outwards by motor vehicles. When these salts or the brine that they produce spread into the root areas of trees in the paving or the verges of roads outside towns, frightful damage is done. In regions of light snowfall, sand should be used instead and where salt is un-avoidable its rate of application should be reduced and the tree pits given a measure of protection by a low lip of concrete to check the seepage of brine.

Atmospheric poisoning arises from industrial plant, from motor vehicles, especially diesel engines, from home fires and other sources. In the classic case of the region around Ducktown, Tennessee, fumes from a copper-smelting plant denuded an enormous area of every vestige of plant life and even now, many decades later,

The London plane
*(*Platanus × acerifolia*)*
on the South Bank, London.

parts are still devoid of vegetation. The foothills west of Los Angeles, which are an important watershed for the city, are being denuded of their native pines, presenting the dual threat of the destruction of reservoirs by siltation and of landslides through loss of vegetation. Happily, the ravages of air pollution have been checked in the London area and other parts of Britain, largely through "clean air" legislation and it is now possible at the Royal Botanic Gardens at Kew to grow certain plants which were on the "hopeless" list twenty years ago. The notorious "smogs" of London and Manchester are almost things of the past. Fortunately also, there are quite a lot of trees that laugh at these awesome hazards and a list of them is included in Part III.

Other hazards to trees in towns are daunting enough but can more easily be overcome with care and attention. City soil is very bad soil; it is lifeless, devoid of plant nutrients and compacted. It is usually a mixture of sterile subsoil and rubble from the

43

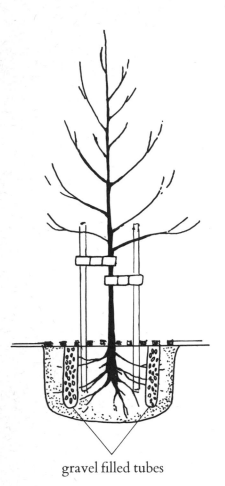

gravel filled tubes

Planting in towns.

demolition of older buildings and from the hard-core beneath roads and pavings. In such conditions the planting pits should be excavated and filled with a good grade of loamy top soil. For standard trees with a bole of up to 3in diameter a planting pit of *at least* 4 × 4ft and at least 2ft deep will be necessary. In Barcelona we have watched a remarkable example of planting which is a model of thoroughness. After digging down about 3ft the planters excavate far *outwards* underneath the paving, to give extra root spread.

Trees so planted are in reality growing in "containers", like outsize flowerpots; therefore the same care should be taken to ensure that the soil in the container will support prolonged and vigorous growth. Soil tests must be made. City soil is sometimes surprisingly acid, particularly where soft coal was burned as fuel for generations. The sulphuric acid washed out of the air by countless years of rain and fogs has resulted in soils as acid as *pH* 3·5 in some areas, far too low for the health of almost any tree. Where this is the case lime should be added to bring the *pH* up to 6·5. Ground limestone, especially dolimitic limestone with its high magnesium content, is preferable to hydrated lime, because it lasts much longer.

Other constituents of the soil mixture also need attention. For trees that in nature grow in stony, rocky ground, the mix must not be too rich, but usually a good level of fertility must be created. Well-rotted animal manure or some other bulky organic matter is all to the good, but should not exceed ten per cent of the mix, for it shrinks as it rots, leaving the tree sitting in a saucer in the paving. In sandy soils, as we have already noted, chopped up turves are excellent. If lime is needed, delay its application for at least a month after digging in manure.

In suburban and village areas there is not as a rule the same necessity to excavate pits entirely and refill, as the native soil is probably in good shape, but analysis is a sensible precaution.

The next danger to town trees is that of compaction of the soil by the constant trampling overhead. The surface of the pit should therefore be covered with a good carpet of gravel with a metal or concrete grill on top.

It should be manifest to anyone that the trees, having been planted, must have a regular supply of water, yet town trees die more from thirst than from any other cause. The tree's struggle for life is made all the more arduous by the heat reflected from pavements and buildings. The need for water is most emphatic for newly planted trees and for evergreens above all. This must be the responsibility of municipal authorities, who ought to give all their trees a thorough soaking at least once a week in the absence of rain.

When rain does shower its blessing the gravel and grid will help it to penetrate, but the chances of its getting really well down to the root tips is assured if vertical irrigation channels are sunk into the pit *before* filling in. This is done simply by setting in two vertical cardboard tubes filled with gravel, on opposite sides of the tree. The cardboard rots away but the gravel channels remain (see illustration above).

5
"Superfluous Branches"

TREES DO NOT NEED the regular and systematic pruning that is the rule for roses and other flowering shrubs. Indeed, it is necessary only for the removal of dead and decadent limbs and for training the tree to a good shape, especially in its youth. The wise gardener of Richard II summed up the matter when, with Shakespearean aptness, he declared:

Superfluous branches
We lop away that bearing boughs may live.

Pruning is governed by a few important precepts, which we shall set out in short order.

The basic one is to prune when one cycle of growth has ceased and another is about to begin. Thus any plants (mostly shrubs) which flower before midsummer are pruned immediately after flowering, when they are beginning to put forth new shoots, and those that flower later are pruned (if at all) in winter dormancy. As you might expect of almost every rule, however, there are exceptions.

For our purposes, the chief exceptions are those deciduous trees (a good many) in which the sap starts stirring early in the year to begin the new "cycle of growth" and which bleed if cut at that time. Hickories, walnuts, silver birches, liquidambars and maples are a few examples. These accordingly you prune after the sap has finished rising, which is about the end of July; but any time from then onwards to autumn will suit. We note these trees in the Register, but, when in doubt one may fairly safely prune all trees at this season. The flowering cherries and their kind can be pruned (if needed) in June, to avoid infection by bacterial canker that may occur after winter pruning. Conifers and other evergreens have their own special rule and these one normally prunes in April. In all cases a little light trimming of branch tips can be done at any time.

The first pruning group – flowering trees that bloom early – includes some bearing flowers in the spring and decorative or edible fruits later in the year, such as the rowans or mountain ashes, the crab-apples, koelreuterias and persimmons. These you do not prune after flowering, but after fruiting, cutting back (if you have a long

45

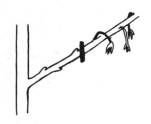

On small flowering trees, prune back to a selected bud below the spent flowers.

Renewal pruning.

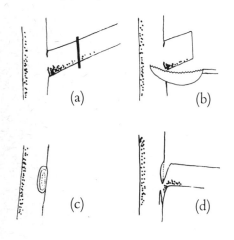

Removing a heavy branch:
(a) saw off the branch at a little distance from the main trunk;
(b) undercut the stub flush with the trunk; (c) complete the amputation from above;
(d) result of not making an undercut.

Removing a rival leader and tying in the selected one.

reach) to a new shoot. In fact, very few trees in this book really need this sort of treatment, unless you are a perfectionist.

The next most important precept concerns the method of pruning. Always cut at a calculated and reasoned point, not at random. If the pruning is for the purpose of getting rid of a length of stem that is withered or broken or that has finished its spell of flowering, cut back to a selected bud behind the withered or spent portion. This is renewal pruning, intended to stimulate the selected bud into growth to replace the old one.

The pruning may, however, be for the purpose of getting rid of a whole branch or a lateral or sub-lateral. The need may arise from disease or because the branch or lateral has become an obstruction of some sort or is otherwise overmighty, or because the whole tree needs thinning out. In such instances you amputate the limb at its point of junction with its parent and the positive commandment is to make the severance absolutely flush with the point of junction.

The amputation of a whole branch or a big lateral may be a fairly considerable job, with a saw. Any attempt to remove a substantial limb at one blow, so to speak, will result in a large and dangerous scar in the main member, because, before the saw gets through, the branch will be wrenched away by its own weight, tearing a strip of the main limb with it. Accordingly, whatever intermediate loppings may be needed for reasons of safety or convenience, you must saw through the branch in two places – one a foot or so away from the main limb and another to remove the stub flush at the junction. In this second and final amputation, you first make an undercut with the saw for an inch or two, flush with the junction, and then a cut through from the top to meet it. Pare off any rough surface with a keen knife or a chisel.

In every kind of pruning, never leave a stump; it will simply be a breeding ground for disease. Paint every cut that is more than about half an inch with one of the tree paints made for that purpose. Surgery of really big trees calls for a professional.

Pruning of one sort or another is often necessary for shaping a tree as you would have it. Much can often be done by a little snipping of the tips of twigs when the plant is small. Specimens of tree shapes are shown on page 32. It is usually best to allow a tree to adopt its natural form, while preventing any interior crowding and any crossing or rubbing together of branches. Many very decorative trees look best when forking low from the ground, as in magnolias, arbutus, the Judaea tree, and (somewhat higher) the catalpa and many others. Bear in mind that low-forking trees will be more wide-spreading than the same species grown as a standard.

Trees that naturally have a central mast, rather than forking, should be encouraged to continue in that habit by the removal of any "rival leader" and by tying in the selected one to a good cane. Specimens of this habit arrive from the nursery as "feathered" trees, with several small branches growing from the central stem. When planting these, shorten the lateral "feathers" by one-third, leaving the

46

*A weeping willow
(Salix × chrysocoma)
sheathed in ice.*

central stem severely alone. This will save the tree, when it starts growing, from transpiring excessively through putting out an area of foliage unduly in excess of the root area. If you subsequently want head-room under the tree, remove the lower branches flush with the main stem to the desired height, a few at a time, perhaps over a period of three years. Do this removal at the proper season, leaving the central leader untouched.

Trees that embellish the garden picture by the beauty of their bark do so all the better if they are grown in multi-stemmed form, or, if standards, by the gradual

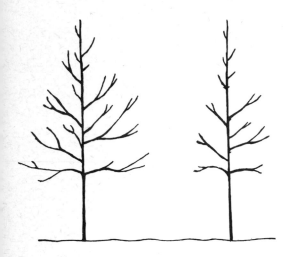

Pruning a newly arrived feathered tree with a central stem.

removal of their lower boughs, as in the snake-bark maples, *Acer griseum*, the cinnamon-hued arbutuses or strawberry trees and the polished mahogany bark of *Prunus serrula*. The gleaming white barks of the eucalypts look extremely well, especially in small gardens, if coppiced every year (cut almost down to the ground) and so putting forth new stems of their beautiful juvenile foliage; the same might (perhaps) be said of the golden forms of the robinias and the catalpa, but, if they are grafted trees, the cut must be made well above the point of union of stock and scion. This coppicing allows a tree to be grown that would otherwise become too big for small places.

Of course, if so ordered, many trees arrive from the nursery not as feathered trees, but as standards, with a head of branches sprouting from the top of a bare "leg" or stem. These may be specimens of a selected species or form, grafted or budded by the nurseryman on top of a leg of wild, vigorous stock, as typically in hawthorns, crab-apples and flowering cherries, or they may be the selected species on their own roots (i.e., which originated as feathered trees). These standards are what one might call tailor-made trees, at once giving some height and form to the garden scene, but they are expensive and not always of the most desirable habit, as in the overdone *Robinia pseudoacacia* 'Frisia'. A few notes on this aspect of things are given in the Register where appropriate. The gorgeous flowering cherries and their kind, usually grown as standards, are often of greater splendour as low-forking, wide-spreading trees, but can be an impediment to man and mower.

On all standard trees keep a sharp look-out for suckers, both from the stem and from ground level and remove them at once. On grafted specimens these will be from the unwanted wild stock, which will quickly overwhelm the desired scion. Some of the larger trees (of any shape) are notorious for throwing out thickets of suckers from their roots.

It will be seen in general, therefore, that pruning is to a large extent applied common sense, based on a little knowledge and observance of how a tree grows.

PART II
A Register of Trees

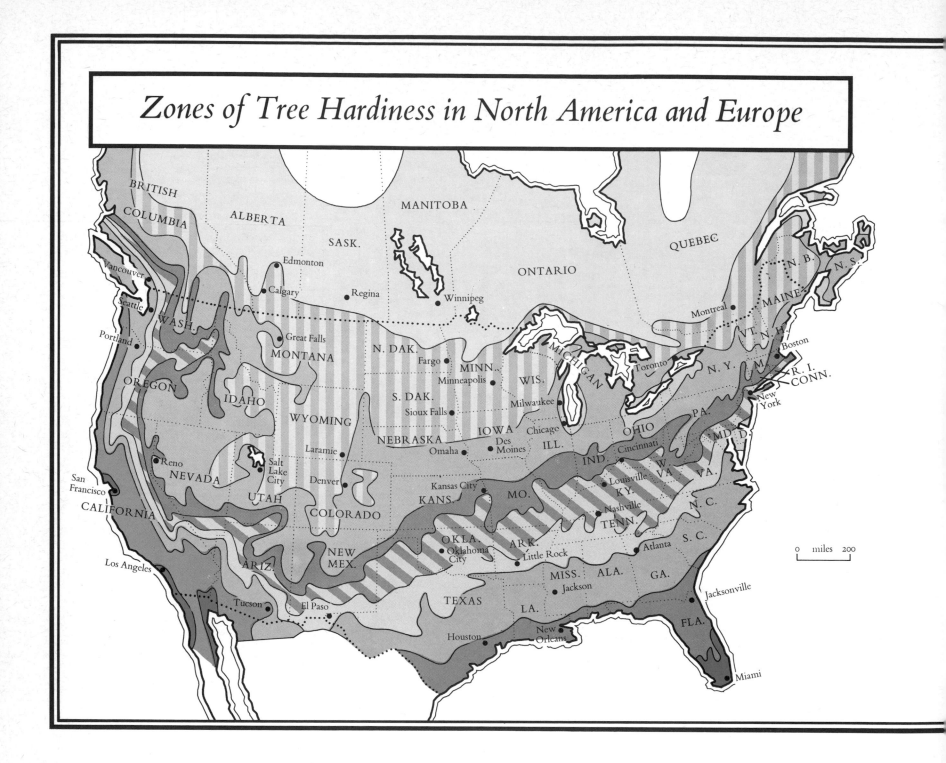

Zones of Tree Hardiness in North America and Europe

BRITISH COLUMBIA
ALBERTA
SASK.
MANITOBA
ONTARIO
QUEBEC
N. B.
N. S.

Vancouver
Seattle
Edmonton
Calgary
Regina
Winnipeg
Montreal
MAINE
VT.
N. H.
Boston
WASH.
Portland
Great Falls
MONTANA
N. DAK.
Fargo
MINN.
MICHIGAN
Toronto
N. Y.
M.
R. I.
CONN.
New York
OREGON
IDAHO
Minneapolis
WIS.
S. DAK.
Milwaukee
PA.
MD. D.
Reno
WYOMING
Sioux Falls
Chicago
OHIO
W VA.
VA.
San Francisco
NEVADA
Laramie
NEBRASKA
IOWA
Des Moines
ILL.
IND.
Cincinnati
Louisville
KY.
Salt Lake City
Denver
Omaha
Kansas City
Nashville
N. C.
UTAH
MO.
TENN.
CALIFORNIA
COLORADO
KANS.
Los Angeles
ARIZ.
NEW MEX.
OKLA.
Oklahoma City
ARK.
Little Rock
Atlanta
S. C.
Tucson
El Paso
MISS.
ALA.
GA.
Jacksonville
TEXAS
Jackson
LA.
FLA.
Houston
New Orleans
Miami

0   miles   200

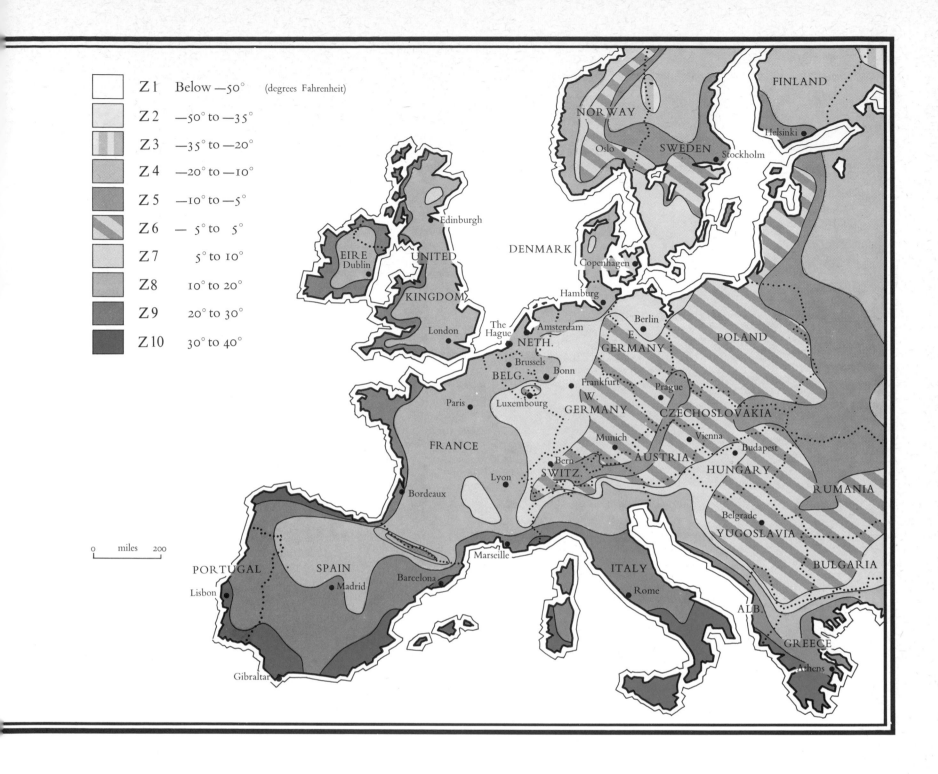

Z 1	Below —50°	(degrees Fahrenheit)
Z 2	—50° to —35°	
Z 3	—35° to —20°	
Z 4	—20° to —10°	
Z 5	—10° to —5°	
Z 6	— 5° to 5°	
Z 7	5° to 10°	
Z 8	10° to 20°	
Z 9	20° to 30°	
Z 10	30° to 40°	

0   miles   200

FINLAND

NORWAY

SWEDEN

Helsinki

Oslo   Stockholm

DENMARK

Copenhagen

Edinburgh

EIRE   UNITED

Dublin

Hamburg

Berlin

KINGDOM

E.   POLAND

London   The   Amsterdam   GERMANY

Hague   NETH.

Brussels   Bonn

BELG.   Frankfurt   Prague

Paris   Luxembourg   CZECHOSLOVAKIA

W.

GERMANY

FRANCE   Munich   Vienna   Budapest

AUSTRIA

Bern   HUNGARY

Lyon   SWITZ.   RUMANIA

Bordeaux   Belgrade

YUGOSLAVIA

BULGARIA

Marseille

PORTUGAL   SPAIN   ITALY

Lisbon   Madrid   Barcelona   Rome   ALB.

GREECE

Gibraltar   Athens

Introduction

THIS REGISTER includes the majority, but by no means all, of the ornamental trees that can successfully be grown in the world's temperate zones, with special reference to the Northern Hemisphere. The species, varieties and cultivars within each genus can be no more than a selection, although that selection has been made as wide as possible.

We include no shrubs. Since a limit has to be set somewhere, we also exclude any plant of less than about 24 feet, but here and there, as in the flowering cherries and the hawthorns, we have exercised some indulgence. Inevitably this involves the exclusion of several of the desirable smaller species, such as *Magnolia stellata*, the dwarf Japanese maples, *Malus sargentii* and all the small conifers, but to have let them in would have opened the door also to the great crowd of cotoneasters, pyracanthas, embothriums, eucryphias, the larger rhododendrons and even some roses, which jostle on the heels of trees proper and which are quite outside our brief.

In so large a subject, covering so wide a slice of the globe's surface, it is obviously desirable to give some sort of hint of a tree's hardiness and acceptability in diverse conditions. As a basis for this we have found it convenient to adopt the zoning system evolved originally by the Arnold Arboretum for North America and we have adapted it to Europe also. This system, however, applies only to temperature – the extent to which a tree will resist cold. This is the most important single factor in assessing hardiness, but several other factors have also to be taken into account, particularly altitude, humidity, the nature of the soil, its water content, exposure to winds and the art of the cultivator himself. A tree that is hardy in an area of good rainfall is liable to succumb in a dry one, even though the zone be warmer, and a tree that prospers at sea level may die at 1,000 feet up at the same latitude.

These temperature zones, hereinafter indicated simply by the letter z and shown in the maps on the previous two pages are, in degrees Fahrenheit.

In the lists that follow the zone given for a tree is that of its northern limit of reliable hardiness. Our usual authority is Rehder. Nearly all trees will succeed in warmer zones also, subject to water supply and other factors, but this is not invariably

OPPOSITE *Winter in the beechwoods.*

so; the sugar maple, the canoe-bark birch, spruces, firs, hemlocks and others that originate from the colder zones will languish in climates warmer than Zone 7. Conifers accustomed to ample moisture in both the atmosphere and the soil, such as many of those from the Pacific Coast of North America, cannot always be relied upon to reach their full statures when grown in drier climates. Wherever important, we have included notes on the various environmental factors.

The heights of trees given in this Register are the normal maxima in what might be called good-average conditions of cultivation and circumstance. Elsewhere they obviously vary and some examples are given of very large specimens. Likewise the times which trees take to reach their maximum sizes vary considerably; thus in ten years the sycamore will grow to about 35ft but the shagbark hickory only 12ft. Gardeners and landscapists must plan accordingly.

The flowering seasons given are also the normal ones in normal conditions for the appropriate zones. Some variation must be expected in other zones and in special conditions of altitude and other environmental factors, but generally speaking there is a remarkable unanimity of opinion among authorities in diverse zones and on both sides of the Atlantic. In the Southern Hemisphere, with its reversal of the seasons, the dates differ.

In the following notes a few of the more famous botanical and horticultural establishments are mentioned in short form. These are:

Kew – Royal Botanic Gardens, Kew, Surrey.
Arnold Arboretum – Arnold Arboretum, Massachusetts.
Edinburgh – Royal Botanic Gardens, Edinburgh.
Westonbirt – Westonbirt Arboretum, Gloucestershire.
Wisley – Royal Horticultural Society's Garden.
Others are usually given in full.

Authorities

IN THE PREPARATION of this Register we have consulted and compared a large number of leading authorities, the chief of which are:

W.J. Bean: *Trees and Shrubs Hardy in the British Isles.* (Eighth (revised) edition as so far published.)
Alfred Rehder: *Manual of Cultivated Trees and Shrubs Hardy in North America.* (Second edition.)
Donald Wyman: *Trees for American Gardens.*

A.F. Mitchell: *Conifers in the British Isles* and his *Field Guide to the Trees of Britain and Northern Europe.*
Dallimore and Jackson: *Handbook of Conifers.*
Hillier and Sons: *Manual of Trees and Shrubs.*
E.J.H. Corner: *The Natural History of Palms.*
William Flemer III: *Shade and Ornamental Trees.*

In nomenclature, where all are not in agreement, we have usually followed Bean, as being the most recent.

The Broadleaves

ACACIA
Wattle

The true acacia, not to be confused with the false "acacia" of popular speech (which is the totally different *Robinia*), only just qualifies for admission into these pages, for none resists a severe frost. But on the warmer fringes of the temperate zones its chosen species present splendid spectacles when, at the birth of the year, they display their foaming clusters of tiny, fluffy, yellow florets, often sweetly scented. In such areas as the French Riviera and southern California they are grown commercially on a large scale for florists' shops. In less kindly climes they are favourites for large greenhouses.

The only desirable acacias come from Australia and Tasmania. Evergreen, they are clothed with elegant, ferny, double-pinnate leafage, but in many species this is replaced after juvenility by a flat stalk, known as a phyllode, which

The feather-like leaves of Acacia dealbata.

continues to perform the functions of a leaf. Abundant sun is the wattle's prime need. Water is less important, for it has good resistance to drought. The less lime the better, though a modicum is tolerated. The wood is brittle, the roots shallow and the span of life restricted. The vernacular name derives from the fact that in Australia the long, pliant branches were used for wattle fences (Old English *wateel*).

Propagation is easy enough from seed or from heel cuttings in sand and peat with some bottom heat. Pruning, if necessary, is done after blooming.

Many wattles form no more than large shrubs and as such are outside our brief. Of the tree forms the following are the most favoured.

A. dealbata, the silver wattle, so-called because of the silvery down that coats the feathery foliage, is the most popular of all and is the main source of those fluffy golden sprays which we oddly call "mimosa" (a quite different plant). In its native Australia it becomes a very large tree and even in parts of Britain it can be of impressive stature. A tree of very fast growth and great beauty, its fragrant flowers associate charmingly with its delicate foliage. z9.

A. baileyana, the Cootamundra wattle. This is a small, exceptionally beautiful, round-headed tree, growing very fast and attaining 30ft or so. The steel-blue foliage may, in ideal conditions, become almost obliterated by the mass of deep golden blossoms. It is more tender than the silver wattle, but drought-hardy and a favourite in southern California. It is short-lived. z10.

A. longifolia, the Sydney golden wattle, is a small tree of about the same size. It develops phyllodes, from the axils of which emerge the slender flower clusters. It is widely planted in California and France and may be grown in the mildest parts of Britain. z10.

Two weeping acacias, both of maybe 30ft, attract our gaze. One is Rice's wattle, **A. riceana**, which is not a true weeper but picturesquely

Acacia riceana.

Acacia longifolia.

architected with slender, pliant, pendulous branches. It is armed with spiny phyllodes, from the axils of which spring little clusters of fluffy, sulphur florets. Admirable for training on pergolas and arbours as well as an open-ground tree. In its native Tasmania it grows beside streams. The other is **A. pendula**, the Weeping Myall. More definitely a weeper and quite willow-like, it becomes a pretty waterfall of soft yellow at flowering time. Both z10.

ACER
Maple

The maples, which spread their handsome and diverse forms over most of the Northern Hemisphere, are a very large genus, from the noble trees of North America and Europe, growing up to more than 100ft, to the elegant Japanese dwarfs. Hilliers of Winchester list some 180 species and varieties, but we can do no more here than make a studied selection of them and must regretfully omit the smaller shrubs, such as the beautiful *palmatum* and its varieties, and the useful *ginnala*.

The main characteristics of the maples are the winged "keys" (or samarae) of their seeds, which flutter to the ground like little helicopters, and their broad, bold leaves with prominent lobes, but the latter is a variable feature, for in *griseum* and *negundo* and others the leaves are compound (consisting of several leaflets), and in *carpinifolium* are just like the simple leaves of the hornbeam. Except in the red, the Norway and the Italian maples, and a few less familiar sorts, their small, clustered flowers are inconspicuous and we grow them for the opulence of their foliage and the majesty of their forms or for the embellishment of the garden scene by the graceful silhouettes and the tinctures of the smaller species. Some are happily adaptable to city settings and all display themselves gloriously in parks. Their repertoire of form and habit is brilliant, including some of the best columnar or otherwise compact trees for cities or private gardens.

For the splendour of the autumn foliage in which most of them are habited they are rivalled only by the nyssas and the liquidambars, though the richness of their colouring is seen at its best only in acid soils and far more vividly in North America than in Europe. In parts of the United States and Canada the red and the sugar maples, often growing in partnership, dominate large areas of the countryside, which, in imagination, they set on fire in the fall with their vivid tinctures.

A characteristic of several of the larger species is that they exude a milky sap, but in *saccharum* the sap is watery and from this sap maple sugar is made. Of the smaller species one of the most picturesque groups is found in the snake-bark maples, in which the coloured bark is engagingly patterned with white stripes and in which, as a rule, the leaves are less prominently lobed. These are grouped together at the end. Bark variations are seen also in the beautiful *griseum*.

All maples are easily cultivated in a fairly rich, moist soil and in a sunny or partially shaded position, though *negundo* is happy also in a dry one. The Norway Maple and the sycamore are

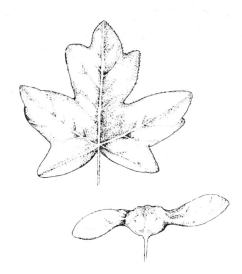

The field maple, Acer campestre.

Acer griseum.

both excellent for reclaiming degenerate ground. What pruning may be necessary should be done from late July to Christmas, for maples bleed if cut in the earlier months.

A. campestre is the field maple of Britain and northern Europe, often neglected, often chopped and laid as a hedge, often, like other European natives (and prophets), held in more honour in countries other than its own. A country lass indeed, but as an isolated specimen she reveals herself as a picturesque rounded tree, rarely more than 40ft high. A native of chalky soils, the field maple is quite at home in others and is excellent in towns and for factory sites. Its most celebrated occurrence is in the gardens of the old Imperial Palace of Schönbrunn, near Vienna, where it makes spectacular hedges 35ft high.

You will know the field maple by its small leaves, which have three widely spaced and rounded lobes, by its small keys spinning down with their wings outspread horizontally, by its grey-brown bark, broken up into squares and shallow fissures, and by the thronged clusters of twiglets that terminate its widespread limbs and serve to identify it in winter nakedness. You will know it also by the milky sap in its leaf-stalks when broken off. Among its several forms 'Postelense' is the most attractive, having golden leaves in spring. 'Schwerinii' has purple ones, which look effective against light backgrounds.

In southern Europe the field maple becomes replaced by the Montpelier maple, *A. monspessulanum*, and it has become popular in parts of America also. All z5.

A. cappadocicum This Asian, growing 50 to 60ft high, is to be recognised by the lobes of its leaves, which are drawn out to fine points like a mandarin's fingernails, the leaf-stalk milky when broken, and by its wide-angled seed keys. Older

trees throw up thickets of suckers. It is known best by some of its varieties, particularly the handsome 'Rubrum', in which the young leaves are blood-red and which reaches 77ft at Westonbirt. In 'Aureum' they are a bright golden yellow for several weeks, then green, then a chromatic yellow in autumn. In the attractive variety *sinicum*, which is smaller in all its parts (about 30ft high), the young leaves are copper-hued and the seed keys bright red. z6.

Of the few maples that are florally spectacular, perhaps the most remarkable is one bearing the forbidding label **A. diabolicum purpurascens**, the colourful "horned maple". This is a round-headed tree of up to 35ft, with pink-flushed bark and slender branches, sheeted from top to toe in April with hanging clusters of small flowers in rich tones of red. At the same time purple leaves burst out from their buds, expanding later into large, broadly-lobed, green blades, which redden in autumn. In the "devilish", broad-winged samarae, also purple at first, the nutlets arm themselves with stinging bristles and throw out two tiny, horn-like projections (which are the persisting styles of the flowers).

Captain Collingwood Ingram, after seeing the horned maple in flower in its native Japanese woodland, likened it to "the smouldering embers of a gigantic bonfire". It is thus a colourful tree of modest size which is very effective in a landscape or private garden. z5.

The senior of the species, *A. diabolicum* itself, has yellow flowers.

A. griseum, the paperbark maple, is one of the most beautiful and fascinating of all small trees, elegant in outline and gracious in bearing. Far too distinguished to be treated as one of a herd, it deserves to be planted in splendid isolation or widely spaced with others of its own kind, so that the beauty of each can be contemplatively admired. The leaves are very distinctive, having three quite separate leaflets, grey-blue on the underside, and in autumn they become dyed with the most glorious orange and scarlet hues. The most distinctive feature of *griseum*, however, is the manner in which the old bark peels back in papery flakes to reveal the brilliant cinnamon of the new bark below.

Few specimens of the paperbark maples are known to exceed 30ft, so that it is one of the choicest trees for private gardens. It is quite happy even in chalk, as seen in the late Sir Frederick Stern's chalk garden at Highdown in Sussex. Unfortunately its seed germinates very poorly, so *griseum* is scarce in commerce and not cheap. z5.

A. heldreichii A handsome and distinctive Balkan tree of medium size, with large, deeply-cleft and coarsely-toothed leaves that give it a resemblance to the sycamore. Normally limited to about 45ft. z5.

A. japonicum Not quite certain whether to become a tree or a shrub, this most distinguished and elegant maple, very diverse in its clothing and deportment, just qualifies for these pages, occasionally attaining 30ft. The leaf is round in general outline, but its edge is fretted as with pinking shears into many short, pointed lobes. Of its varieties, the most compelling in the composition of the garden picture is 'Aureum', the leaves of which, cut into eleven notches, are pale gold throughout the season if grown in partial shade. Restrained to 20ft, particularly effective in a setting of light woodland, or etched against a background of dark green, it gives light and life to any scene, but in full sun its tender-hued leaves are liable to scorch.

Quite different is the japonicum variety 'Vitifolium', remarkable for the splendour of its multi-coloured foliage in autumn and recognisable by its large leaves, which are 6in in diameter and with multiple notches as in 'Aureum'. It is faster growing than others of its kind. All z5.

A. lobelii An Italian species (or possibly a hybrid) much neglected in Britain but rated at its true value in the milder parts of the United States. Its great merit is that it assumes a narrow, columnar bearing, so that it is very handy for towns or for confined places. It grows very fast indeed and will reach 50ft, occasionally higher, as at Westonbirt and Edinburgh. The leaves are broad and five-lobed, each lobe drawn out to a fine and slightly twisted point, and the young bark is prominently striped. z7.

In **A. macrophyllum**, the Oregon maple, we find a big tree, occasionally 100ft high, with enormous leaves, sometimes a foot broad and deeply incised but of thin texture, and profusely

Acer lobelii.

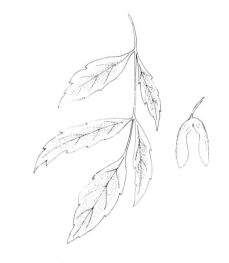

Acer negundo. '*Variegatum*'.

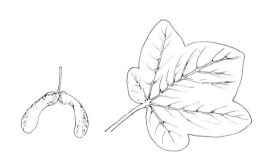

The rounded lobes of the Italian maple, Acer opalus.

ornamented with clusters of yellow, scented flowers that hang down in the manner of laburnum. Afterwards come dense, heavy bunches of large keys. The leaves droop also. An elegant tree, forming a tall, narrow dome, it is best in a somewhat moist atmosphere, as near the sea or a lake. z6.

A. negundo, the so-called 'box elder' (very odd) is an ultra-hardy tree (z2), prospering in very cold areas, in dry ones, and, unexpectedly, in hot ones also. To all but purists it is most popular, and justifiably so, in those of its forms that have variegated leaves, for they are highly decorative in the garden scene, embellishing it with light and grace-

ful foliage, obedient to the impulses of the wind. The true species, native to North America, may develop into a large and rather dull tree 60ft high, but the coloured and variegated forms are very rarely anything like so large. The elegant leaves, carried on long stalks, are sharply divided into three or five quite separate leaflets, not at all characteristic of maples at large.

The most popular variety is undoubtedly 'Variegatum', in which the leaflets are broadly margined with silvery white. In 'Elegans' the margin is bright yellow and in 'Auratum' the leaves are wholly yellow, retaining that colour all the summer and constituting one of the very best of the golden-leaved trees.

In all these eliminate at once any all-green shoots and any suckers.

A. opalus, the Italian maple, is distinctive for the abundance and showiness of its floral display. The flowers, of a good, clear yellow, are borne in large, crowded clusters (corymbs) on the leafless stems in April, to such good effect that it is one of the most ornamental of all early-flowering trees. Long, dangling bunches of samarae follow. In size it varies enormously from a big shrub to a 60ft tree. The leaves have three broad, rounded lobes and two small basal ones. z5.

A. platanoides, the Norway maple, is one of the great splendours of the genus, growing fairly fast to some 90ft and thrusting out its powerful limbs to form a most impressive mass. The thronged yellow flowers, almost as conspicuous as those of *opalus*, break out on the bare stems in April, visible a mile away. The large leaves have the characteristic maple form with five lobes, each lobe drawn out to several fine points, the whole having a distinctly spiky outline, and in the fall they age graciously to a primrose hue. The roots range close to the surface. The Norway maple is thus pre-eminently a tree for parks and for the large landscapes, but it also, where there is room, gives nobility to a townscape. It is utterly hardy (z3) and will prosper in almost any soil. Some of the finest specimens are to be found in Scotland, as at Dawyck and Keillour Castle, and it is a great success in America also.

The Norway maple has been the sire of many variations. None is really better than the primal form, but a few have their special virtues in various situations. Thus 'Columnare' and 'Erectum' declare their characters. The former is a broad column to about 50ft and nearly half as wide, and the latter, though it has larger leaves, is very much narrower, rarely more than 7ft after many years. Both are excellent for streets or to form a screen.

'Schwedleri' is a colourful, robust and compact maple, but rather slow to attain its 60ft. The buds

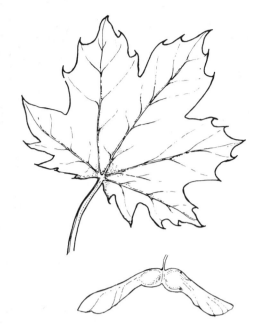

The Norway maple, Acer platanoides.

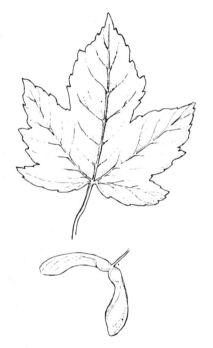

The sycamore, Acer pseudoplatanus.

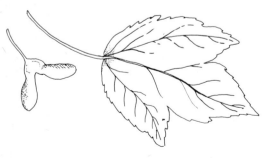

The red maple, Acer rubrum.

are bright red and the leaves that emerge are encarnadined purple. A wholly reliable tree, much favoured by public authorities. The German 'Reitenbachii' behaves in much the same way, but the young leaves are red and the tree smaller.

The plump 'Globosum' has a character all its own. It makes a short, dome-shaped tree, twice as wide as high, its out-thrust bulk crowded with foliage, opulent and cheerful.

'Summershade', an American variety, also has a strong individuality. It is a fast, elegant tree, tapering to a pronounced leader and has the special quality of prospering in hot localities. The large, green leaves have a leathery and durable texture.

'Drummondii' looks very attractive when its young leaves open with a yellow flush, later turning green with a white margin, but it is liable to revert to its ancestral all-green.

A few Norway maples are robed in foliage that is ruddy or coppery all summer. The best is 'Crimson King', a great favourite, raised in France, and certainly spectacular against a blue sky in spring, but this bright crimson fades towards the end of summer to a less exciting purple-brown. It is a better tree for colour than the dusky 'Goldsworth Purple'.

Other varieties of the Norway maple bear leaves that are deeply incised or lacerated, somewhat in the manner of the dwarf Japanese maples. The best of these, but very slow, is 'Lorbergii', a small, broad tree; or, if you want a curiosity, grow the eagle's claw maple, 'Laciniatum', a slender, upright tree.

A. pseudoplatanus, the celebrated English sycamore or pseudo-plane, is one of our grandest trees, often exceeding 100ft and, when in isolation, developing into a huge dark-green dome, broader than high, impressive in bulk and carriage. One of the quickest off the mark, it reaches 35ft in its first ten years. The finest sycamores in the world, we apprehend, are grown in Scotland (where they are known as "planes"). Plenty exceed 100ft, but perhaps the most historic of all is the "Reformation sycamore" which was planted during the Reformation in the sixteenth century at Newbattle Abbey, near Edinburgh, and now measures 90ft with a trunk girth of 16ft 4in.

A nuisance in towns, where its large leaves and their tough foot stalks clog drainage and hinder the motorist in the autumn, and no less a nuisance in small gardens, the sycamore is essentially a parkland tree if to be seen in its full splendour, yet, so tough is it, that it readily fulfils the harshest utilitarian tasks and is one of the finest of all shelter plants against salt-laden gales along the coast. It scatters its right-angled samarae with boundless liberality, and the little nut-seeds take root eagerly

anywhere. In wartime London the bombed ruins quickly became spinneys of sycamore.

The English "sycamore" and the French "sycomore" have a curious derivation. From the shape of its leaf it was formerly thought to be the fig *Ficus sycomorus*, which Zaccheus climbed to see Jesus over the heads of the multitude. So Zaccheus's tree lent its name to the pseudo-plane. "Sycamore" occurs several times in the Bible. In America the name is often applied to *Platanus occidentalis*.

The pseudo-plane has a pale grey bark, which peels off in large flakes in the manner of the true plane. The broad leaves, five-lobed and variably toothed, have the typical maple construction, but do not blaze into the exquisite chromatics of the other maples. The flowers, of a mustard yellow, tumble from the branches in abundant drooping bunches. z5.

The sycamore has produced a large number of varieties, of which we select the following as the most handsome.

'Atropurpureum' (or 'Spaethii'), the purple sycamore, is a large and regal creature. The leaf-blade is green on the upper surface and purple below, so that, when tossed by the wind, it ripples with a fine blending of colours. 'Worleei', raised in Germany, is a very useful variety of only moderate size but mantled in richly golden leaves for a long season before turning green, better in this respect than the old 'Corstorphinense'.

Several other sycamores have various leaf mottlings, stripes, or colour suffusions, but the jewel of them all is 'Brilliantissimum'. In this the young leaves are a lovely soft-pink, then old-gold, then bronze-green. Slow of growth and not often seen more than 20ft high, it needs to be grown in partial shade, unless in a damp climate zone, as in the lovely specimen at Knightshayes, Devon. 'Prinz Handjery' is a pretty little tree with a rather wider, more open crown, but of similar personality, the leaves, when young, being golden above and purple below.

A. rubrum, the red or Canadian maple, is one of the great glories of North America, where it often exceeds 100ft, colouring superbly in autumn where the soil is acid and moist, but more soberly in other soils, though in other respects it is highly tolerant of diverse conditions. It justifies its name by its rich red flowers, which profusely adorn the bare branches in early April in dense clusters. The leaves have inconspicuous lobes, usually only three with a silvery reverse, and the pale-grey bark is seen to good advantage if the trunk is cleared of its lower branches to 8ft or more gradually as the tree develops. Growth is very fast. In Britain the tallest specimen, at Westonbirt, measures 75ft. z3.

There are several selected clones of the red

RIGHT Acer rubrum, *the red maple, in the garden of Mr William Flemer II in Princeton, New Jersey. This is the parent tree of 'October Glory'. The smaller tree with the grey bole is* Halesia carolina.

maple. 'Schlesingeri' is noted for the extra brilliance of its autumn colour. 'October Glory', raised at the Princeton Nurseries, has lustrous foliage of vivid crimson, displayed in any type of soil. 'Columnare' and 'Scanlon' are close-packed column, valuable for constricted places.

A. saccharinum, the huge and splendid silver maple, owes its vernacular name to the silvery down on the reverse of the long-stalked leaf-blade, picturesquely revealed when the leaves, cleft into long, slender, elongated pointed lobes, are ruffled by wind to contrast with the tender green of the obverse. In autumn they blaze in scarlet and gold. This tree is extra hardy and without doubt a dominant choice in any cold locality that can accommodate its ample proportions, for it grows at express speed, reaching 25ft in ten years and finally well over 100ft in North America and almost as much in England and Germany (a full 100ft at Westonbirt). Choose a fairly moist loam for it in a place not exposed to severe winds. It likes the riverside. The wings of the samarae are broad and shaped like a sickle.

In its native country the silver maple is less popular than it was, because of the propensity of its timber to split in high storms, but in Europe it is the most successful of all American maples, quickly forming a broad-crowned tree, especially in Germany, where it surpasses all other deciduous trees. Its natural form is varied in the handsome, broadly columnar 'Pyramidale' and another good variation is *laciniatum*, which has deeply cut lobes on pendulous branches. z3.

A. saccharum, the sugar maple, is a large and spectacular tree, another of the glories of the North American scene in autumn, when it bursts out into a blaze of crimson, scarlet, gold and orange in different specimens. It grows pretty fast, reaching 20ft in its first ten years and going on to 110ft or more. Its aspect in spring and summer closely resembles that of the Norway maple, but the points of its leaves are blunt, not spiky, and it is particularly famous for its watery (not milky) sap, from which maple syrup is manufactured. A native of a cool, moist climate, it languishes in hot ones. In nurseries it is usually raised from seed, so that there is a good deal of variation in habit. A few selected clones have been perpetuated, those that please us most being 'Temple's Upright' and 'Newton Sentry', names which sufficiently describe their deportment.

In Britain the sugar maple is not generally a great success, but it is happy in northern Scotland and there are specimens at Westonbirt and Blenheim Palace of about 70ft. z3 to z7.

Closely allied to the sugar maple, and by some regarded as a variety of it, is the black maple, *A. nigrum*, so called because of its darker (and more

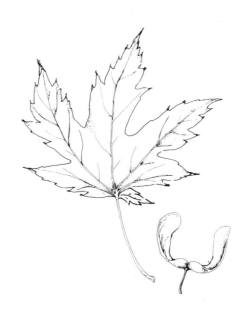

The silver maple, Acer saccharinum.

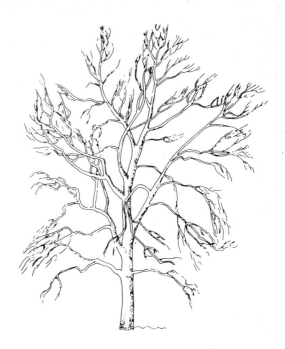

Winter aspect of the silver maple.

furrowed) bark and rather darker leaves. Here also we have a good erect variety in 'Slavin's Upright'. z3.

THE SNAKE-BARK MAPLES

These, having their own particular characters and uses, can conveniently be grouped together. They display their decorative limbs most effectively in winter nakedness, planted on the edge of light woodland and among contrasting forms.

In **A. capillipes** the young bark is red before turning brown and becoming streaked with white. Red is also in the young leaves, the leaf-stalks and the mature keys. The leaves are faintly three-lobed and a rich, shining green. 30ft. z5.

A. davidii, of 45ft, is diverse in character, separate seed strains having been imported from China. The young bark is green or mauve, becoming decorated with white stripes, and the leaves are only obscurely lobed, if at all. The most commonly seen form, introduced by George Forrest, is a loose and open tree with large, polished, leathery, very dark-green leaves (6in by 4in); that introduced by Ernest Wilson being a low, spreading tree with small, pale-green leaves. z6.

Though it rarely exceeds 20ft, we must include **A. grosseri** because of its much larger and more imposing natural variety *hersii*, which reaches 40ft at Westonbirt. The bark is olive-green, striped white, the leaves large and partially lobed, the keys very large, dangling in thick clusters. z6.

A. pensylvanicum is the very hardy moosewood, of about 35ft. The young wood is smooth

The sugar maple, Acer saccharum.

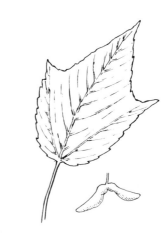

Acer capillipes.

PREVIOUS PAGES, LEFT *The silver maple,* Acer saccharinum.
PREVIOUS PAGES, RIGHT Acer pseudoplatanus *'Brilliantissimum' in spring.*
LEFT *The horse chestnut,* Aesculus hippocastanum.

ABOVE *A snake-bark maple,* Acer davidii.
BELOW *The unlobed leaves of* Acer davidii.

Acer pensylvanicum.

and jade green before becoming grey and streaked, and the leaves are large, broad and dangling, with three long, tapering lobes. A spindly and sparsely branched tree, best seen in light woodland. There is a rare variety in which the winter twigs are brilliant red. z3.

A. rufinerve is very similar to the moosewood, but distinguished from it and others by its grey and pink bark and by the slate-blue flush of its young growth. 30ft. z5.

AESCULUS
Horse Chestnut or Buckeye

The horse chestnuts are among the handsomest of our deciduous trees, adding to their bold foliage the splendour of their great bouquets of flowers in a profusion not equalled by any other tree of their size. Characteristically, they are very large, broadly spreading trees, but several are quite small and even, as in *A. parviflora* and others, no more than large shrubs. Most species are natives of North America, but what are usually considered the most lordly originate from Europe and Asia. The generic name is the ancient Latin appellation for an oak or other nut-bearing tree.

The leaves of the horse chestnuts are large, of rough texture and bold design, being arranged in digitate or finger-like fashion, like the podgy, outspread fingers of an enormous hand. The fingers (or lobes) are usually spatulate and may number anything from three to nine, but are usually five. The flowers, borne in May in most species, display themselves in bold pyramidal trusses that evoke the image of the multitudinous candles of a giant Christmas tree. Well-read children will remember that it was the horse chestnut which kept its "candles burning" to light the fairies safely home after their dance.

The true or "common" horse chestnut is *A. hippocastanum* and one associates most of them with those big, tough-skinned, lustrous-brown "conkers" beloved of combative small boys, encased in a fleshy, somewhat spiky sheath, but not all aesculus are so provided. In contrast, the edible fruit of the sweet or Spanish chestnut, which is *Castanea sativa*, is distinguished by its bristly, hedgehog-like sheath, clustered among the single, uncomplicated leaves.

All the aesculus are of the easiest culture in temperate climates from Zones 3 to 10, provided they are given a good, deep, loamy soil not liable to dry out; drought can be very damaging. The true species, and even some of the hybrids, are easily raised from the big seeds, if sown as soon as they fall. Growth is fairly quick. They transplant well up to about 14ft as a rule and prosper in towns, but should be carefully sited, for, apart from the conkers, there are heavy falls of bud-scales in spring, spent flowers in summer and tough leaves in autumn. The leaves are difficult to compost.

Thus the best use for the larger horse chestnuts is in parks, in select isolated positions in towns and large gardens and, above all, in boulevards and broad avenues, where they have no peer. Celebrated examples are seen in many places, notably Paris and in the parks of Hampton Court Palace, a favourite resort of Londoners on Chestnut Sunday. Particularly good choices for such avenues are *hippocastanum*, *indica* and *plantierensis*.

For all places and purposes where the scene is spacious, priority of choice is accorded to **Aesculus hippocastanum.** Though seemingly belittled (in Britain) as the "common" horse chestnut, this is really *the* horse chestnut, the original one so called, emperor of them all, lifting its imperial head in time to 100ft or more and illuminated with an enormous candelabrum, each candle perhaps a foot tall. Its origin has been traced to the mountains of Greece and Albania, but the seed first came to western Europe from Turkey, in the time of Queen Elizabeth I, and at once proved itself hardy in England and northern Europe and later in the northern American settlements also. Its specific name is a mongrel Latin combination of "horse" and "chestnut" and derives from the curious story that the Turks used to feed the nuts to ailing horses. Self-respecting horses today seem to have no enthusiasm for them, but deer and cattle certainly have.

The bark of this original horse chestnut is a

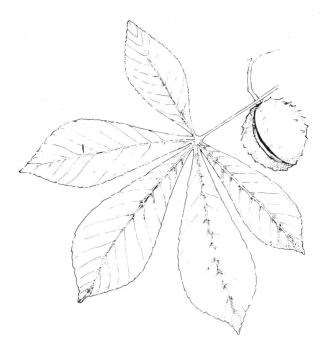

The "common" horse chestnut, Aesculus hippocastanum*; leaf and opening fruit.*

greyish-brown, breaking up into little squares as it ages and later becoming ribbed. Young trees grow a good 2ft a year. The big digitate leaves have five to seven fat, spatulate fingers, which are stalkless. Unlike most other trees, their autumn colour is better in Britain than in America, becoming an orange-tinted rust. In winter the plump, brown buds of next year's leaves become encased in sticky sheaths, which are one of its recognition signals, and if you put the twigs in water the leaves unfurl their crinkled emerald lobes.

The flowers are white, with a coloured eye which is at first yellow and then red. The conkers follow, tumbling like showers of garnets from an imperial hand. There is, however, a variety of very special merit with flowers which, being double, not only last an extra long time but also are sterile, so that there is no litter of conkers. This excellent variety (the best of several) is named 'Baumanii' after its discoverer, who found it as a sport of the true species in Switzerland.

The oldest living horse chestnuts in Britain, and still in fine shape, were planted in Surrey in 1664. Large specimens sometimes throw out erect, "epicormic" shoots from the branches. These may spoil the balance of the tree and should be cut out while still small. z3 to z10.

A very close runner-up to the common horse chestnut, and even superior in some situations, is **A. indica**, the Indian horse chestnut. This is a smaller tree of graceful and aristocratic bearing.

Everything about it is slender – its outline, its leaflets and its candles, which are not lit until late June, their florets white with pink and yellow tints. The tree grows to 60ft in England, much more in India. It is not, however, as hardy as its Greek brother, the young shoots being somewhat susceptible to late frosts, and it has a more positive need for a damp climate, though it prospers in chalk. The conkers are glossy black.

Altogether, the Indian horse chestnut is a grand tree for avenues and parks. Some fine specimens quickly catch the eye of the visitor to the Royal Botanic Gardens at Kew, where there is a new, very attractive clone, with very large flowers and olive-green leaves, named 'Sydney Pearce' after a deputy curator. z7.

Our next choice might well be **A. × carnea**, the so-called red chestnut, though its flowers are really deep pink. It will grow to 75ft, branching close to the ground and forming a dense canopy. Large burrs often form on the bark and these should be left alone, for disease may follow the knife. It has not the majesty of *hippocastanum* and is, perhaps, a rather over-rated tree, except in its very handsome French offspring 'Briotii', a clone which delights the eye with its large, exhilarating, ruby-red candles and its opulent branches sweeping right along the ground. The leaves are dark and crinkly, the leaflets overlapping. It has the great merit of only occasionally producing any fruits. Altogether it is one of the finest avenue or parkland trees. z3.

A. chinensis This rare and elegant Chinese horse chestnut, with long, slender, white trusses, may attain 80ft if it survives spring frosts in its adolescence. A tree listed as *A. wilsonii* is almost identical, but has larger leaves. z5.

A. californica declares its origin. A distinctive tree (sometimes only a shrub) of low, very wide-spreading habit, some 35ft high on a short trunk, densely cloaked in small leaves with a metallic tint. The white or blush-pink flowers are scented and generously produced in dense, slender candles from June to August. z7.

A. flava (or *octandra*) is the sweet or yellow buckeye, a big tree widely distributed in nature throughout the United States. The yellow flower candles are rather short and the husk of the nuts is smooth. The leaflets are slim, pointed and elegant. It flourishes in the milder parts of Europe, including England, and grows to 100ft (85ft at Kew). A pink form grows wild in West Virginia. z3.

A. glabra The Ohio buckeye. A small 30ft tree of handsome form and foliage, a brilliant orange in autumn, but let down by its undistinguished flowers, which are a pallid yellowish-green. Has a rugged, much-fissured bark, but the

variety *leucodermis* is remarkable for its smooth, off-white bark when young. z3.

A. × plantierensis The pink horse chestnut. A grand and spectacular tree with very big candles of pale pink. Not as big a specimen as *hippocastanum* but bigger than *carnea*, which were its two parents. It produces no nuts. Often listed as a variety of *carnea*, but Bean elevates it to the standing of a hybrid group. z3.

The Indian horse chestnut, Aesculus indica.

A clone of the red horse chestnut, Aesculus × carnea *'Briotii'.*

For something almost unique we could go to **A. neglecta**, in which we find the uncommon variety 'Erythroblastos' ("red bud"). Its leaves often open a bright pink, mature a golden-green and age to orange. Grows to 30ft, and more. z5.

AILANTHUS
Tree of Heaven

Seldom seen at its best, gaunt and skeletal in winter, **Ailanthus altissima** is nonetheless a very dependable jack-of-all-trades in awkward spots. Tough, tenacious, disease-free, fast, thriving in rough and derelict soils, it puts up with any amount of pollution and even allows its feet to be washed in sea water. Very good for reclamation of spent industrial sites.

No wonder, then, that we see it used so often in towns (especially in America), where it throws a dappled shade from its large, loosely-borne, pinnate, sumach-like leaves, which may be anything up to a yard long. It grows readily to 70ft (reaching maturity in 55 years) and, when in isolation, can become a noble specimen of shapely, oval profile. Indeed, a specimen at Endsleigh, Devonshire, measures 95ft.

The dog-Latin of its generic name is a perversion of the Chinese, meaning "strong enough to reach heaven". Female plants only should be grown, for the flowers of the male stink. The female bears large, pyramidal clusters of flowers in June, followed by pretty, winged, fluttering seed-envelopes rather like those of the maples.

Sometimes one sees the tree of heaven cut to the ground every spring, when it throws up a sheaf of vigorous new shoots. If these are reduced to a single stem it will bear enormous leaves and look rather like a palm-tree. In Oxford University Botanic Gardens you can see a towering specimen planted in 1800 and a cut-back specimen hard by. z4.

See also under *Cedrela*, a better tree in some conditions.

ALMOND See under PRUNUS

ALBIZIA

Albizia julibrissin, the Korean "silk tree", is a small, dainty, flat-topped tree that looks like a pink acacia, having the same sort of delicate, filigree foliage and tiny powder puffs in July and August, followed by flat pea-pods. Growing to about 30ft, it is one of the very best for resisting city pollution. Superb in southern Europe, but in Britain rarely a success outside the southern counties. 'Rosea' is a brighter pink, smaller, rather hardier variety. z6. Wherever the mimosa fungus may be rife, as in the southern United States, the cultivars 'Charlotte' and 'Tryon' can be grown. z7.

ALNUS
Alder

The alders, formerly made into charcoal for gunpowder, are of particular value on the banks of rivers and ponds and in other wet soils, though some will flourish just as well in ordinary garden conditions. Indeed, the three species that we mention are good even in industrial areas. Usually they have a slender, lightly-branched silhouette, dressed with small, oval or rotund leaves and decorated with catkins, the female catkin turning into a firm growth like a cone, known as a strobilus. Their carriage is given elegance if the lower branches are pruned away, at the end of summer.

The outstanding species is **A. cordata**, the Italian alder, a large and splendid tree of conical shape, with bright, glistening foliage, growing rapidly to 80ft or so. Though happiest near water, it will succeed on drier places also, even in chalk. It has been much used to provide the piles upon which Venice is built and is a fine roadside tree. z5.

Foliage and strobili of the common alder, Alnus glutinosa.

The tree of heaven, Ailanthus altissima.

Few other alders are really garden-worthy, but **A. glutinosa**, the English "common" alder, marked by sticky buds and twigs, shining, pear-shaped leaves and almost black bark, is valuable for planting in boggy places and elsewhere to stop erosion, growing 90ft in 80 years. z3. Its offspring 'Imperialis' is lobed in cut-leaf, feather-like foliage.

A. incana, the grey alder, extra hardy, the lower surface of its leaves coated with a grey down, serves well for places that are very cold as well as wet and is very valuable for the reclamation of degenerate soil. It grows 60ft in 60 years. z2.

AMELANCHIER
Snowy Mespilus or Serviceberry

This is a pretty race that consists mainly of shrubs, but with a few small trees, giving a very fleeting but prodigal display of snowy masses on naked branches in early spring, and a colourful one of foliage in the fall. Very hardy, they are best suited by damp soils and look well on the edges of woodland. The nomenclature has a very confused history.

Of the tree forms, the one usually grown is generally, but wrongly, called *A. canadensis*. Its legitimate name is now **A. lamarckii.** This is a

pretty tree of 25ft, on which the leaves unfurl bronze-pink in April below clusters of tiny, white stars which are held erect, smothering the tree for perhaps ten days. z4.

According to Bean the genuine *canadensis* is a shrub frequenting the bogs of North America.

AMUR CORK See PHELLODENDRON

APRICOT See under PRUNUS

ARBUTUS
Strawberry Tree

Perhaps the best of our evergreen broadleaf trees, certainly so in the glorious *Arbutus menziesii*. The arbutus, however, are not quite as hardy as we should like and are slow starters, having to be planted out from a pot while very small. The foliage is small, dark green, glossy and abundant, the trusses of flowers resemble those of the lily of the valley and the fruit that follows looks rather like a small strawberry. The trunks, which usually fork above ground level, are delightfully tinted, so that the whole tree presents a handsome picture of broadly bushy build. The fruit is edible but not very palatable; in fact the specific name *unedo* is hybrid Latin for "I eat one only". All except the "Madrona" will prosper in limy

soils as well as in acid ones. All z7.

Fortunately all the strawberry trees respond well to the pruning saw and knife. Thus the lower branches can be amputated to reveal a good stretch of the handsome bark. So also any branches, or even the main stem, can be cut hard back after damage by storm or by severe frost. As for most evergreens, April is the time.

The four usually cultivated are:

A. andrachne, the small Grecian strawberry tree. White flowers in spring, small smooth-skinned orange-red "strawberries" later. The old chestnut bark sheds to reveal the new one of pale orange. Tender when young, becoming hardier if planted in a well-chosen position. Rare in cultivation and seldom more than 25ft high.

When *andrachne* became espoused to *unedo* a beautiful child was born in **A. × andrachnoides** and it proved pretty hardy. Plants sold as *andrachne* are usually this one. It has a bark of a deep, glowing ruby or tawny orange, and the flowers come in late autumn or late winter. The fruits are red. A lovely tree in all its parts, it may attain 35ft in the most favourable spots. It grows well in chalk.

A. menziesii is the gorgeous "Madrona", growing wild over a large tract from British Columbia to California. Its vivid cinnamon-red or tawny-orange bark, its burnished leaves, ice-blue on the reverse, and its erect pyramids of

Arbutus × andrachnoides, *one of the "strawberry trees", in flower.*

The Madrona, Arbutus menziesii.

The most familiar strawberry tree, Arbutus unedo.

Arbutus unedo *in fruit.*

white flowers in April, followed in summer by fruits that vary from orange to crimson, make it a stunning spectacle, the essence of elegant strength. In its native territory it soars up to 100ft, in Britain merely to 60, growing about a foot a year when established.

The Madrona needs an acid soil and is reckoned the least hardy of the strawberry trees, but will resist several degrees of frost when established. It is pretty safe in the southern counties of England, and on the mild west coast. Propagation is by seed.

A. unedo, sometimes called the Killarney strawberry tree, though native to the Mediterranean also, is probably the most generally grown arbutus, being the hardiest of the lot and resisting 30° of frost. It has the engaging habit of displaying its drooping, white flowers, which come out in the autumn, at the same time as the rough-skinned

"strawberries" that result from the flowers of the previous year. The tree grows about 15ft in 25 years and may reach 40ft in 100 years, forming a dense, rounded crown. The bark is chestnut-brown, and becomes cracked with age. Prune, if necessary, in late April. There are a few varieties or forms, the most desirable being the pink *rubra*.

ASH See FRAXINUS

ASPEN See POPULUS

BAY See LAURUS

BEECH See FAGUS

BETULA
Birch

Found wild over large areas of the earth's surface for millions of years, the birches, which derive their name from the Old English *birce*, still paint the countryside with a brush of particular delicacy, and, when the forest air is alive with the "lisp of leaves and ripple of rain", they still whisper their devotions with undiminished faith. Much have they seen and much endured, surviving the rigours of the last Ice Age, and prospering still in the harshest conditions. You will find the little, shrubby *Betula nana* growing cheerfully within the Arctic Circle and the silver birch, the hairy and the canoe-bark will overcome even the handicaps of industrial sites. They excel at the waterside, in which their reflection has a dream-like quality, as well as in dry, sandy heathlands. All soils come alike to them, though they do not relish unalloyed chalk. Indeed, there is almost no situation which they will fail to adorn with their feminine grace and poise. None does so more elegantly than our native *B. pendula* and well did Coleridge proclaim it as the "most beautiful of forest trees".

The beauty of the birches lies not only in their coloured barks, but also in their small, widely spaced leaves carried on thin, whippy branches which, in combination, result in an open, airy crown that admits plenty of light and etches the background with delicate tracery. Though their roots are often said to be "hungry", grass and many flowering plants prosper beneath their branches and a silver birch springing up from a carpet of heathers is one of nature's most alluring pictures. Their life, alas, is short, seldom exceeding man's own allotted span, but they regenerate in abundance by their winged seeds. These seeds result from a mating of the minute flowers in

their catkins, the male catkins displayed in dangling clusters, like lambs' tails, the females short and stubby.

The most characteristic feature of the birches, however, and the one which perhaps most impresses itself on the landscape, is their bark. Most of us think of them as having a gleaming white bark, and so they have in *pendula*, *papyrifera*, *pubescens* and *jaquemontii*. But we can have sherry-coloured barks in *utilis*, pink in *albo-sinensis*, cream in *ermanii*, dark grey in the water-loving *nigra*, orange in others and an aromatic bark in *lenta*. These colourings are, however, subject to some variations.

Propagation by seed is easy but may result in mongrels. Plant out the saplings when very young, if possible in fairly close clusters against a background of evergreens. Birches bleed profusely if cut at the wrong time and any pruning that might be necessary – as particularly to remove some of the lowest branches and so expose a good length of trunk – should be done between August and Christmas. In Europe birches are reasonably free from troubles, but in North America borer insects often afflict them, especially the species of European lineage.

We choose the following species:

B. albo-sinensis is a beauty from China, grows to about 70ft and has a shaggy bark of brilliant orange, which peels off in successive sheets, each glistening with a silvery-green bloom. Its natural variety *septentrionalis*, has bark of a duller orange, peeling to fawn-pink, sparsely clothed with very large, slender leaves. z5.

B. jaquemontii, a big Himalayan. If the specimen is a good one, this is the most dramatic of all for its bark, when it is a dazzling chalk-white, but specimens may be seen in cream, ochre or pink. This species is a great favourite of photographers, especially when clad in the soft gold foliage of autumn. z7.

Asia has given us several other beautiful birches. **B. costata** is a smooth creamy-white, tinted gold through all its branches, fascinating in winter and 100ft high. **B. ermanii** is somewhat similar, but tinted pink and reaching only 60ft. Both z5.

Alone among the birches we name here, **B. lenta**, the cherry birch, has no rich colour in its bark, which is grey-brown, with some chestnut zones as in the cherry. If you care to chew it, it is sweet and aromatic. An oil is extracted from it. What is more important is that it is a handsome tree of denser foliage than most birches, pyramidal when young, round-headed later. It grows to 70ft and colours extra well in autumn. z3.

B. lutea the yellow birch, is the biggest of the North Americans, running up to more than 100ft,

RIGHT *The silver birch,* Betula pendula, *in winter.*

The cream and pink bark of Betula ermanii.

in which the old, chestnut bark peels back to reveal the gleaming amber or deep gold of the young. A very handsome birch with relatively large leaves, up to 4½in long. z3.

B. maximowicziana, another giant, broad and strong, possibly reaching 100ft, is from Japan. This triumphs in cold, exposed places, in dry, sandy soils and over chalk if well cushioned by other soil. Its large, heart-shaped leaves may be up to 6in long and are borne on an orange bark that ultimately turns grey. z5.

B. papyrifera, the paper birch or canoe birch, is one of the most striking of all trees and familiar (by inference) to small boys of all ages as the material for the canoes and wigwams of North American Indians. The bark usually becomes glistening white, smooth and waterproof and it strips off in large sheets; but this snowy patina is slow to develop. The leaves are a dark, matt green on stout, hairy stalks. It makes a large tree of perhaps 90ft (nearly 100ft in a specimen in Maine) and is another dweller of the waterside but is extremely versatile, being happy also in dry, sandy soils, in industrial areas and even over chalk if there is a good coverage of other soil. It does not, however, care for hot climates and is unhappy in southerly latitudes.

The crown of the canoe birch is commonly very open and sparse, so that, overall, it is not quite as good a tree as *pendula*; but, prospering even as far north as the frozen wastes of Hudson's

Bay, it is a prime choice for any cold and exposed position. Nor is it so liable to be plagued by borers. In nature it keeps close company with conifers, especially the white pine, and the association of its silvered stems with the dark green of the conifers is a thrilling spectacle. z2 to z7.

B. pendula, the silver birch, is in common estimation the best and most graceful of all birches, taken overall. The white bark, mottled with dark patches, the disposition of the slender branches, the tremulous small leaves and the gently drooping tips combine to make the silver birch a well balanced tree of the most graceful poise; and in forests the multitude of white trunks, often growing in companionable clumps from seeds that have floated down together, creates a sense of peace and remoteness and is of particular beauty in the winter. It prospers almost anywhere, in damp or dry soils, in acid or limy ones, in cold and bleak ones and on industrial sites. Its elegance is as beautifully displayed in quite small gardens as in the great birch forests of Finland, by the waterside or on high moorland. In parts of North America, alas, it is often preyed upon by boring insects.

A native of Britain and of Northern Europe, *B. pendula* reaches 25ft in 15 years and 60ft in about 60 years, when, in the milder countries, it begins to die. It has several excellent variations, of which quite the best is 'Dalecarlica', the Swedish birch. A tall, slender, graceful tree, growing to 90ft in Perthshire, it is known by its prettily lobed leaves on elegantly drooping branch tips. In 'Tristis' (or 'Elegans') we have a slender, erect

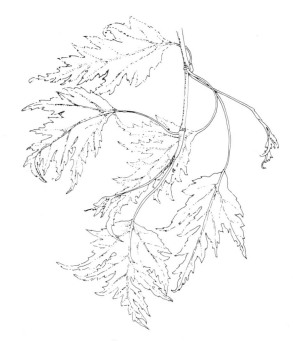

The Swedish birch, Betula pendula *'Dalecarlica'.*

tree with twisted branches drooping sharply, not at all "sad". In 'Youngii' we have a tree adequately expressed by its popular name of Young's weeping birch, a beautiful mushroom-shaped tree when well trained, 25ft high and colourful in autumn. All z5.

B. pubescens, the hairy or white birch, is no beauty but is useful for wet places and is of extreme hardiness in its natural variety *carpatica*, which does well in Iceland but in such latitudes is usually seen as a large shrub. z2.

B. utilis, the Himalayan birch, is a handsome tree of up to 60ft or so, in which the bark, which peels in horizontal flakes, varies considerably according to the provenance of the seed. It may be golden-brown, mahogany or nearly chocolate as at Westonbirt, or, as in the lovely specimen at Grayswood, Surrey, pale cream with a pink flush. In the variety *prattii* it may be bright pink. z7.

BOX ELDER See *Acer negundo*

BROUSSONETIA

Where a soil is poor, sterile, gravelly or otherwise unpropitious, the paper mulberry, *B. papyrifera*, is just the thing. Of neat habit, it grows to 45ft with dense, variable, irregularly lobed, rather coarse foliage and small red fruits on the female trees. In China the bark is used for making paper and in the Polynesian islands for cloth. A venerable specimen can be seen near the Governor's Palace in Williamsberg, Virginia. A good town tree. z6.

BUCKEYE See AESCULUS

Broussonetia papyrifera.

CARPINUS
Hornbeam

The hornbeams, so often mistaken for beeches (*Fagus*), owe their vernacular English name to their old Anglo-Saxon one, which meant "the horny or hard-wooded tree", their timber being very tough, durable, resistant to abrasion, yet not difficult to work. Obviously this name applied at first to the hornbeam that was native to southeast Britain and Europe, which is *Carpinus betulus*, but by association became applied also to the species from the Orient and from North America.

However impressive the beech may be, especially when robed in copper or purple, the hornbeam is at least as good. It will prosper in any reasonable soil, including heavy, wet clays and, as a rule, has a more erect carriage. Visually, the hornbeam differs from the beech in three main features: the leaf is saw-edged and deeply ribbed or corrugated by its sunken veins, the young bark is faintly striped and later deeply fissured, not smooth and skin-tight, and in autumn the branches are laden with their scaly nuts, hanging in dense, leafy bunches, showing kinship with the hazels. In isolation the European or "common" hornbeam (as called in Britain) is suitable only for large, open landscapes, which it embellishes with its sturdy grace, but in less ample spaces the oriental or American species are more suitable. We select the following species:

C. betulus, the "common" hornbeam, is a lowland tree of valley levels. We have noted its overall resemblance to the beech, but it also has some affinities with the birch; hence its specific name. Its growth will average a foot a year up to its ultimate 70 or 80ft on a grey trunk, often beautifully and curiously fluted. The growth at first is rather upright, but it then fans out until the older branches are about horizontal, with drooping terminal twigs. The leaves are relished by some mammals and the little nuts, unless borne away on the wind by their three-pointed wings, are equally relished by birds, squirrels and mice. When the autumn air sharpens, the tree becomes alive with flocks of small birds. In our forefathers' days, as may still be seen on old, high-branched specimens in Epping Forest and elsewhere, the hornbeam was often pollarded to provide poles and its timber was also used for ox yokes, mill wheels and many other purposes; it is still used in the working parts of pianos. It transplants well up to 15ft or so.

Again like the beech, the hornbeam makes a superlative hedge, dense and sturdy, its leaves defying the winter with their russet shroud, not quite so rich a colour, indeed, but more closely woven. Likewise, it is first-class for pleaching and

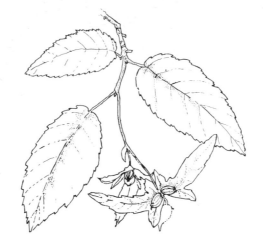

The hornbeam, Carpinus betulus.

as such is seen at its finest in the celebrated quincunx at Hidcote Manor in Gloucestershire. For all such purposes clip it back at the end of July.

Several variations of the common hornbeam are to be found in the erect 'Fastigiata' (or 'Pyramidalis'), a fine tree of formal carriage and excellent for streets, the 'Pendula' and several cut-leaved forms, such as 'Incisa' and 'Asplenifolia'. z5.

Other hornbeams are usually smaller. Thus the graceful American **C. caroliniana** is a bushy tree about half the size of *betulus*, but is extremely hardy, with a well-muscled trunk and fine autumn colours. Known as the ironwood or blue "beech", its wood is extremely tough. z2.

C. japonica is a handsome wide-spreading, broadly pyramidal tree, averaging 40ft in height, with long, tapering, deeply wrinkled leaves and densely crowded fruit-clusters. z4.

C. orientalis is a pretty tree of only 30ft, distinguished by its small leaves, its purple-tinted bark streaked with buff and the bushiness of its fruit clusters, explained by its leaf-like bracts. z5.

Scarcely to be distinguished from the hornbeam is its close cousin the **Ostrya**, the hop-hornbeam, which we place here for convenience. The dangling clusters of nuts are less leafy and look just like bunches of hops. In *O. carpinifolia* (50ft) the bunches hang on all winter and in summer are white. A pretty tree of z5. *O. virginiana* also known as the ironwood, is similar but only 40ft. z4.

CARYA
Hickory

The hickories are in the very first rank of foliage trees, thrusting high up towards the heavens with power and grace, draped with beautiful and luxuriant pinnate foliage and producing quantities of nuts. A characteristic adornment of the eastern United States, where most of them originated, they are very close (and much more graceful) cousins of the walnut; indeed the name *Carya* is Greek for a walnut tree, while the vernacular name comes from the Virginian *powcochicora*, an oily liquor expressed from the kernels. Outside the United States they have not been grown with that freedom that their excellence deserves, though there are a few fine specimens, close on 100ft high, in England and the continent of Europe.

The leaves of the hickories are refined versions of those of the walnut, being sometimes as long as 18in overall, with the pointed leaflets sparsely arranged on either side of the midrib. In autumn they become various shades of yellow. The flowers are borne in catkins and the fruits that follow are round or oblong husks, which split open to reveal the nuts, the kernels of which are sweet and edible in some species, but bitter in others. In fierce storms hickories are apt to split, despite the toughness of the wood.

Like the walnut, the hickory has a deep tap-root. It is therefore very difficult to establish it satisfactorily unless planted very young. The best method, indeed, is to grow it from seed from an American nursery immediately after the seed is ripe in the fall. The sowing may be done in the position chosen for the tree, or alternatively the seed may be over-wintered ("stratified") in a container of moist sandy soil and planted singly into 6in pots in spring, for final planting out in late May. Small, young plants can also be bought from good nurseries. As the upper branches multiply, prune away the lower ones, a few each year in July/August, so as to form a clear trunk of about 7ft in height.

Hickories prosper best in a deep, fairly moist, well-worked loam and their full grandeur is seen when planted in isolation. One or two species, such as the sweet-flavoured *C. cathayensis*, are found in China, but those we select are American.

C. cordiformis, the bitternut, is perhaps the hardiest and easiest, viable as far north as Quebec, but the least ornamental. It becomes a rather open, broad-headed tree, reaching 90ft in England as in America, with leaves 6 to 12in long, usually divided into seven leaflets. It is easily distinguished from other hickories by its bright yellow winter buds. As the vernacular name implies, the kernels are bitter. z4.

C. glabra, the pignut, is a handsome and symmetrical tree that may grow slowly to 120ft high. The bark is purple-grey and fissured and the leaves are about 10in long, arranged in five or seven finely pointed leaflets, the terminal one

long. The kernel is astringent. Takes kindly to dry, rocky soils as to others, but is not good for streets. z4.

C. illinoensis, the pecan, is the grandmaster of all, a strapping tree growing faster than any other hickory to an ultimate 150ft, with massive branches and particularly renowned for the sweet kernels of its oblong nuts. In its long elegant leaves there may be anything up to seventeen leaflets, each maybe six inches long. This luxuriance of foliage, which almost hides its deeply furrowed bark, distinguishes it from all other hickories. There are several named varieties and hybrids with *cordiformis* and *tomentosa*.

The pecan must have a rich, moist soil, never a dry one. Though hardy in Zone 5, it nevertheless needs a more southerly one to be sure of ripening its fruits. In Britain it is rarely a success, falling a prey to fungus diseases after a hard winter, but it does very well and fruits in southern France. z5.

C. ovata is the big shagbark hickory, so called

ABOVE *The Pecan,* Carya illinoensis.
BELOW *Bark of the shagbark (*Carya ovata*).*

(a)

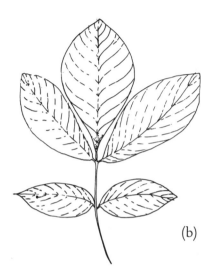

(b)

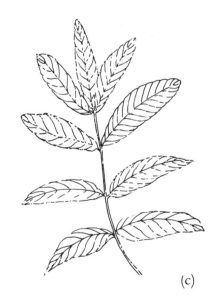

(c)

Hickory leaves:
(a) *the mockernut (*Carya tomentosa*);*
(b) *the shagbark (*C. ovata*);*
(c) *the bitternut (*C. cordiformis*).*

because, after some thirty years, its grey, ragged, tattered and loosely attached bark curls away crazily in large strips, though remaining attached to the trunk, an oddity which is its chief sign-manual. Another sign is the leaf structure, in which there are only five leaflets but the three terminal ones are very large, particularly in young trees, when they may be 12in long, shrinking to half that size when aged. The tree has a rather narrow, upright stance, irregular but picturesque. The kernels are much prized. The shagbark may attain 120ft in its native land. It does well also in Europe, specimens of up to 85ft in height being recorded in southern England, but seldom fruiting well. z4.

C. tomentosa, the mockernut or big-bud hickory, is not such a giant as its brothers, seldom exceeding 80ft. It has, however, a particularly stately and symmetrical carriage and is gifted with aromatic foliage, which is densely furred underneath with a starry down, as are the young branchlets, the male catkins and the winter buds. It is called mockernut because the nut is deceptive and big-bud because of its fat, velvety winter buds. Fine specimens of the mockernut grow in southern England, and in North America it is hardy up to Ontario at least. z4.

Similar in general appearance to the shagbark is the shellbark, **C. laciniosa**, the trunk of which is overlaid with long, loosely-adhering scales. Its pinnate leaves are the largest of all the hickories, maybe 30in long, but with only about seven widely-spaced leaflets. z5.

Other good hickories are *aquatica*, useful in swampy ground, *myristiciformis* the nutmeg hickory, and the variable *ovalis* or red hickory, resembling the pignut but having sweet kernels.

CASTANEA
Sweet Chestnut

The sweet chestnuts have no relationship with the horse chestnuts (reviewed under *Aesculus*), being in fact members of the beech family. They are specially splendid trees, easily distinguished from the aesculus by their more refined leaves, which are single and separate, long, glossy and conspicuously toothed along their margins. Also very distinctive are the very bristly, hedgehog-like burrs in which the nuts are enveloped. The castaneas are fairly hardy, especially noted for their resistance to drought, but need hot weather to ripen their delicious nuts.

To most people the sweet chestnut means the Spanish chestnut, *Castanea sativa*, the finest of all, but in North America it has been virtually annihilated by disease. So has America's own native chestnut, *dentata*, though the few grown in England are healthy and happy. This was Longfellow's "spreading chestnut tree", beneath which the "village smithy" stood. The loss is grievous to America for it is a tree of noble bearing; only a very few remain in their native soil. North America has thus had recourse to the Japanese and Chinese species, which are good but not so good.

The noble **C. sativa** is common to several areas of the Mediterranean, not merely to Spain, and is said to have been brought into France and Britain by the Romans. Give it light, well-drained loam, not heavy clay, peat or strong chalk, when it will overtop 100ft in 90 years, averaging 12ft every 10 years, and is valuable not only for its nuts, but, for us, even more for its splendour when standing as an isolated specimen, massive and stately. In a full-grown specimen the trunk will have an enormous girth, sometimes of 40ft. It is thus pre-eminently a tree for large gardens, for parks or for the ample landscape. The bark is at first smooth and grey, then becomes deeply fissured and finally develops spiral ribs. The shining, toothed, oblong leaves may be 9in long. In spring the whole tree becomes a fuzz of very long, creamy catkin-flowers, very agreeable to the eye but not to the nose.

The Spanish chestnut lives to a great age. In the north of Scotland can be seen a remarkable pair planted in 1550, the tallest of which, despite the cold climate, measures 85ft. The tallest in Britain, 120ft high, is at Ashford, in Kent. More remarkable still was an enormous specimen, now defunct, growing on the slopes of Mount Etna and said to have been some 2,500 years old. Indeed, for any hot, dry, stony or sandy soils the Spanish chestnut has no superior. z5.

Several leaf variations have arisen as sports; as in 'Albomarginata', edged white, 'Aureomarginata', edged yellow, a handsome form, 'Laciniata', the teeth stretched out into long, fine threads, 'Purpurea', the leaves very large and purple when young, and others in which the leaves are narrow and finely dissected.

There are also a few clones specially selected for the quality of their nuts, such as 'Marron de Lyon' and 'Paragon'; these are unreliable from seed and are grafted on to seedlings of the parent species.

A good runner-up to *sativa*, and resistant to chestnut bark disease, is **C. mollissima** the Chinese chestnut, a handsome tree of 50ft or more, now much cultivated in the States. Dense and round-headed, it looks like a small version of the Spanish chestnut, but can be distinguished by the fur on its young shoots, by its more bristly leaf margins and by the straw-coloured spines of the husk enclosing the nut. It needs an acid soil

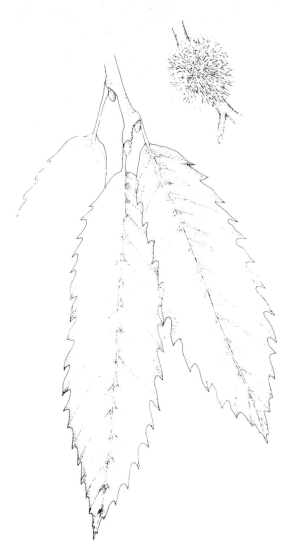

Leaves and a fruit of the sweet or
Spanish chestnut, Castanea sativa.

and, being self-sterile, two or more should be planted. z4, but fruits better in warmer zones.

Thirdly, there is the Japanese chestnut, **C. crenata**. A small tree or large bush of 30ft or less, often widespread, it is fairly resistant to disease, but its nuts are not so tasty as those of its Spanish and Chinese brothers. z6.

CATALPA

The big-leaved, strong-limbed catalpas are among the best of trees for private gardens and for small open spaces in towns. Not usually tall, but spreading widely, they combine grace with strength, display their bold foliage in the handsomest way, create a pool of shade and are richly arrayed in high summer with large and beautiful bouquets of flowers in the manner of the horse chestnuts. For town conditions (but not street-sides) there is no better tree, one well-known group being at the foot of Big Ben in London. As isolated specimens on lawns or in courtyards they are exceptionally fine. *Catalpa* is the American Indian name, not Latin.

Catalpas come from America and China. They succeed in any reasonably good soil that is well drained, but best of all in a generous, deep, moist loam. They dislike being shut in by other trees and want an open, sunny home, not exposed to fierce winds. Their natural habit is to fork out broadly from near ground level, so that, if not bought from a nursery in standard form, it may be as well to train up a trunk to perhaps 10ft, after which the tree will spread out naturally. In mature trees the branch tips often sweep the ground elegantly, but some bracing, propping or pruning is often needed for over-heavy branches. Cutting induces new growth readily and forked specimens may, if desired, be cut back hard each winter, when they will become bold bushes, a practice very effective on the beautiful yellow-leaved 'Aurea'. The fruits, borne after warm summers and more curious than beautiful, are carried in long, bean-like pods, though the catalpa does not belong to the bean family. It should be planted in spring.

C. bignonioides, known colloquially and unnecessarily as the Indian bean (i.e., American Indian) and originating from the eastern United States, is the most favoured species. Its big, handsome leaves, which do not open much before June, are heart-shaped and it flowers (after some years) in July to August, when its large, pyramidal trusses form a glowing spectacle, each bell-shaped floret in the truss sprinkled with purple and yellow spots and frilled at the margins. It is a low-altitude tree, which you must not expose to strong winds. Expect it to grow to 40ft in 50 years.

The most admired form is 'Aurea', in which the leaves are a rich and persistent yellow throughout the summer, making a beautiful spectacle. The dwarf 'Nana' is often grafted at the top of a tall stem, not always with happy results. z4.

C. × erubescens. This designation embraces various hybrids, the most noteworthy of which is the stalwart, fast-growing 'J.C. Teas', which originated in Indiana from a marriage now known to have been between *bignonioides* and the Chinese *ovata*. The leaves are enormous, flushed with purple when young and divided into three lobes. The floral display is prodigal, with anything up to 300 florets in a truss. In England there are specimens 60ft high but the floral display is indifferent. Other good varieties are 'Japonica' and 'Purpurea'. z4.

Catalpa speciosa *displaying its long bean pods in an American setting.*

C. speciosa, the extra-hardy western catalpa, far overtops all its brethren, reaching 100ft in the territories of its origin west of the Alleghenies and about 65ft at Kew in England. Its form is pyramidal, its large leaves more or less heart-shaped, drawn out to a fine point and coated with a downy growth underneath. The flower trusses are loose, but the florets large. A difficult tree to place except in an ample scene. The timber is valued as being remarkably durable in water and in wet soils. z4.

Two other species cultivated, both from China, are the small *bungei* and the slender, erect, pink-flowered *fargesii*. z5.

CEDRELA

In Paris, Philadelphia and some other cities one meets an aromatic street tree that looks like an improved tree of heaven, and was, indeed, for-merly classed as an ailanthus. This is the Chinese toon, now called **Cedrela sinensis.** Its ash-like foliage is luxuriant, colours well in autumn, has an onion flavour and, when young, is eaten by the Chinese. The cream flowers come in panicles a foot long and are not malodorous. In China the tree normally grows to almost 70ft, but a specimen at Heligan, Cornwall, reaches 90ft. It is not as hardy as the ailanthus. z5.

C. odorata provides the aromatic wood of cigar boxes.

CELTIS
Hackberry or Nettle Tree

The hackberries or nettle trees, which have leaves like those of the elm, have no great claim to distinction but two species are of value in towns and for their drought resistance.

C. australis, the European hackberry, is a dark-green, elm-like tree of up to 75ft, exceptionally tolerant of drought and heat. Recognisable by its long, slim, twisted leaf-points, it is widely used in southern France, in confined places with little room for root development, making an excellent shade tree. z6.

C. occidentalis, the American hackberry, of 60ft, gets much disfigured in its native country by a twig disease, but the selected clone 'Magnifica' is immune. This species is gifted with a resistance to both intense cold and drought and is known by its rugged, knobbly and ribbed trunk. It grows naturally in rocky ridges with very little soil, conditions that are very similar to those of streets. z2.

Other species of *Celtis* of usefulness and generally resistant to the twig disease are the Chinese *G. bungeana*, with shiny leaves, and *C. laevigata*, the sugar hackberry, widely used as a street tree in the southern United States. Both z5.

CERCIDIPHYLLUM
Katsura Tree

In this somewhat reserved Japanese family, much debated by botanists, we meet only one member.

This is **C. japonicum**, the Katsura tree of Japan. Though it can boast no particularly distinguished feature – no gorgeous flowers, no spectacular foliage, no immensity of stature, no quirk of habit – yet it has a well-bred grace, an elegance and a symmetry that make it one of the most decorative of hardy trees for the garden of moderate size and for any woodland environment. It resists disease, but not drought, very hot sun, nor exposure to bitter winds.

In its native country the Katsura may grow to 100ft but elsewhere is usually much less. The trunk, which in nature usually forks from close above ground level, is spirally twisted, becoming furrowed, and from this its slender branches are deployed in a somewhat pyramidal formation, drooping at the tips as they age. The leaves are small, almost round, dark blue-green above, sea-green below, suggestive of the common nasturtium; in this they are a small-scale version of the *Cercis* (Judaea tree), from which the Katsura's generic name is derived. In autumn, given an acid soil, they become dyed with all sorts of gay colours.

There are some fine specimens of the Katsura in the Arnold Arboretum in Massachusetts and in the old imperial gardens of Germany. In Britain the new growth is liable to be damaged by frost, yet in Cornwall, Gloucestershire and Southern Ireland there are specimens of 60ft and more. z4.

RIGHT Catalpa bignonioides:

A Chinese variety, *sinense*, is almost identical with the Japanese. In *magnificum* the tree is smaller, the leaves larger, the bark smoother – a fine, rare tree and probably the easiest.

CERCIS

These are pretty, small, fairly hardy trees remarkable for the little pea flowers that cluster like butterflies all along the stems and branches in May, often before the unfolding of the foliage. The leaves, too, are very characteristic, being much like those described for the cercidiphyllum, but a good deal larger, or, in some species, broadly heart-shaped. They belong to the pea and bean family and their fruits are flat bean-pods. The long, thick roots dislike disturbance and the patient gardener will get the best ultimate results by growing from seed; otherwise the trees must be planted very young in late spring. They must then be put out in full sun in a deep, generous, well-drained loam, preferably one on the sandy side. The ancient Greek name, which might well have been kept by the botanist, was *Kerkis*.

The best-known is **C. siliquastrum**, the "Judas tree", so called because of the fanciful legend invented in England that it was on this tree that Judas hanged himself after betraying Christ. It came to England in the sixteenth century via France, where it was quite aptly called the Tree of Judaea, but by Shakespeare's time "Judaea" had already somehow become corrupted to "Judas", an unhappy name that clung to it when it went to North America and elsewhere.

Originating from the eastern Mediterranean, the Judaea tree (as we shall call it) is a charmer, enamelled in spring with clusters of rosy-mauve pea-flowers all along the naked stems and branches. The nearly-round leaves are blue-green. It is an admirable tree for private gardens and for courtyards, forking close to the ground, spreading rather broadly and seldom more than 30ft high, but an arresting 40ft in the Royal Botanic Gardens at Kew. Fine specimens are seen in Cambridge gardens and it is a great favourite in Italy. There is a charming white form, *alba*. z7, or z6 on a wall.

A hardier cercis is **C. canadensis**, the eastern redbud, usually seen as a very big, wide-spreading shrub. The flowers are purple-pink and the leaves broadly heart-shaped and pointed. A favourite in New England, it is not at its best in Britain. There are a white form, a pretty, double form and a selected clone 'Wither's Pink Charm'. z4.

C. racemosa is a distinct 30ft redbud introduced from China for Harvard University. It

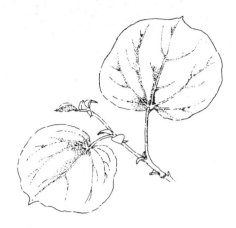

The Judaea tree, Cercis siliquastrum.

differs from its brethren by adorning itself, while the branches are still leafless, with dangling clusters 4in long, crowded with tiny rose-pink florets. The leaves are broadly heart-shaped and a shiny dark green. In England it grows to 40ft. z7.

Others of the genus are *chinensis*, with exceptionally large and dense flowers, *occidentalis* (the shrubby western redbud from California) and *reniformis*, a slender tree from Texas and New Mexico.

CHERRY See PRUNUS

CHESTNUT (Sweet) See CASTANEA

CHINABERRY See MELIA

CLADRASTIS
Yellow-wood

These are most handsome trees of medium size and rounded form with dense, luxuriant, pinnate foliage and white or pale pink, scented flowers. Members of the pea family, their seeds hang in long pods. They need a rich, loamy soil with plenty of sun. The botanists' mongrel-Greek name indicates that the branches are brittle. Make sure to retain the leader and keep the tree growing without check. Prune, if necessary, in late summer or the tree may bleed.

The usual choice is the very hardy **C. lutea**, which grows normally to about 50ft rather slowly, with a similar spread; a good specimen in isolation forms a perfect dome of vivid green. The leaflets in the compound leaf are broadly oval and from among them, partially hidden, hang white, scented panicles in the manner of the wisteria, 10 to 16in long, in late spring, but unfortunately not every spring. The bark, grey and smooth, re-

sembles that of the beech. The timber is hard, close-grained and yellow when freshly cut. Specimens in southern England reach 60ft and a giant grows at the Perkins Institute for the Blind at Cambridge, Massachusetts. z3.

C. sinensis obviously comes from China. Not quite so hardy as the American, but its blush-white scented flowers are erect, conical panicles, like big, glowing candles. They are lit in late summer – a useful achievement in nature. It is all too rare a tree in cultivation. z5. *C. wilsonii* is a closely related species, still more rare.

CORDYLINE

These small, evergreen trees from New Zealand do very well in some parts of the Northern Hemisphere and conveniently fill the bill for anyone seeking to paint what is often called an "exotic" picture, for they have a seeming kinship with palms.

The most easily wooable is **C. australis.** On the west coast of Scotland, even almost as far north as Cape Wrath, and in Cornwall, Ireland and similar climates, it grows with relish and seeds itself freely, often reaching 30ft. It forms an erect stem for several feet, then forks into several equally erect branches, each crowned with a dense cluster of narrow, scimitar-like leaves, which may be 3ft long, accompanied by large panicles of creamy, scented flowers. An acid soil and a moist atmosphere seem to be the conditions that it most favours, but it does not refuse other quarters, including hotel lounges. It can be grown quite easily from seed. z8.

C. indivisa is more tender, yet even this sustains ten degrees F of frost. An imposing small tree, with luxuriant foliage, it needs a rich soil and careful planting when young. z9–10.

CORNELIAN CHERRY See *Cornus mas*

CORNUS
Cornel or Dogwood

This well-loved family is under threat from certain argumentative botanists, who would break it up into separate cliques. We shall resist this aggression and retain the old, familiar name; but certainly the dogwoods are of great diversity, from tiny, creeping shrublets, as in *C. canadensis*, through the osier-like *alba*, grown for its vivid stems, to trees of small or medium size. Only with this last group shall we be concerned here.

PREVIOUS PAGES, LEFT *The canoe-bark or paper birch,* Betula papyrifera.
PREVIOUS PAGES, RIGHT Cercidiphyllum japonicum *in autumn*.
LEFT *The Judaea tree,* Cercis siliquastrum.

79

The first "recognition signal" that we shall observe is that all the veins in the leaf converge to meet together at the tip. Then we shall observe, except in *C. mas*, their decorative behaviour of splaying out their branches more or less horizontally, though resolving themselves overall into a roughly rounded silhouette, and bearing their floral decorations facing upwards or outwards. These floral decorations consist of multitudes of tiny florets in *controversa* and *mas*, but in the others that we review they are pseudo-flowers, formed of large bracts which, as in the poinsettia, display themselves immediately below the insignificant true flowers to attract the pollinating insects by their bright colours.

The place to see cornels at their best and in their greatest quantity is in the United States and their most impressive manifestation is in Valley Forge, Pennsylvania, where thousands of *Cornus florida* are planted as a memorial for the dead in the Revolutionary War.

All cornels prefer a fairly acid, fertile and reasonably moist soil; in arid conditions they fail. Contrary to general belief, many are quite happy in limy soils, even chalky ones. Not suitable as street trees, on account of their spreading arms, but lovely in one's private garden, in a landscape or as neighbourhood trees.

The word "cornel" is the Old English name, originally applied to the common hedgerow shrub, *Cornus sanguinea*, also known as the dogwood, indigenous to Britain and parts of the European continent; later it became applied also to *C. mas* (Latin for male), the Cornelian cherry, described below.

Most dogwoods are pretty hardy and are deciduous, but in **C. capitata** we have a 40ft tree of z8 only which is evergreen in favourable conditions. Its bracts are deep cream, followed by strawberry-like fruits, quickly gobbled up by the birds. The leaves are a lustrous dark green. It is a handsome tree at all seasons.

C. controversa, from Asia, is a tree of rare originality and beauty, for, departing from stereotyped tree form, it stretches out its arms in slender, sweeping horizontal tiers, or, as architects would say, tabulations, with a beautiful *chiaroscuro* of alternating light and shade. It is, indeed, an architectural tree and a definite leader should be retained to form a trunk. In June and July, when it is old enough, it becomes sprinkled with very small, true, white flowers, like snow-flakes, in flat clusters. It may grow to 60ft and does very well in chalky soil. It attains its richest beauty but not its largest size, in its variety 'Variegata', in which the leaves are decorated with cream margins. z5.

C. florida, which must have an acid soil, is a much loved tree of memorable beauty, which in its most favoured places can reach 40ft. Its arms, arrayed with shining leaves, spread out widely and fast in the most elegant manner and are smothered in May with large white bracts or, in the form *rubra*, red or pink. A natural woodlander, *florida* is quite accustomed to shade and looks stunning on the fringes of a wood or even deep within it. Few plants, indeed, flower more generously in the shade; but it will flower even more abundantly in full sun if the soil is moist and the rainfall ample, and if it is not exposed to searing winds. The autumn display of the foliage is a brilliant crimson or claret and the clustered fruits then glow like red sealing wax.

It is best to start with rather small plants and with natural multi-stemmed ones, for the beauty of the branch structure is thus displayed far better than in a grafted standard. Growth is quite rapid.

Though classified by Rehder as for Zone 4, the Florida dogwood is really variable in its hardiness as in its native distribution, which spreads from Florida to Massachusetts, so that only forms from northern sources are hardy in Zone 4, and indeed *rubra* is timid further north than Zone 5. Sadly, *florida* seldom justifies itself in Britain outside the south-eastern counties, though it has been cultivated here for 250 years. Late spring frosts damage the shoots, and the bark does not ripen unless there is plenty of summer sun.

Several attractive clones of the Florida dogwood have been established, including 'Cherokee Chief' and 'Spring Song' (both from *rubra*), 'White Cloud' and 'Tricolor' (in which the leaves are tinted cream, rose and bronze). There are also

Cornus florida *var.* rubra.

The Japanese dogwood, Cornus kousa.

a pendular form and a disappointing fastigiate one.

C. kousa, the Japanese dogwood, is of great beauty and in autumn a brilliant spectacle, especially in the variety *chinensis*, which is larger in all its parts, reaching 30ft in some climates. The large, star-like bracts, with long, pointed, twisted tips, are white and so abundant that in June (succeeding *florida*) the lustrous leaves are almost completely obscured. Bracts and flowers face upwards in serried ranks, engagingly poised on the tips of short, erect stems, and the raspberry-red fruits that follow add to the adornment. It is an easy tree in any good, loamy soil with a fair share of sun and has been a great success in Britain. The form 'Speciosa' grows erect and the bracts of 'Summer Stars' glow until mid-August. z5.

The noblest cornel of all, however, is assuredly **C. nuttallii**, the Pacific dogwood, which is one of the lime-haters. A great splendour towering up to 60ft or more, it is covered in May with very large bracts in four to six segments, that begin green, turn white and then blush pink and in the autumn the forests from British Columbia to California seem to be on fire from its falling, flame-like leaves and its red fruits. It clearly pre-prefers a fairly humid atmosphere, for while doing well in parts of Europe also, it disappoints in the eastern American States. In Britain it does really well only in the milder, moist counties of the south-west and even there is usually short-lived. A marriage arranged in British Columbia with *florida* has produced 'Eddy's White Wonder', which is hardier and more adaptable. z7.

From these spectacular dogwoods we turn to one of much humbler floral performance in **Cornus mas**, the ancient Cornelian cherry. It was well known to the Romans and has been cultivated in Britain and parts of Europe for many centuries, growing to 25ft with a spread of about 15ft and doing well in chalk. It has a character all its own. While the earth is still in the grip of winter, often as early as February, it breaks out into a brave froth of tiny, golden, true flowers all along the naked branches, as though stippled with gold paint, and later it develops small red, edible fruits that have a pleasantly acid flavour.

When the little flowers have all gone the Cornelian cherry loses its beauty, for its foliage is commonplace. This weakness is overcome, however, in its cultivars 'Variegata', in which the leaves are prettily margined white, and 'Aurea Elegantissima' in which yellow and pink tints appear; both make handsome small trees. z4.

The Japanese *officinalis* is much like *mas*, but perhaps more interesting in winter because of its exfoliating bark. Though somewhat coarse, it enlivens the autumn with gay leaf tints and little red "cherries".

CRAB APPLE See MALUS

CRATAEGUS
Hawthorn or May

The hawthorn, you would suppose, is a pretty humble creature, yet botanists enumerate more than a hundred separate species. In fact, most hawthorns, or mays, have a pretty close resemblance to one another and all we have to do is to pick out the best. Hoary with legend in England, France and Ireland, all are easy to grow and pretty tough, succeeding in poor soils, acid or limy. Dense, twiggy and thorny, most of them make splendid hedges or screens, submitting to hard clipping, as exemplified particularly in *monogyna*, so pronounced a feature of the English landscape for many centuries. Hawthorns are highly successful in towns, resisting pollution and de-icing salts; but in parts of America are much plagued by insects and diseases.

In nurseries thorns intended for garden adornment are usually raised with a clean stem of about 6ft, with a branching, bushy head, creating an "instant" tree. As a rule, however, a better proposition, especially in the larger sorts, is to get a tree with a clean stem but a central leader. If unobtainable, the gardener can order "feathered" trees (see Glossary), allow the central leader to extend and, as the crown forms, prune away the lower branches by degrees.

We have limited our selections to those that have some character distinctive from the general run of thorns and we have omitted all the smaller, shrubby ones, except when outstanding. Our first choices would probably be 'Paul's Scarlet' and the Washington thorn.

C. crus-galli, the cockspur thorn. A tree of picturesque, flat-topped, wide-spreading habit, up to 35ft high, fiercely armed with thorns 3in long. Flowers white, borne abundantly in June, autumnal display brilliant scarlet, haws deep red, persisting usually throughout the winter. Leaves oblong, broadest near tip ("obovate"). Good for hedging. The variety 'Pyracanthifolia' is thornless and smaller in all its parts. z4.

C. × lavallei (or *carrierei*). A notable French hybrid of only about 22ft, distinguished by large, glossy, obovate leaves. Flowers white, in prodigal abundance, haws orange, persisting through the winter. Few thorns. Particularly resistant to air pollution and a first-class street tree. z4.

C. oxyacantha, the historic "common hawthorn" of England, which has broad leaves slightly lobed, is usually a mere shrub of 15ft and so would find no place here but for a few of its arresting varieties, particularly 'Paul's Scarlet Thorn', a spectacular little tree, which originated in England in 1858. The brilliant flowers are double and have a very long season of bloom but set no fruits. Another splendour is the sparkling American hybrid 'Crimson Cloud' with a white star set in the centre of the red flower. Of the several pink forms 'Rosea flore pleno' might be chosen, and 'Plena' from among the whites. In *aurea* the haws are yellow.

C. phaenopyrum, the handsome Washington thorn, is very distinctive, not flowering until July and having lustrous, almost maple-like foliage,

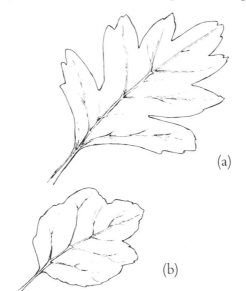

Hawthorns or mays (Crataegus):
(a) *the may or quickthorn,* C. monogyna, *the lobing varies;*
(b) C. oxyacantha.

white flowers and a fine autumnal display, bright red haws all the winter and long, fierce barbs. One of the very best and a good hedger. There is a columnar form. z4.

C. pinnatifida is a Chinese thorn, of which there is a particularly fine variety in *major*. The leaves are large, and a rich, dark, shining green. The lustrous red haws hang in clusters. There are few thorns. A well-furnished tree is a fine spectacle up to 25ft. z5.

C. monogyna is the true may or quickthorn, forming mile upon mile of the hedgerows characteristic of so much of the English countryside. The may is a tough country lass but, grown as a specimen, is a wonderful sight, sheeted with white, strongly scented flowers, followed by red haws. The leaves are lobed, rather like those of oaks, but are variable. Three cultivars deserve mention for different reasons. One is the slim and erect *stricta* (or 'Fastigiata'), very unusual but very helpful where a small sentinel tree is wanted, though usually reluctant to flower well. Its structural opposite is a luxuriant weeping tree of small stature, *C.m.* 'Pendula Rosea', a waterfall in red.

A third variety of the may is the fabled Glastonbury thorn ('Biflora'), said to have sprung magically into flower from the staff carried by Joseph of Arimathaea on his mission to convert the heathen English. All z4.

C. 'Toba'. An extra-hardy Canadian hybrid, resembling *monogyna* in general. It has thick and leathery leaves and large, blush-pink double flowers. z3.

DAVIDIA

D. involucrata is known variously as the handkerchief tree, the dove tree and the ghost tree, by reason of the pair of very large and conspicuous white bracts that surround the small cluster of paltry florets. They flutter just like dangling handkerchiefs.

The tree grows to about 60ft, with large, heart-shaped leaves drawn out to a fine point and covered with silky hairs, except in the variety *vilmoriniana*, which is the one usually seen. In all, it is a very handsome tree if not crowded by others, as it too often is.

Give the davidia a moist soil and, if it forks when young, prune it to form a single bole. z6.

DIOSPYROS

This Greek name means Zeus's corn, on the supposition that the god's basic food could be nothing

The "date-plum", Diospyros lotus.

less than a succulent fruit. Most trees of this genus are tropical or sub-tropical, such as the ebony tree. The flowers are unisexual, but solitary females can produce seedless fruit. Full sun is needed. They make good town trees.

The best known is the persimmon, **D. virginiana.** In temperate climes this grows to about 60ft, often with pendulous branches, draped with oval leaves of a glossy green. The bark is picturesque, deeply cut into rectangles. Although this tree is tender when young, it becomes quite hardy. The orange fruits are much appreciated but only when fully ripe. The persimmon is rare in Britain, but big specimens are at Oxford and Kew. z4.

D. kaki, the Chinese persimmon or kakee, grows to about 40ft, producing very good orange fruit about the size of an apricot. It fruits well in warm situations in England and has glorious autumnal foliage of orange and purple. It is cultivated extensively in southern Europe and in California as a commercial fruit crop. z7.

As a tree, however, the handsomest is **D. lotus**, known as the "date-plum". This builds up in a lustrous, luxuriant, evergreen, 40ft mound, composed of long, polished, dark-green leaves, densely borne. The female tree produces small, colourful but unpalatable fruits. z5.

DOGWOOD See CORNUS

DOVE TREE See DAVIDIA

ELM See ULMUS

EUCALYPTUS

The eucalypts, or gum trees, of Australia and Tasmania have only fairly recently become known outside their homelands, so that our knowledge of their behaviour in the various sectors of the Northern Hemisphere is still incomplete. However, as a result of much intensive research of recent years, we can now grow certain of the species with considerable confidence.

This we should certainly do in private gardens, in countryside plantations and in towns (where they prosper), for the blue or sea-green bloom on their attractive and versatile leaves and the remarkable beauty of their young barks – chalk-white, cream or pink in the hardy ones, outshining the silver birches – are exclusive to the eucalypts and can dramatically influence the garden picture. In company with golden conifers and Gleditsia 'Sunburst' they are stunning. To boot, all are evergreen and begin flowering when about three years old. They are the fastest of all trees and, having no resting buds, stop growing only in cold spells, and are the tallest of all broad leaves. The flowers, which burst out from tiny capsules, consist of dense tufts of stamens, looking like toy powderpuffs, usually white, and are grouped in clusters. The foliage is sparse and the trees are of open, ascending carriage.

What is of the first importance is to realise that, in its home countries, a single species of eucalyptus may grow in a wide-ranging variety of climates – from close above sea-level to perhaps 7,000ft. Obviously, those that come from a high altitude are more tolerant of cold weather than others, so that the provenance of the seed vastly influences its performance. Furthermore, seed from trees grown outside their native regions is better all-round than imported Australian seed. The average gardener's guarantee is to go only to a first-class nursery that knows its business. The gums must normally be propagated from seed – quite a tricky business – and they must be planted out, when very young, in late spring or early summer, for their sensitive and impatient roots rarely abide disturbance.

Demand specimens not more than 2ft high. Give them the utmost sun, the least possible exposure to fierce winds, a soil that is fairly acid, not too rich and of not too heavy a texture but retentive of moisture, with abundant rain or watering in the first year.

Given these conditions, put out the young plant without disturbance of roots in a saucer of soil (to hold water) and plant the root-ball so that the top of it is 2in below ground level. Water copiously and tie the shoot or shoots to a cane not more than

18in tall. In most species the young trees will grow with express speed – often more than 7ft in its first season, and faster still in hot climes. It is thus fatally liable to being blown over by any strong wind. Accordingly, plant three stout, equidistant stakes about a foot away from the tree and secure the tree to them by canes or otherwise for the first three years, unless they are to be coppiced. For the first winter or two (except in warm zones) put on a protective mulch of straw or such-like. Never put hoe or fork within two feet of the trunk.

Most cultivated eucalypts have at least two forms of foliage – the blue juvenile of the first year or two and the adult subsequently. The juvenile leaves look quite round and seem to have been skewered by the branch in the manner of a kebab, though in fact they are pairs of leaves closely clasping the branch. These are replaced by the adult foliage, which comes in the forms of dangling sickles or lance-points or broad blades, which may still be a waxy blue or sea-green or a darker green. They have an oily fragrance. As the bark ages it becomes grey or brown (in most species) but peels off to reveal fresh young bark below.

Juvenile foliage is much appreciated by flower arrangers and a ready supply of it is provided by pruning the tree anywhere, for it will then produce such leaves however old it is. Indeed, a highly effective way of growing the eucalyptus, especially in smaller gardens, is to cut it down close to the ground every year in mid-May; it then becomes a delightful, blue-tinted shrub of 4 to 7ft. Refrain from severe cutting back, however, until the tree has developed a woody swelling ("lignotuber") just below ground.

E. niphophila, the small snow gum, is a high-level alpine. Though not long in commerce outside Australia, it is now established as one of the two hardiest of all and a gem among trees. A slow starter, it then shoots up 3ft or more a year until it reaches its maximum, which will probably be only about 25ft in cultivation. The newly opened leaves are chestnut, turning to sea-green, and the young stems shine with a silvery bloom, later beautifully dappled in pale grey, cream and green. In July there is a spectacular show of dazzling white flowers. It is best left alone to attain its full beauty, for it lacks the round, juvenile leaves of other species. z8.

E. gunnii, the cedar gum from Tasmania, is of equal hardiness but far better known, having been in cultivation in the Northern Hemisphere for more than 100 years. The leaves are rinsed in blue, the older ones sage-green and the young bark is ice-white ageing to grey. In Britain, growing 6ft a year, it has exceeded 100ft, is altogether reliable and excellent for coppicing. It succeeds in chalk. z8.

Foliage of the snow gum, E. niphophila: *the stalks are red.*

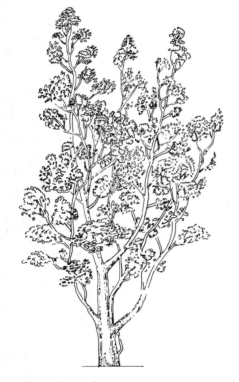

Typical open habit of most eucalypts; this is E. gunnii.

E. coccifera, the Mount Wellington pepper-mint, is reckoned to grow to 70ft, but is much taller in Scotland – a tribute to its resistance to frost and snow, though it can succumb in southern England. The leaves are blue-green, the young bark white becoming grey. It is planted as a street tree in Ullapool, in Scotland, and is excel-lent when coppiced. The crushed adult leaves smell of peppermint. z8.

E. urnigera, the urn gum, so called from the shape of its small fruits, rears up to 120ft in Ireland and nearly as high in Scotland. The bark is streaked in various colours. The young leaves are ice-white, the adults dark, glossy green. z8.

E. glaucescens, the Tingiringi gum, grows to about 40ft and is a highly ornamental tree, with

Juvenile foliage of Eucalyptus gunnii; *many other eucalypts are similar.*

glistening, chalk-white bark ageing to grey, and blue-green leaves. Excellent both as a tree and when coppiced. z9.

E. pauciflora, the cabbage gum, grows to about 50ft and is very reliable. Its white bark ages to grey. The adult leaves are large, leathery and glossy green. z9.

E. globulus is the magnificent Tasmanian blue gum, 180ft high in the wild and 130ft even in County Cork, with blue adult leaves up to a foot long, and a bark streaked in diverse colours. It grows very fast, with shallow roots, so is easily blown over, but is excellent when coppiced for its almost ice-white young leaves. This is a very widely planted tree in such climates as California and Italy, with huge specimens in Ireland. z9.

Other eucalypts that are proving hardy in parts of Britain are the imposing, chalk-stemmed *dalrympleana*, the long-leaved *nitens*, the grace-fully drooping *mitchelliana* and *parvifolia*, which is one that can safely be planted in chalk.

FAGUS
Beech

No need to extol the virtues of the beech, one of nature's noblest creatures. Its majestic form is best seen in great parklands or in the enchanting, cathedral-like woods and groves planted by our far-seeing ancestors, notably in England. Except

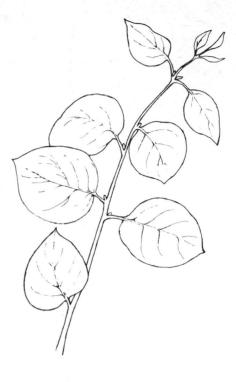

Eucalyptus pauciflora.

for the soldier-like Dawyck Beech, its wide-flung arms usually forbid its admission to towns, but it is quite town-hardy and, where there is room to plant a single specimen, it adds grandeur to the scene, moulding itself into a great green dome in summer and an impressive spectacle of branch and twig structure in winter. It looks delightful on a village green. When planted in groves its carriage is more erect.

The foliage is very dense, so that a deep, cavern-like umbrage is created, beneath which very little else will grow unless some lower branches are removed – a form of surgery which may disfigure the specimen. In winter the foliage spreads itself over the ground in a rich, russet blanket, but when the beeches are planted thickly to create hedges, as they do with willing obedi-ence to the gardener's demands, the leaves cling on to the twigs all winter if pruned in late summer.

All thrive in any light or medium soil, and, except for the Americans, do very well in lime; in Europe they are particularly associated with chalklands. In heavy wet clays the hornbeam is to be preferred. They can be planted up to 15ft high.

As we have seen under *Carpinus*, the beech has a close resemblance to the hornbeam, the main difference being that in the natural species of the beech the leaf has a flowing margin, scarcely toothed (except in the American and Japanese species), and the indentations made in the leaf-blade by the veins are shallow. We shall see,

RIGHT *The weeping red may,* Crataegus monogyna '*Pendula Rosea*'.

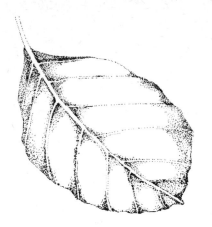

The leaf of the common beech, Fagus sylvatica.

The fern-leaved beech, F. sylvatica *'Asplenifolia'.*

however, that the beech exhibits an enormous diversity of leaf forms and colours. The bark is smooth, soft-grey, tight-fitting, rarely crenellated. The fruits are small, bristly husks enclosing little nuts, collectively called beech mast. Except as stated below, all are Zone 4 trees.

Dominating the genus is the European or "common" beech (as it is called in Britain), **F. sylvatica**, growing 20ft in the first 15 years and occasionally soaring up to well over 100ft. It prospers in chalk, as elsewhere. The young foliage is exceptionally beautiful in the shimmering, soft, pastel green in which it unfurls to the spring, before assuming the dark-green of its maturity. The lower branches retain their russet leaves all winter. There are, however, quite surprising variations in the leaf, both of colour and of pattern, and unfortunately there is much confusion in their names, but we shall follow W. J. Bean, as being the most up-to-date authority.

The most popular of all these varieties come

rightly under the general heading of **F.s. purpurea**, the purple beech. This embraces not only the original colour form from central Europe, the young leaves of which unfurl a beautiful light red, but also other hues, as in *cuprea*, the copper beech (a term often loosely applied), which has leaves of a paler hue than the original purple, and the remarkable 'Riversii', a very fine form in which the purple is so dark as to appear almost black. There is also the weeping purple beech, 'Purpurea Pendula', a superb, very small, mushroom-headed tree.

Other colour elaborations are seen in the pretty

A beech tree robed in snow in Alice Holt Forest.

'Roseomarginata', which has purple leaves striped and margined in rose and pale pink, in the yellow-leaved 'Zlatia' and in variables that have white or gilt margins.

Besides these diversities in colour, *Fagus sylvatica* exhibits some very surprising variations in the form of the leaf. Finest of all is the fern-leaved beech, **F.s. Asplenifolia**, of which there are various forms. This develops into a magnificent and stately tree, of the highest ornamental value. Most of the leaves are long and narrow (sometimes 4in long but only $\frac{1}{4}$in wide) and deeply but irregularly incised or feathered, quite fern-like.

LEFT *The "snow gum",* Eucalyptus niphophila.

The weeping purple beech, Fagus sylvatica *'Purpurea Pendula'.*

open carriage, and by its suckering habit, so that a single tree will form a colony if allowed. It is rarely successful in Britain. z3. The variety *caroliniana* has a rather simpler, finer-toothed, thicker leaf, but is reckoned for z5.

Other beeches that we may need to notice come from Asia, of which the choicest is the Chinese beech, **F. englerana**, a singularly beautiful little tree of no more than 35ft. Everything about it is slender and the autumn colour is delicious. z5.

FRAXINUS
Ash

The ashes with which we shall be concerned are rugged trees which build themselves up into fairly large, strongly branched structures, very well known for their long, pinnate leaves. Indeed "ash-like" is a term often used for other trees with pinnate leaves. In autumn the ash is further recognised by its bunches of samarae, or winged seeds, which the wind scatters where it listeth and which, rooting readily and growing very fast, can become a nuisance to the gardener and the groundsman. A few seedless varieties thus deserve our patronage. A small group, known as the *ornus* section, adorn themselves with very decorative clusters of white or cream flowers.

Cultivation is easy, but soil requirements vary with the species. The gardener should preserve the leading growths as long as possible, cutting out rival leaders. Having dense, fibrous roots, ashes transplant well up to about 18ft. They excel in limy soils as in acid ones. Several prosper as town or coastal trees. Leaf-fall, accompanied by the tough midribs, is a nuisance, however. The following is a brief selection.

F. americana, the white ash, has pendulous leaves, of seven broad leaflets, silvered below. It grows fast anywhere and easily to 120ft, sweeping the ground with the tips of its branches. It is enriched with good autumnal colour, especially in the less vigorous cultivars 'Autumn Purple' and 'Rosehill'. These have the additional merits of being seedless and tolerant of lime and of de-icing salts. z3.

F. oxycarpa (a sub-species of the narrow-leaved *angustifolia*), has given us a distinctive and exceptionally good cultivar, named 'Raywood', raised in Australia but marketed in England by Notcutt's Nursery. It begins as a slender tree but opens up with age and so will need ample space in time. Its blue-rinsed, pinnate leaves are arranged in whorls, or circular clusters, which, in favourable conditions, give us a glorious autumnal display of plum-purple. 'Raywood' is also

The overall effect in a well-grown specimen, maybe 80ft high, is one of luxuriant strength. 'Incisa', *laciniata* and the rare purple "Rohanii" are other similar variants.

Other leaf variations are seen in the shell-like 'Cochleata', in the cock's comb beech ('Cristata'), which bears its leaves in dense clusters, and in the attractive, small-leaved 'Cockleshell' and 'Rotundifolia'.

Yet more variations in the common beech are seen in the deportment of the whole tree. The most striking of all is the celebrated **Dawyck beech**, which adopts the carriage of the Lombardy poplar – erect, fastigiate, columnar, narrow, and is indeed a much finer tree than the poplar. Given root room, it is quite suitable in small spaces and a pair of Dawycks at a gateway

make the most impressive sentinels. The original specimen at Dawyck, in Scotland, is now well over 80ft high.

The dead opposite of the fastigiate form is seen in weeping or pendular ones. We have noted the weeping purple beech. That which is known as plain 'Pendula' is green-leaved. A more elegant one, as a rule, is 'Aurea Pendula', which develops as a tall, slender tree with the branches hanging down almost perpendicularly, with its young leaves yellow.

From this extraordinarily versatile European we turn to the American beech, **F. grandifolia.** This is another big fellow, distinguished from the European by its longer, narrower, bluish-green, coarsely toothed leaves (up to 5in long), much paler and more decorative bark, more slender and

RIGHT *Winter aspect of the "common" ash,* Fraxinus excelsior.

exceptional in preferring a fairly dry soil and it is a very good street tree. One of the original specimens at Notcutt's is 8oft high. z6.

F. excelsior, the common ash of Europe, is one of the Old World's most venerable trees, much teased for its laziness in coming into leaf. It soars up to 140ft in favourable places, growing 15ft in the first ten years, sparsely arrayed in leaves that may have eleven leaflets, disposed on an equally sparse, open and ascending branch structure. Though scarcely a beautiful tree, it can have great dignity when in isolation in rich soil. It favours a deep, moist, loam, thrives in lime, including chalk, excels at the salty seaside and is immune to pollution but is not a good town tree. z3.

The common ash has produced a quantity of cultivars and forms, of which the best is 'Pendula', the weeping ash, one of the finest weeping trees, forming a wide-spreading crinoline or tent. It needs to be grafted high on stems of the common ash. It originated in Cambridgeshire some 200 years ago and several spectacular specimens are now to be seen in various places. There are other weeping ashes also, which are often mistaken for the genuine article.

Another picturesque cultivar and of definite beauty is 'Jaspidea', golden in both leaf and branch, sometimes incorrectly called 'Aurea', which is a dwarf.

F. pennsylvanica, the exceptionally hardy red ash, much resembles the white, but grows to only half the height. More valuable is its natural variety *subintegerrima* or *lanceolata*, the green ash, from which have sprung the outstanding 'Marshall's Seedless', a male clone with thick, glossy leaves, and 'Summit', nearly seedless, with leaves not so leathery. Both withstand lime, salt, drought and become handsome, oval-headed or pyramidal trees. z2.

The so-called Oregon ash, *F. latifolia* (or *oregona*) is now regarded as a sub-species of the Pennsylvanian, with stalkless leaflets. z6.

F. velutina, the velvet or Arizona ash, is exceptional for its toughness in standing up to arid, almost desert conditions and to alkaline ones. Its leaves are velvety to the touch, except in the variety *glabra*, which is the glossy but less desirable Modesto ash. z5.

From these large ashes with scarcely discernible flowers, we turn to a group of ten or so that lavishly decorate themselves with white or cream flowers. Known as the *ornus* section, they are more luxuriant in their foliage than those that we have been considering, but usually smaller and of slow growth, some being mere shrubs, as in the charming *F. mariesii*.

F. ornus itself, the manna ash, will, however, grow into a large tree, smothering itself in May with a profusion of white flowers in 4in panicles, though not of agreeable scent. Trees of great splendour, up to 75ft high, grow in Hyde Park and Kensington Gardens in London, but in the States they are often ravaged by borers. z5.

The manna ash is the source of manna sugar, a mild laxative obtained from the sap. It is unlikely to have provided the manna of the Old Testament, which more probably came from *Tamarix gallica mannifera*, the honey-like exudation of which falls to the ground and solidifies during the night.

GEAN See *Prunus avium*

The common ash, Fraxinus excelsior.

Gleditsia triacanthos *'Sunburst'*.

GLEDITSIA

The gleditsias, known colloquially in North America as "locusts" (as also are the robinias), are a race of trees curiously neglected in England; undeservedly so, for the best of them are of great beauty, being clothed with small, delicately fashioned, fern-like, pinnate leaves, dancing with the wind, and are deployed on a loose, open and informal structure of branches, so that there is a graceful pattern of light and shade. They are grown more freely in France and Italy and even more so in the United States, where several species are native and where they are now reckoned among the most important of ornamental trees and a valuable replacement of the casualties caused by the elm disease. Nearly all make big trees. Most are very fiercely armed with thorns, often triple thorns, as in the formidable Caspian locust (*G. caspica*), and were formerly considered unsociable trees, but thornless forms have been developed, largely through the work of Mr John Siebenthaler, of Daytona, Ohio. For the term "locust", see under *Robinia*.

Gleditsias grow well in any good, loamy soil which is not excessively acid, preferring it light, rich and rather moist. Many are tolerant of shade. They may be grown as standards or as ground-sweeping trees. Whatever pruning may be necessary must be done after July, or they will bleed. Being members of the pea family, they produce in warm zones big, brown dangling seed pods which hang on a long time.

The sovereign choice of all the gleditsias is to be found among the several cultivars and forms of the "honey locust", **G. triacanthos** ("triple-thorned") and above all in the form which, in flat repudiation of its parentage, is called *inermis* (thornless) thus making a nice contradiction of botanical terms. This has given birth to a whole covey of clones, which are among the most highly ornamental of cultivated trees, all virtually thornless and free of the undesirable seed pods. They resist air pollution and drought and can be transplanted at 15ft or more. Plant in spring. z4.

The one that has been greeted with the most spirited acclamation is 'Sunburst', the leaves of which, airy and elegant, glitter with a golden sheen when they first salute the garden and then slowly change to a light, olivine green, but never entirely losing the golden touch. The raisers (Cole Nurseries) say that it will grow to 35ft. Other very good selected clones of *G. triacanthos inermis*, all but one green-leaved and nearly all untried in Britain, are:

'Moraine', a broad-shouldered, four-square tree to 60ft.

'Rubylace'. The leaves open a bright ruby-red gradually turning bronze-green. The American raisers put its height at 40ft.

'Shademaster', an erect form with strong central leader, 70ft.

'Skyline'. Narrow, pyramidal, neatly tailored for streets, 50ft.

'Imperial' challenges 'Moraine' where the need is for a full, broad-crowned tree; 60ft.

'Continental', ultimately forms a 70ft, narrow, rectangular crown, with exceptionally large, dark green, pendulous leaves.

The "honey" appelation of *G. triacanthos* in the vernacular derives from the succulent pulp in which the seeds are embedded in the pod. A few other cultivars are of interest besides the form *inermis*, such as the weeping 'Bujotii', the shrubby 'Elegantissima' and 'Nana', which at Kew is anything but dwarf.

Another thornless gleditsia is the hybrid *texana*, a big, bold fellow that will grow to 120ft. *G. aquatica* is the water locust (z6). The big *G. japonica* is unsurpassed for the elegance of its ferny leaves, but fiercely armed (z5). *G. sinensis*, from Pekin, is a smaller tree, prospering in France and Italy (z6).

For other breeds of "locust trees", see *Robinia*.

GUM TREE See EUCALYPTUS

GYMNOCLADUS
Kentucky Coffee Tree

G. dioicus is unmistakable in its huge, multipinnate leaves, often 3ft long, crowded with 60 to 70 leaflets, which emerge pink and turn a fresh, clear green. A good foliage tree, which can grow

The big, bi-pinnate leaf of the Kentucky coffee tree, Gymnocladus dioicus, *with 60 to 70 leaflets in each complete leaf.*

to 120ft with an open, strong system of branches. The leaf stalks persist after leaf-fall. The tree is unisexual and the female produces long seed pods. The seeds are said to have been used by the early settlers in Kentucky and Tennessee as a substitute for coffee. Good examples are in France and Germany and a few in southern England of about 50ft. Give it plenty of sun and a deep, rich soil. Prune in July–August if necessary. z4.

HACKBERRY See CELTIS

HALESIA

The "snowdrop trees" or "silverbells", as they are sometimes fancifully called, are charming when, for a brief period in May, they are enamelled all along their branches with their small, white, pensive flowers, imaginably like snowdrops; but for the rest of the year they are of little account. They need an acid soil, moist and well-drained. Prune, if need be, after flowering.

H. carolina grows maybe to 30ft as a tailored tree, but is perhaps best when branching naturally

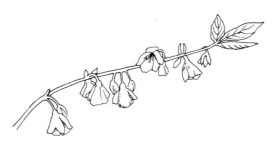

The hanging bells of Halesia carolina.

Halesia monticola.

from the base, when it forms a big, widespread shrub, with oval, pointed, downy leaves. z4.

In **H. monticola**, the beautiful "mountain silverbell", the flowers are a trifle larger and, in very favourable conditions, the tree, which grows very fast, may reach 100ft (40ft in Britain). There is a pink-flowered form called *rosea*. z5.

HAWTHORN See CRATAEGUS

HICKORY See CARYA

HOHERIA

These beautiful, summer-flowering New Zealanders, some of them evergreen, are hardy only in the warmer fringes of the temperate zones. The most readily wooable are the delectable *glabrata* and the almost identical *lyallii* (of Zone 7), but they are too small for our pages. Of the larger species we have to notice two, both evergreen, both probably not hardy north of Zone 9, unless given the shelter of a warm wall.

The more resilient of the two, *H. sexstylosa*, is a lovely small tree, usually of slender, erect carriage, growing fast to 25ft, clad with slim, saw-edged, fine-pointed light-green, glossy foliage and lavishly decorated with bouquets of small, white flowers in July and August. May be defoliated in sharp winters, but quickly recovers.

H. populnea grows to 45ft, with larger clusters of white flowers at the end of summer and rounder leaves. An elegant tree, of which there are several cultivars, such as 'Osbornei', which has purple stamens and a purple tincture on the lower side of the leaf.

Plant hoherias in May and prune in April.

HONEY LOCUST See GLEDITSIA

HORNBEAM See CARPINUS

HORSE CHESTNUT See AESCULUS

INDIAN BEAN See CATALPA

JUDAEA or **JUDAS TREE** See CERCIS

JUGLANS
Walnut

Nature has sprinkled walnuts over a wide expanse of the Northern Hemisphere but, whether from Europe, America, the Himalayas or Japan, they differ in little else than their stature and the quality of their nuts. To the world at large the nuts hold paramountcy and to the Romans the walnut was "Jove's acorn" (*Jovis glans*). The English name originates in the Old English *walhhnutu*.

Our main concern, however, is in their value as trees, which is considerable but below that of the hickories, to which they are closely allied, having a similar tap-root and large, pinnate leaves. Their branch structure is bold, strong and open.

Having a tap-root, walnuts object to displacement, so they have to be planted when small (or, better still, grown from seed) and this is their danger time, for they do not immediately acquire hardiness. If cut by frost they develop new shoots of a bushy character and the gardener must then select a good leader and tie it up. Thereafter he may need gradually to prune away the lower branches of the larger species to a height of some 15ft, year by year, for the tips of the branches will sweep the ground even from this height. Be sure to do this, and any other pruning, in late summer or early autumn, for the walnut is one of the worst trees for bleeding at the touch of the knife at other seasons.

The time to plant is in the spring. They do best in a deep light loam over limestone. Thin acid soils will not do, and in heavy loam the walnuts are too slow.

J. ailantifolia, the Japanese walnut, grows to a moderate 50ft with very large leaves of up to 17 leaflets and male catkins a foot long. It is known also as *sieboldiana*. Its variety *cordiformis* (the heartnut) has striking yellow catkins but is less free-fruiting. z4.

Closely related to the foregoing are the rather larger but less hardy *hindsii*, a favourite street tree in California, and the lush Texan walnut, *J. microcarpa major*, a 50ft, rather narrow tree, the leaves of which have innumerable small leaflets. z7. It is sometimes given the status of a species.

J. nigra, the black walnut, usually begins life as a shapely, pyramidal tree before developing its great, commanding, outflung arms, reaching 100ft high with an 80ft spread in its native America. It is marked by a nearly black, deeply furrowed bark and much-divided leaves. Its roots are very toxic to other plants in close association. As a tree, it is the most handsome of all walnuts, especially in its cut-leaf variety 'Laciniata', the texture of which is more refined and luxuriant. The large nuts are not of the highest quality, except in a few selected clones such as 'Thomas'. The dark wood is enormously valuable. z4.

The venerable **J. regia**, variously known as the English, Persian or (in Britain) common walnut, is the most popular of all, having been cultivated for certainly more than 2,000 years, chiefly for the excellence of its nuts. A large commerce flourishes in Southern Europe, Asia Minor and California (where more than 125,000 acres are planted). This was the original "Jove's acorn" of the Romans. Its timber is extremely valuable, so that many trees that would otherwise flourish for many centuries never attain a full life. The bark is silver-grey, at first smooth, becoming deeply fissured after many years. The leaves, which unfurl a tawny orange, are thick and leathery and, unlike any other walnuts, have no serration on the margin. z5.

The common walnut is not so fine a tree as the black, except again in its cut-leaf variety 'Laciniata', a handsome and ornamental creation. Other varieties abound, including a weeper, and of special interest is the Polish variety 'Carpathian' which endures −40°F. The French have led the field in the production of fine fruiting varieties, as in the oval, fruity 'Franquette'.

Marriages have inevitably been made between the English walnut and the black. They are known collectively as *J.* × *intermedia*. The most famous, about 100ft high, is in the garden of M. de Vilmorin, near Paris, bearing the aspect of *regia* and the fruit of *nigra*.

The "butter-nut", **J. cinerea**, is a rather slender tree of nearly 100ft, with leaves 3ft long, divided into maybe 17 leaflets. It is very hardy, but not as handsome as *nigra*. z3.

KATSURA See CERCIDIPHYLLUM

KENTUCKY COFFEE
See GYMNOCLADUS

Pinnate foliage of Koelreuteria paniculata.

Perhaps the finest examples to be seen are in France; other good ones are in the grounds of Hampton Court Palace, at Syon House, London, and in the Ohio Valley.

Its erect cultivar 'Fastigiata' is perhaps the slimmest broadleaf tree in creation, being only about 24in wide when 25ft high, but very shy in flowering; a perfect tree for very narrow streets or very small gardens, yet very rarely seen. Another rarity is *apiculata*, in which the leaves are doubly pinnate and more refined, making a very ornamental, broad-crowned specimen. All z5.

The koelreuteria has a diversity of fancy names, such as the China-tree, Golden Rain, Pride of

KOELREUTERIA

These agreeable and much neglected trees from China have a high garden value, whether in town or country, especially where there is no room for a big horse chestnut, linden, maple, gleditsia or the like. They prosper in any reasonable soil but are at their best in a good deep loam, with plenty of sun.

The only species successfully grown is **K. paniculata**, which extends to about 30ft with a broad, spreading crown, draped with attractive, pinnate leaves, each leaflet lobed rather like an oak's. Its floral adornment is a large, pyramidal cluster of small yellow flowers, in the style of a horse chestnut, flowering in July and August, when so few other trees are in bloom. In a warm spot it rewards the gardener by flowering in great profusion, and afterwards it gives a showy display of coloured, bladder-like seed pods, first green, then pink, then brown. It grows quickly and easily from seed.

The denser leaflets of the fastigiate Koelreuteria.

India and so on, all rather pointless. It is named after the eighteenth-century Professor Koelreuter.

KOWHAI See *Sophora tetraptera*.

LABURNOCYTISUS
Included under LABURNUM

LABURNUM

Sometimes unnecessarily and ambiguously called "golden chains", laburnums are some of our prettiest small flowering trees, their branches massed with hanging, grape-like bunches of glittering, yellow, pea-flowers in May or early June, amid trifoliate leaves. They are of the easiest culture, fast growth, and prosper in any reasonable soil, acid or limy, in sun or partial shade, in smoky towns or in seaside breezes. Leaves and seed are poisonous to man and animals.

Laburnums are usually grown as standards. If any branches threaten to unbalance the shape of the tree or to overcrowd its centre, remove them while young in late July or August. Spring pruning may cause bleeding.

The charming **L. alpinum** is for some reason known as the Scotch laburnum. It makes a pretty, small, broad-headed standard, possibly attaining 30ft and flowers in early June in long, slim, scented bunches of small florets. A form with erect branches is called 'Pyramidale' and its antithesis is found in the stiffly weeping 'Pendulum'. z4.

L. anagyroides is the "common" laburnum, still sometimes known as *vulgare*. As compared with the Scotch, it has shorter bunches, larger florets, blooms a fortnight earlier and is a trifle less hardy. It lends itself readily to manipulation by the skilful gardener to cover pergolas and archways with stunning effect, for it responds well to spur-pruning. z5.

L. × vossii (of catalogues) is the most splendid of the lot, with long, slim clusters of flowers, prodigally borne, forming a glittering, golden waterfall in June. Happily, it produces few seeds, so there is little danger of poisoning. Responds very well to spurring. It is really a selected clone of *L. × watereri*, a hybrid born from the marriage of the two preceding laburnums. Another variant of *watereri* is 'Alford's Weeping', which explains itself. z5.

Laburnocytisus is another variation of the theme of laburnum which we may conveniently consider here, regardless of botanical orthodoxy. Its seven-leagued name derives from the fact that it is a "chimera" or graft hybrid (as against a hybrid produced by cross pollination) of the common laburnum and the broom *Cytisus purpureus*. The result of this remarkably contrived marriage is that some flower clusters are yellow, others purple and others again a mixture of the two. It is now known by the orthodox as +*Laburnocytisus adamii* (after its Parisian marriage-maker). z5.

LAURUS
Bay or Laurel

The true laurel or bay tree, employed by the Romans to decorate the brows of heroes and by the modern cook to impart a pungency to casseroles is *Laurus nobilis*, the "laurel" of popular speech being usually the broad-leaved aucuba or else a species of prunus (which cook must not use).

The bay is one of our most handsome evergreens. In complete freedom and in a fairly warm place it will form a broad, lustrous pyramid 40ft high, but is more often seen as an outsize shrub, or else as a prim little toy outside the doors of restaurants. Its small, glossy, dark-green, aromatic leaves are companioned in April with small yellow florets, rather like those of the "mimosa", which cluster gaily along the stems, and on female trees (for the bay is unisexual) the flowers are followed by black berries.

If cut by a particularly hard frost, the bay sprouts again readily, even from ground level. It thrives in coastal gardens and if the leaves become seared by cold winds the stems can be pruned back as far as necessary without fear. For the noble bay submits willingly to the knife and is easily trimmed to any shape you like. Prune patiently with the secateurs in early May, after flowering. z6.

LIME or **LINDEN** See TILIA

LIQUIDAMBAR

The liquidambars are some of the most beautiful of our trees, with maple-like foliage, picturesque form, handsome bark and lively autumn colours if in acid soil. They are for private gardens, parks and the countryside rather than for towns, unless in choice, isolated positions and in a deep, rich, moist loam. Plant in autumn or spring; they transplant easily enough when quite young and get away well. Any pruning that may be necessary (such as the removal of lower branches to expose the trunk), must be done in August or early autumn, or they will bleed.

In North America the liquidambars are com-

The true laurel or bay, Laurus nobilis, *in flower.*

Liquidambar styraciflua.

monly known by the much less melodious name of "sweet gums". Of the few species, easily the sovereign choice, and the hardiest, is **L. styraciflua**. A real forest beauty in North America, where it frequents river valleys, it reaches 15ft in ten years and is capable on occasions of reaching 125ft, densely packed with its shapely leaves, which become a great scarlet glory in autumn. It retains a balanced symmetry in all circumstances and its splendour is best displayed when placed in isolation, though it is effectively used as an avenue tree in Washington. The maple-like leaves have five to seven lobes, deeply cleft, but are distinguished from those of the maple by being alternate in their disposition, instead of opposite (see

Glossary). A few clones have been selected for their own special tastes in autumnal dress, such as 'Lane Roberts' (rich dark crimson), and in America 'Burgundy', 'Festival' (pink and apricot) and 'Palo Alto' (orange). z5.

Two other excellent liquidambars can be grown in slightly milder climes. **L. orientalis** is closely related to the American, but not so lusty and has a more rugged bark. Fine specimens are in Bologna, in Italy. **L. formosana** is a beautiful tree of slender form and rapid growth, as big as *styraciflua*, distinguished by having three-lobed, sharp-pointed leaves which unfurl purple, become bronze-crimson, then green and finally crimson in autumn. Both z6.

LIRIODENDRON
Tulip Tree

Liriodendron tulipifera is another great forest splendour and one of the very few large trees that is conspicuously adorned with flowers. If the soil is rich, rather cool and moist, the tree may grow 150ft high, decked in summer (after some years) with large, yellow-green, solitaire flowers that are vaguely tulip-shaped, the six petals enclosing a mass of stamens and carpels. The sign-manual of the tree when not in flower is its odd leaf, which looks as though the tip has been bitten off. In autumn these leaves turn a bright butter-yellow.

The tulip tree behaves very well in a town environment and is quite hardy, though liable to be nipped by hard frost in its childhood; protect and cherish it accordingly. The roots are fleshy and need careful planting; do this in spring. It dislikes very hot and very dry spots.

Young feathered tulip trees grow well and the lower branches should be gradually amputated to a height of about 8ft. If ready-made standards are bought from a nursery, make sure that they have a good central leader. If strong, upright shoots grow out from the lateral branches, cut them right back. z4.

There are a few variant forms. Outstanding among them is the quite magnificent 'Fastigiatum', which builds up into a broad, dense column and so forms a green architectured pillar of the most distinguished bearing until it ages and splays out. Here you do not, of course, remove the lower branches. Other variants have gilt-edged leaves ('Aureomarginatum'), undulating leaves ('Crispum') and leaves without lobes (*integrifolium*).

L. chinensis is an oriental tulip tree, very nice indeed, but smaller in all its parts.

ABOVE *The "bitten-off" leaves of the tulip tree,* Liriodendron tulipifera.
BELOW *Flowers of the tulip tree.*

LOCUST TREES See GLEDITSIA and ROBINIA

LONDON PLANE See *Platanus acerifolia*

MADRONA See *Arbutus menziesii*

MAGNOLIA

Only the cherry can challenge the claim of the magnolia to be queen of all flowering trees. The opulent, waxen flowers, fashioned in the semblances of goblets, bowls or tulips, erect or languidly pendant, often scented, adorned with highly ornamental stamens and pistil, glitter like crown jewels in the garden and the landscape, whether as small, starry shrubs or as huge trees in the sumptuous splendour of Campbell's magnolia. In their due seasons they adorn the scene from early spring to autumn, their blossoms sometimes bursting out on naked branches or gleaming later among luxuriant leaves. A fully grown *campbellii* in flower, whether in Cornwall or in its native Himalayas, is a sight that brings the beholder to a halt.

Within the waxen heart of the flower is a dense circlet of coloured stamens, in the fashion of a monk's tonsure, but often of a brilliant scarlet or crimson, to catch the eye of the pollinating insect, and, thrusting up through this mass is a short pillar crowded with carpels, which form part of the female pistil. In due course this pillar becomes elongated into a queer seed pod that resembles a small cucumber and when the pod splits open at last it reveals a new treasure of brilliant, red, jewel-like seeds.

There are, however, certain provisos and certain short-comings. Except as we remark below, an acid soil or at least a neutral one, is very desirable and sometimes mandatory. Many magnolias will demand from you a vision of the future and a faith to pursue it, for they do not come into flower for many years; indeed, for *campbellii* you may have to wait for 25 years and for *kobus* and *mollicomata* at least half that time. Those species that blossom early in the year may become blistered in the bud by late spring frosts and those with large leaves may be riven by the blasts of rude winds. The roots of all are fleshy and sensitive, so that they must be planted when very young, and with care. Except in the warmer climes and in sheltered nooks elsewhere, it is as well to regard all as of suspect hardiness in the first year. However, among the rich treasure of magnolias there are many glories to satisfy both the impatient gardener and the one who has command over small territories, if elementary precautions are taken. Most are very good town trees.

American species of magnolia are usually unable to face lime in the soil, but many of the Asiatics can, as demonstrated particularly by Lord Rosse in Ireland. Indeed, the late Sir Frederick Stern successfully grew *delavayi*, *sinensis*, *wilsonii* and the hybrid *highdownensis* even in his celebrated chalk-pit garden in Sussex.

Except in the warmer places, choose a spot sheltered from whatever wind prevails in the winter. A south-facing wall gives good protection in doubtful circumstances. A woodland setting also gives good shelter and magnolias look

*Winter aspect of a mature deciduous magnolia;
this is* M. denudata.

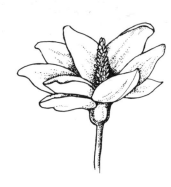

The Yulan, M. denudata.

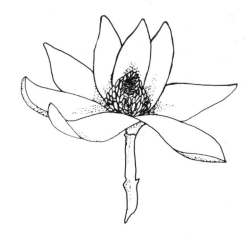

Magnolia kobus.

charming when so situated. In the cooler climes the best time to plant is the middle spring.

A good start means nearly everything. Prepare a hole of ample proportions – at least 5ft wide and 18in deep – and enrich it with organic material and with plenty of peat in order to hasten the penetration of the soil by the roots. Handle the roots of the young plant carefully and do not plant it deep, for the roots grow close to the surface. When returning the soil, firm it with care but *do not* harshly stamp it in with the heel, as so often wrongly advised. Water copiously (in itself a good method of firming). Thereafter never harry the nearby soil with hoe, spade or fork. Apart from a scattering of the seeds of a few annuals or perhaps a few small bulbs, allow nothing to encroach on the immediate root area, but mulch generously.

Naturally, magnolias fork low above the ground, branching out broadly, often to the embarrassment of people with small suburban gardens. This can be avoided, when essential, by pruning away the outermost branches low down at a point where they join some inner branch. Magnolias respond well to pruning and regenerate readily if damaged wood has to be cut or if a plant has become ungainly. Do the pruning at the end of July and protect with a suitable dressing all cuts of more than half an inch thick. Several species, especially the very strong ones such as *campbellii*, *grandiflora* and *delavayi*, can with profit be trained to a central lead.

After this somewhat lengthy introduction we must set out our few chosen varieties sparingly and in short terms. As before, we exclude all that are little more than shrubs, such as *stellata*, *highdownensis* and *watsonii*, and we exclude also those that are mainly foliage plants, such as *acuminata* and *cordata*. The easiest and most accommodating of all are *soulangiana* and its varieties, though they make only small trees. For gardens of modest size

other top choices are: *wilsonii, loebneri, denudata, salicifolia* and *sieboldii*.

M. campbellii The monarch of all, rising in favoured places up to 60ft. Huge, shell-pink goblets open out like water-lilies in very early spring (end of February in some places), with long leaves. It usually takes 25 years to flower. z8.

Of its several varieties, cultivars and colour forms, all taking about 12 years to flower, we may note:

mollicomata, a very fine natural variety (Bean). Mauve, 50ft.

'Lanarth' (or 'Borde Hill'). Deep lilac-purple. 50ft so far in Cornwall.

'Charles Raffill'. Petals deep purple without, white within. 'Kew's Surprise' is very similar.

'Darjeeling'. Vinous pink; valuable for late flowering.

M. delavayi Evergreen tree to 30ft (55ft in Cornwall). Large, fragrant, creamy, cup-shaped flowers, rather fleeting. Large, dull-green leaves. Accustomed to lime. In mild climates even better than *grandiflora*; a good wall plant elsewhere. z8.

M. denudata is the celebrated, beautiful and hardy Yulan of Chinese temple gardens. Give it a moist, acid, woodland soil, where it will reach 15ft in twenty years, ultimately perhaps 40ft, with a wide, rounded crown. The flowers are ivory-white, erect, outspreading, scented, but rather variable in form, borne with prodigality from late March to May, according to the season. In Britain it responds too eagerly to premature warmth and its buds may be spoilt by subsequent frost. Good varieties – 'Purpurascens' and 'Purple Eye' – describe themselves. z5.

M. grandiflora This lordly, evergreen, pyramidal tree is seen in great splendour in Italy and the French Riviera as well as in its native southern states of the USA, where it reaches 80ft; in Britain it can be a splendid 50ft. The white, scented, very large flowers begin to open in late

May, embowered among handsome, polished, dark-green leaves, and continue spasmodically for several weeks. In climes where it may be risky to plant in the full exposure it makes a very fine tree for a warm wall. Excellent in towns, it is surprisingly resistant to pollution. The best form is 'Goliath', but 'Exmouth' and 'Ferruginea' are also first-class and flower early if propagated by good nurseries. z7.

M. kobus var. **borealis** is a straight, sturdy tree of strong constitution, growing 30ft or more. It takes twelve years or so to flower and then, in April, breaks out abundantly into slender, narrow-petalled flowers of ivory white. Lime is no deterrent. z5.

M. × loebneri is an easy and hardy species of 35ft. Its white, fragrant, starry flowers appear when the tree is very young and in great profusion in April. It takes readily to all soils, including chalk. Two cultivars are of special merit – the rosy-lilac English 'Leonard Messel' and the white, fast-growing American 'Merrill'. z4.

M. hypoleuca (obovata), of 50 to 90ft, is of open, pyramidal habit. The very large, white, scented flowers hold back until early June. The large, obovate leaves are tinted blue on the undersides and its prominent fruits resemble cones. z5.

M. salicifolia (the "Anise" of America) grows to 40ft, with an elegant, closely pyramidal carriage. Large, white, spicily scented flowers are massed on naked branches in April and the narrow, willow-like leaves are also scented. It blooms when quite young and is beautiful in all its parts. z5.

M. sargentiania This very handsome tree reaches 60ft with very large flowers, mauve without, pale within, borne on leafless branches in April and opening out like large water-lilies. The leaves are glossy and dark-green. The variety 'Robusta' is the one to have. Flowers appear after about 12 years. z7.

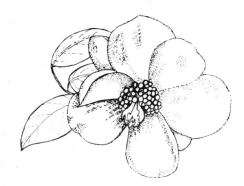

Magnolia sieboldii.

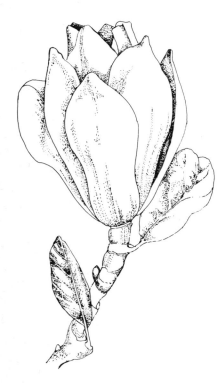

Magnolia × soulangiana.

Magnolia virginiana.

M. sieboldii (or *parviflora*) is a small tree of rounded habit. Its fragrant, white, cup-shaped, nodding flowers with brilliant red stamens bloom in early June, with a scattering throughout the summer, followed by spectacular crimson fruits. A fine tree for small gardens. z6.

M. × soulangiana, a hybrid originating in France, is the easiest and most popular magnolia, growing under best conditions to 25ft, broad and opulent, with a likeness to its noble parent, the Yulan. Pale pink, erect, tulip-form flowers begin to appear in April. For town and suburban gardens, it is one of the best. z5. Of its varieties, the choicest are as below. The petals of all are ivory-white on the inside.

'Lennei', of Italian origin. Petals a rich, deep rose-purple without borne for six weeks in April–May, escaping spring frosts. The most popular.

'Alexandrina'. White, flushed purple. Erect.

'Brozzonii'. Very large white flowers, opening 10in wide.

'Rustica Rubra'. Rose-red.

'Speciosa'. White, faintly flushed purple. Late. Erect.

'Verbanica'. Rose-pink. Late, usually escaping frost. Fine, erect habit.

M. sprengeri This beautiful tree may grow to 60ft, somewhat resembling *campbellii*. Large, saucer-like, scented flowers, rose-pink without, pale-pink within, blooms in March before the leaves. Its habit is pyramidal. The best form is *diva*. z7.

M. × veitchii is valuable for flowering when very young. A tree of 70ft and of open habit, it bears pink flowers, flushed with mauve, most of which appear in April before the leaves. The branches are brittle. z7.

M. virginiana (or *glauca*), is the "sweet bay" of America. It grows to 60ft, evergreen in warm zones, shrubby and deciduous in colder ones. Small, white, globular, very sweet flowers appear in late May, continuing all summer. Remarkable for flourishing in swampy soils. This was probably the first magnolia to be grown in England, in about 1675. z5.

M. wilsonii is a beautiful, small tree to 25ft. Large, fragrant, pendulous, white flowers with brilliant stamens appear in May and June. This is a lovely Chinese species much neglected in America. Successful in lime. z6.

MALUS
Apple, including Crab Apple

The botanical name *Malus* applies to all apples but we shall be concerned only with the crabs, which are not eligible for the fruit bowl but are grown for their value as ornamental trees. Their name comes from the old Norse *skrab* meaning sour wild apple.

As such (with few exceptions), they are not perhaps endowed with quite the same distinction and stylishness as the flowering cherries (Prunus). For the greater part of the year their foliage is dull, except in the copper-tinted varieties. Most of them are liable to be preyed upon by diseases and insects (especially the deadly fire-blight disease), though more so in North America than elsewhere. Nevertheless, the crab apples have their own special merits. Many are much hardier than the cherries (the Siberian crab enduring even sub-Arctic conditions); they are ideal little trees for very small gardens and several of them, having finished their floral display, which most of them do in May, reward the gardener again with the handsome fruits that ornament the boughs in autumn. In very cold climates the crabs are the most reliable of all flowering trees.

Fortunately for us, apples have promiscuous morals, much encouraged by man, so that from their crude and bitter origins there have been evolved not only the succulent fruits of the dessert bowl and the pot, but also the colourfully flowered crabs, the fruits of which are too bitter for us to eat but which may be as ornamental as the flowers, besides providing us with cider and jellies. For the floral splendour of the crab apples of today we are mainly indebted to those species which have come from the Orient and which have made happy marriages with the plainer natives of Europe and America.

Cultivation is easy enough. They will flourish in any reasonable soil that is not waterlogged, but must be watched for suckers sprouting from specimens that have been grafted and for pests and diseases. Species from China and Japan and their hybrids are, generally, less prone to disease, especially the scab disease, than those born in America. In the lists that follow we have separated the species from the named clonal varieties and we have omitted from both those found to be particularly prone to disease in various localities or to exhibit other faults; this means excluding for example, the otherwise beautiful Bechtel crab and the "Rosybloom" group raised in Canada and the States for ultra hardiness, such as 'Hope' and 'Almey'. As before, we exclude very small ones, such as the choice *sargentii* and *halliana* 'Parkmanii'.

Of the natural species that may be expected to attain about 25ft or more we select the following:

M. floribunda is florally the pride of them all. A strongly built tree of up to 30ft, with widespread, densely twiggy arms, it becomes massed in May with fragrant blossoms that begin deep pink, and gradually wane to palest blush. The whole tree is totally enveloped by the prodigality of the flowers. Other crabs may have more brilliant colours, others have more handsome fruit, but this one has class. z4.

Beyond all doubt **M. hupehensis** also has class. It shapes itself picturesquely in the form of a vase, with similar blossoms to that of *floribunda*, but it has a very loose, open framework of branches, not plentifully clothed in leaves. Never more than 25ft high, it is an ideal tree for small gardens, and makes a splendid espaliered tree on a wall. z4.

M. baccata, the white-flowered Siberian, richly scented crab apple, is not a great beauty but is important as being exceptionally tough, prospering even in the icy wastes of Zone 2. It may reach 50ft, with small slender leaves and abundant small fruits. Its two best varieties are *gracilis* and 'Jackii'. It is often confused with its hybrid off-spring *M. × robusta* which itself has a varied progeny, two of which are commonly known as the 'Red Siberian' and the 'Yellow Siberian'.

M. spectabilis is a fine old species long cultivated in Britain, where it can reach 30ft. It is most valued, however, for its double, deep-pink cultivar 'Riversii', a handsome tree of open habit. z4.

In **M. tschonoskii** we have a tree which is distinguished for neither its flower nor its fruit but for its fine, erect, almost pyramidal carriage and for its dazzling display of multi-coloured autumnal foliage. Reaching some 40ft, occasionally more, with a broad leaf, it is a first-class tree for roadside or screen planting. z5.

None of these species so far has been distinguished by its fruits, but in *M. toringoides* and the hybrid *M. × zumi* 'Calocarpa', we have two graceful trees of 25ft, pyramidal in design, which are hung in autumn with rather small but brightly enamelled little apples, much enjoyed by birds. Alas, fruiting usually occurs only every other year, but both are delightful trees. The leaf of the former is deeply cut with lobes, almost like a maple's.

Leaving the species, we turn to the hybrid clones, or selected individuals, mostly with vernacular names. Here we find many of the most popular sorts, desired for the prodigality of their bloom, the brilliance of their fruits or the colouring of their foliage. The flowers are often brightly coloured and often double; those that have double flowers are in bloom for a long season but rarely produce any apples. We have allowed the admission here of a few that are below our minimum of 25ft. All are z4 unless stated otherwise.

'American Beauty'. Red, double flowers, bronze foliage, upright habit. 20ft.

'Dorothea', large, semi-double flowers in

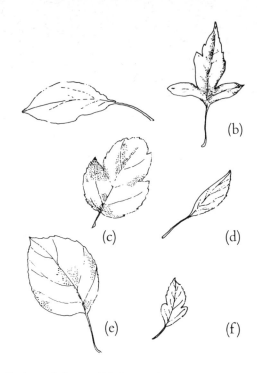

Crab-apple leaves (Malus *species*):
(a) spectabilis; (b) toringoides; (c) sargentii;
(d) halliana; (e) baccata; (f) sieboldii.

blends of crimson and silvery rose; plentiful yellow apples. A beauty. 25ft.

'Flame'. Pink flowers, red fruits. Ultra-hardy. 25ft. z2.

'Golden Hornet'. Large, rich-yellow apples in bunches all along the heavy-laden branches and persisting till Christmas. Spectacular dwarf tree to 20ft.

'Gorgeous'. New from New Zealand. Red buds, white flowers, prominent red fruits. 25ft.

'John Downie'. Best of all fruiters. Large, brilliantly coloured, ovoid, tempting apples in profusion. Edible though sharp. Good for jelly. Buds pink, opening white. Leaves rich, glossy green. 30ft.

'Katherine'. Very large, pale pink, fragrant flowers, red-cheeked fruits, both in crowded abundance. Open habit. 20ft.

'Lemoinei'. Flowers red-purple, leaves coppery, fruits dusky purple. Very popular. See 'Profusion'.

'Montreal Beauty'. Large white flowers, large yellow apples overlaid crimson. z3.

'Pink Perfection'. Double, scented flowers in startling abundance.

'Profusion'. Flowers rosy-purple, waning. Leaves copper-purple, changing to bronze-green. Small, blood-red fruits. A handsome child of Lemoine's crab. 'Liset' is a new grandchild, with improved colouring, flowering when very young and perhaps a little better than both.

'Red Jade'. Of picturesque, pendulous, often asymmetrical habit. Flowers white. Apples glowing red, small but profuse and lasting. 20ft.

'Red Sentinel'. Perhaps the best of the winter fruiters. The roseate apples come in large clusters all along the branch and challenge the snows of mid-winter.

'Snowcloud'. White, double flowers in great profusion. Narrow, upright habit, good for streets. An American. 16ft.

MANNA ASH See *Fraxinus ornus*

MAPLE See ACER

MAY See CRATAEGUS

MAZZARD See *Prunus avium*

MELIA

In areas not severely frost-bitten **Melia azedarach**, the chinaberry or bead tree, is a charming small tree of very easy cultivation in warm, dry places, tolerant of poor, starved soils and especially valuable as a town tree. The delicate, airy, doubly-pinnate foliage is accompanied by loose clusters of scented lilac flowers, followed by yellow berries formerly strung into rosaries, hence bead tree. Popular as a street tree in southern Europe and the southern United States, where it grows to about 40ft, but of no use in Britain. It grows very easily from seed, which germinate quickly when they fall from the tree. The natural variety *umbraculiformis* suggests a flat-topped umbrella. z8.

MESPILUS SNOWY See AMELANCHIER

MOCKERNUT See *Carya tomentosa*

MOOSEWOOD See *Acer pensylvanicum*

MORUS
Mulberry

Mulberries have been cultivated from time immemorial, some for their succulent fruits, others (particularly the white mulberries), as a feed for the voracious silkworm caterpillars. In the West mulberries are essentially trees for private gardens and a rugged old black mulberry poised on a lawn is one of the most delightful garden spectacles.

We have the choice of the black, red and white

mulberries and a few others. Most have broad, heart-shaped leaves and will grow in harsh, stony soil but better still and faster in a good, rich loam. They are excellent town trees, immune to poisoned air. The roots are brittle and must be handled with care when planting. They need sun.

The first choice for most people is the black mulberry, **M. nigra**. It is rather slow but in time develops into a gnarled and picturesque small tree of up to 30ft. Its fruits, resembling large blackberries, are quite delicious if left until they become almost jet black, but they do create an untidy litter on the ground. z7.

The white mulberry, **M. alba**, will grow quite quickly to 40ft and more narrowly than the black, but lacks its quaint charm. There is, however, a delightful weeping form in *M.a.* 'Pendula'. Not at all common in commerce and certainly not common in character. Place it in prominent isolation and it will turn a commonplace picture into a distinguished one as its broad, dense, rustling crinoline sweeps the ground. To get a good speci-men you must tie up a leading shoot year by year in order to form a fairly tall trunk, of 10ft or so. Other varieties of the white mulberry include those with large leaves, with deeply cut ones, a pyramidal one and a dwarf. z5.

The biggest of the mulberries is the red, **M. rubra**, valued in America for its timber and for its excellent resistance to drought.

MOUNTAIN ASH See SORBUS

MULBERRY See MORUS

NETTLE TREE See CELTIS

NOTHOFAGUS

Greek *nothos* plus Latin *fagus* adds up to "spurious beech", yet these fine, big, delicately textured trees from the Southern Hemisphere, which are closely allied to the beeches of the Northern, are not in the least spurious or false. They have their own positive identity as the southern expression of the northern tree. An Australian, indeed, might well put it the other way round. Change *nothos* into *notos*, meaning "south", and you have a true description of the "southern beech".

The southern beeches, however, are not nearly as hardy as the northern, being of doubtful validity in any climate colder than Zone 8. In the milder zones they are very welcome for their very fast growth and, in several species, for their densely set, evergreen foliage. In the best conditions – which means an open, acid, well-drained loam, not exposed to bleak winds – some will grow more than 100ft high. Their chief visual differ-ence from the *fagus* of the north is in their very much smaller and glossier leaves, often very much like those of the box, but saw-edged, their rich autumn colours and their slightly drooping branch tips. Their flowers are of no account and are followed by small, beech-like nuts. Most of them do well in southern England, especially in Cornwall, and there is a notable collection at Rowallane, in Northern Ireland.

All in the following list, except *fusca*, are Chil-ean species, which are hardier than those from Australasia. We prefer *obliqua* and *procera*.

N. antarctica, the deciduous Antarctic beech, has rich, dark, crinkled, glossy leaves and often resolves itself into a very large, loose, multi-stemmed bush. In autumn it robes itself in a gay Joseph's coat of many colours. This is an easy one, which may reach 100ft. Occasionally evergreen.

LEFT *The Raoul,* Nothofagus procera.

RIGHT *A young example of* Gleditsia triacanthos 'Sunburst' *in late summer.*

The antarctic beech, Nothofagus antarctica.

N. betuloides is evergreen, with very small, glossy, oval, densely packed leaves, forming a tight, compact tree to 80ft.

N. dombeyi Evergreen, with very dark, shining close-set doubly-toothed leaves. A most attractive tree of upright carriage. 75ft. May lose its leaves in a cold winter.

N. fusca, the red beech. Beautiful, evergreen, medium-sized tree, with rather round leaves, which often turn copper in winter. From New Zealand. Somewhat tender until established, yet flourishes in Edinburgh.

N. obliqua, the Robel beech. Large, handsome, of very fast growth, quickly making a fine specimen of 100ft or more, the slender branches fanning out and down. Dark-green, toothed leaves of about 3in.

N. procera, the Raoul. Another very fast mover, reaching 45ft in ten years and later some 90ft. Stoutly built and broadly pyramidal. Pale leaves veined and toothed to resemble rather those of the hornbeam. Fine autumn colours.

In mild, moist, maritime localities the evergreen New Zealanders *solandri*, *cliffortioides* and the tiny-leaved *menziesii* are quite at home.

NYSSA

To the ancient Greeks, Nyssa was a nymph of watery places, enjoying wet feet, and her tree still frequents similar haunts. To us her glory comes in the autumn, when, if in acid, moist soil, she puts on dazzling robes of scarlet and orange. Wherever an opportunity allows she should be planted *en*

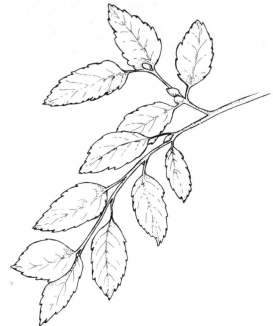

The Robel beech, Nothofagus obliqua.

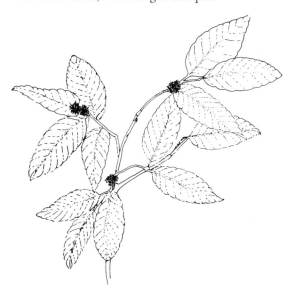

The Raoul beech, Nothofagus procera.

The New Zealand black beech, Nothofagus solandri.

masse, when she will create the impression that the panorama is on fire.

The popular choice is **N. sylvatica**, known (in America) variously by the less euphonious names tupelo, glack gum or sourgum. Like other nyssas, it is in nature a creature of swampy places and looks loveliest where massed close to water and reflected in it, but justifies itself elsewhere if the soil is moist and acid, succeeding in wet clay.

In its native parts of America the tupelo will reach 90ft, but nothing like that in Britain, with a pyramidal or broadly columnar deportment. Before its grand autumnal climax it is a rather commonplace tree, one would say, though its plain, oval leaves are of a dark lustrous green. It is classed z4, subject to the provenance of the seed, those of southern origin being very tender.

Of smaller and variable size – seldom more than 35ft high, and sometimes not more than a very large shrub – is the Chinese **N. sinensis**, a very handsome tree indeed, of which the young shoots are red and the autumnal array a glowing red and yellow. z7.

All nyssas object very much to root disturbance and should be planted when very young, with a good ball of soil, preferably container-grown.

OAK See QUERCUS

OSTRYA See under CARPINUS

OXYDENDRUM
Sorrel Tree

Oxydendrum is botanist's Greek for "sour tree", thus seeming to give some justification for its other, but unattractive popular name. But there is nothing sour about the oxydendrum unless it be the acid flavour of the leaves, which you are under no obligation to chew. On the contrary, **O. arboreum** (which is the only species in the genus) is a tree of great beauty, tall and fair and shapely, a choice decoration for a lawn or some other solitary station, rather than being planted *en masse* like the nyssas.

In the rich forest soil of its native Appalachian mountains the oxydendrum will reach 70ft, in a pyramidal or broadly columnar style, but elsewhere is rarely seen at much more than half that height. It needs an acid soil, moist, rich and humusy, and a fair measure of sun. In the spring the young leaves reveal themselves in an amber translucence and as they unfurl grow elegantly long, slender and lustrously green, congregated in crowded richness. Then in high summer come pendulous clusters of small, pretty lily-of-the-valley flowers and finally, as the Zodiac declines, the tree bursts out in a glory of scarlet. In all this one sees its kinship with the pieris, for, together with the rhododendrons and the heathers, it is a member of the same botanical Family.

The gardener should give the oxydendrum full licence to develop with its lowest branches sweeping the ground; to grow it on a "leg" reduces its natural beauty. z5.

PAGODA TREE See SOPHORA

PAPER MULBERRY
See BROUSSONETIA

PARROTIA

Parrotia persica is another tree known chiefly for the blaze of its autumn colours, but it has other beauties also. Its bark, after first youth, becomes a delightful patchwork of grey and buff, as in the London plane. Furthermore, its lateral branches and their broad, glossy leaves, being spread out in horizontal tiers before their tips begin to droop, create beautiful contrasts in light and shade, in the manner that artists call *chiaroscuro*.

The parrotia is usually seen as a tree of about 25ft, but if it likes the gardener can grow twice as high. Its branches splay out widely and strongly from close above ground, giving the effect of a large, powerful shrub. Some gardeners like it so, but indeed its beauty increases if it is trained to a clear trunk for a good six feet, when its mottled bark is seen the better and, when draped with a dense canopy of foliage, it makes a pleasant arbour for the hours of repose. In time the branches touch the ground and proceed to crawl along it. Let them do so, and be careful with the lawnmower. The flowers are clusters of crimson stamens, opening in March.

Give the parrotia full sun and plenty of elbow room. It succeeds and colours in lime, even occasionally in chalk. z5.

PAULOWNIA

Named after the Dutch princess, Anna Paulowna of the last century, these Chinese creations are among the most beautiful of flowering and scented trees, much neglected in Western gardens. In their strongly (but sparsely) branched structure, their carriage and their large, broad leaves, they much resemble the catalpa and are among the

Flowers of Paulownia tomentosa.

most ornamental of trees when set in a lawn in private or public gardens. They grow exceptionally fast, to about 40ft, and in May produce large, erect, pyramidal, scented flower trusses of most unusual and distinctive character, each floret shaped like a foxglove and painted in hues of violet, heliotrope or lilac.

The drawbacks, however, are that they usually hold back their flowers for a few years and that, as their furry, brown buds (which are themselves picturesque) are formed in the autumn, they may be shattered by a harsh winter. The tips of the fast-growing, sappy growths may also be nipped in winter and their brittle branches broken by storms, but there is no problem in cutting back to sound wood. Avoid cold, wet soils, in which the soft wood of whole branches may die back. A rather dry soil over sand or gravel gives good results and full sun is essential.

The best known of the paulownias is **P. tomentosa** (or *imperialis*). The florets are pale violet, 2in long, and unfurl on naked boughs before the leaves. It is usually reckoned a z5 tree but z6 is safer for the buds. An exceptional tree at Westonbirt reaches 85ft. Avoid the rather crude practice of cutting it down to the ground every spring, as it will never flower but will produce suckers with enormous leaves.

Rather less common is **P. fargesii**. A trifle less hardy, but in Britain often considered to be a better plant, this flowers at an earlier age than *tomentosa* and its heliotrope funnels, which are a

little larger, are freckled with purple spots with a dab of cream in the throat. z7.

The other two desirable, but rarer paulownias closely resemble *tomentosa*. In *P. fortunei*, the flowers are lilac on the exterior with a creamy throat heavily splashed with purple. In *P. lilacina* the flowers are lilac with a yellow throat.

PEAR See PYRUS

PECAN See *Carya illinoensis*

PERSIMMON See DIOSPYROS

PHELLODENDRON

Phellodendron amurense is the Amur cork tree from North China, of value for its resistance to town pollution, its sufferance of harsh conditions and its freedom from disease. Growing only to 40ft, but spreading widely, it has a gaunt, massive branch structure, a deeply furrowed, corky bark and handsome, compound foliage. It needs special training in the nursery to get a good, clean trunk. Grafted or budded male plants are preferable for public places, because the fruits from female trees are messy underfoot when they drop. z5.

PHILLYREA

Wherever a small, evergreen and umbrageous tree is the need, *Phillyrea latifolia* is an excellent choice. It develops into a 30ft tree, billowing with luxuriant masses of slim, lustrous leaves of a very dark green. At a little distance it might be taken for a full-grown strawberry tree or for a small evergreen oak. The crown is a dense dome, often broader than high. It succeeds in any reasonably good soil and is a happy choice for village greens. *Phillyrea* is its ancient Greek name. z7.

Other phillyreas are evergreen shrubs.

PLATANUS
Plane

Platanus is the ancient Greeks' name for this lordly tree, the species that they knew being the Oriental plane. Disregarding the fact that in Scotland the name "plane" is often applied to the English sycamore, we now have three others at our command.

They rank among the foremost of the world's

Platanus orientalis, *a favourite in France.*

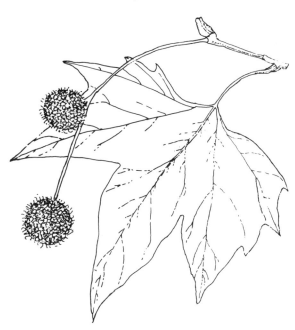

The London plane, Platanus × acerifolia.

big trees, being tall, strong and hardy, clothed with maple-like leaves, and having bold, straight trunks decoratively patchworked as the old, grey bark peels off to reveal a new layer of deep cream. The leaves are rather larger than those of the maples and are borne on the boughs alternately instead of oppositely. The round, bristly fruits, an inch in diameter, dangle like bobbles in small clusters in autumn and winter until they break up into a quantity of small, winged seeds, which sail away with the wind. Planes transplant particularly well, even up to 25ft high, and grow very fast, so creating an "instant landscape".

At the head of them all is the London plane, **P. × acerifolia** ("maple-leaved"), which is a hybrid between the Oriental and the American planes, and may have originated at Oxford about 1633. Shooting up to some 120ft in the open, straight, proud and strong, it is the king of all city trees, for it is impervious to pollution, heat and drought, thrives in impoverished soils and scorns the wounds caused by knife and saw. Acid and alkaline soils come alike to it, if not extreme. An ideal tree for boulevards, squares and other open spaces, it now adorns not only London but many of the great cities of Europe and America, its best known manifestation being in the most renowned of all avenues – the Champs Elysées in Paris. It has settled happily in many a village and far afield in New Zealand and North Africa. Thousands are planted every year. The pity is that it is so often planted in streets that are far too narrow for its wide-spreading branches, to the impediment of traffic and the obscuration of nearby houses, so that the municipal authorities have to prune them hard, and not all do it well.

The maple-form leaves of the London plane are variable, having anything from three to seven lobes (usually five) and are distinguished from those of the sycamore by being smoother and less coarsely toothed and from the Norway maple by being much larger. In the open the tree grows much larger than in streets, where its roots are constricted. There is a magnificent specimen beside the ponds at Carshalton, Surrey, 132ft high. Those in Berkeley Square and other London squares are more than 200 years old and reach to 100ft. The oldest known tree is in the grounds of the Bishop's Palace of Ely, believed to have been planted in 1674.

The London plane should always be raised from cuttings deriving from the original clone, for seedlings vary considerably and most are decidedly inferior.

We are now expected by the botanist to call it *P. × hispanica*, an unhappy choice of name; Rehder gives *hispanica* as merely a variety of *acerifolia*. There are a few other varieties, of which the most useful for street planting is the moderately narrow, erect 'Pyramidalis'. Others merely have variegated leaves, as in 'Suttneri'. The London plane is rated z5.

The Oriental plane, **P. orientalis**, comes a very close second to the Londoner, but is a trifle less lusty and definitely less hardy. The trunk is short and stout, the leaves deeply cut and five-fingered. It has been cultivated in England since the days of Henry VIII, but is not very often seen nowadays. Its natural variety *insularis* is a smaller, easily accommodated tree with prettily sculptured leaves. z6.

Beside these, the American plane, **P. occidentalis**, known there also as the buttonwood or American sycamore, is usually a rather poor third, being highly susceptible to the twig-blight disease. However, it is extra hardy and so is useful in such climates as the northern United States and southern Russia, and fortunately there are some rural localities where it is healthy and it then makes an enormous tree, with the young bark almost pure white. It produces only single fruit-bobbles instead of clusters. Disappointing in Britain. z4.

roots not only send up thickets of suckers but also grow so close to ground level and even on top of it, that the mowing of grass is impossible unless a good layer of soil is spread over them. A more serious charge is the danger that the roots may cause to houses and drains. Required to supply water to the mass of large-pored wood above, the roots range far and wide, sucking moisture greedily from the earth, so that, in areas of low rainfall, and especially in clay, the soil dries, shrinks and subsides, causing the collapse of walls above them. In the same search for moisture the roots also penetrate drains. Therefore poplars should never be planted within 60ft of any solid structure and their use in towns should be forbidden. In wet soils the danger is much less.

Several poplars are also dirty trees. Male and female flowers are borne on separate trees in catkins and the females, having been pollinated, set their seed in small fruit pods, which split open about midsummer and release their seed to the wind. These seeds, equipped with tufts of fine, white hairs, float down to ground in untidy drifts of white fluff, to the distress of the gardener. Accordingly it is usually best to plant male trees only.

On the credit side, poplars can show that they are very hardy, fast-growing and resistant alike to pollution, the wind and to salt-laden gales from the sea. They thus make very good shelter belts and rapidly form screens to hide factories or other objectionable features. In the main, therefore, we have to consider them as utility trees rather than ornamental ones, though those of fastigiate or columnar form, besides their value as screens, can also be very impressive embellishments of the landscape.

In the main the leaves of poplars are small and deltoid or diamonded. A few are lobed. The species and hybrids are very numerous and identi-

fication is often very difficult, even for the expert. In the short list below we have chosen those that are generally found to be most useful. Pruning, if necessary, is done in winter dormancy.

The most familiar poplars are the slim, fastigiate or columnar varieties of the black poplar, **P. nigra**, especially the fast-growing Lombardy poplar (*P.n.* 'Italica'), which marches for mile upon mile alongside Napoleon's roads in France. Beside its uses as an avenue tree, it can be used also with great effect to provide a picturesque sky-line or as a windshield or as a screen against some objectionable feature. It has the virtue of being a clean, male tree, but, being in some areas plagued by canker, is to a large extent being replaced by the similar but slightly plumper 'Plantierensis'. For a screen, plant both 10ft apart. The parental *P. nigra*, native to Britain and parts of Europe, is not a choice tree, but appropriately furnished the garden of Persephone in Hades. z3.

Similar to the Lombardy poplar, but far more unusual, is **P. simonii 'Fastigiata'**, an extremely hardy poplar from North China. Slim and very dense, it is a useful screening tree in very cold regions, with glossy, red-tinted twigs and shining oval leaves rather like a plum's. z2.

Also similar, but considerably plumper, is the Berlin poplar, **P. × berolinensis**. Decidedly ornamental, with a burred trunk, it is exceptionally hardy and a male to boot. Much used on the continent of Europe and in the North American prairies. 70ft. z2.

P. alba is the conspicuous white poplar, easily recognised by the creamy patches on its bark, the white down on the winter twigs and the white, downy undersides of the lobed, rather maple-like leaves, which sparkle with excitement when ruffled by the wind. A large, wide-spreading tree up to 90ft and of random carriage. It prefers a moist, light loam, resists salt sea winds and suc-

POPULUS
Poplar

Whatever their origins, the sign-manual by which you shall know most of the poplars is the lively dancing of their foliage at the wind's least command. This trick they perform by balancing their leaves, which are usually small, on stalks that are long, slim and flattened. The aspens and the white poplar are particularly noted for this pretty dance.

Poplars may also be known, however, by less agreeable habits. With some distinguished exceptions, they have a random, ungainly posture, are very prone to a bacterial canker and their

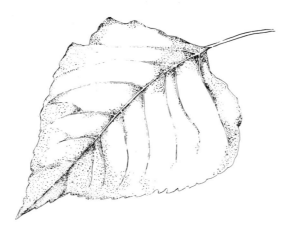

The black poplar, Populus nigra, *from which is derived the Lombardy poplar.*

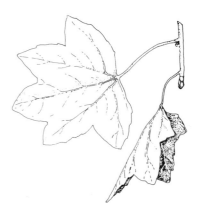

The white poplar, P. alba, *showing the conspicuous white of the reverse, which glitters when agitated by the wind.*

ceeds in chalk. It is the old Abele of Britain and is not so large or well shaped as the grey poplar. Suckers grow freely and form a thicket if allowed. It is an excellent tree where a mass of silvery foliage is wanted and effective as a shelter belt or to stabilise poor soil. z3.

Two good varieties of the white poplar are the columnar 'Pyramidalis', a rival to the Lombardy poplar but short-lived, and the picturesque, smaller 'Richardii', in which the upper surface of the leaf is bright yellow instead of green – a pretty combination.

P. lasiocarpa is an unusual Chinese poplar not exceeding 70ft, with an open crown, long, upswept branches and few laterals. It is distinguished by very large leaves (often exceeding a foot), bright green, red-ribbed and carried on red stalks. z5.

The lively, excitable aspens, with their small leaves delicately attached to thin, pliant stalks, are exceptionally hardy and picturesque trees when in a wide landscape, being particularly responsive to the slightest whim of the wind and fluttering like flocks of tiny, dove-grey birds as their pale undersides are revealed. At their best when planted with a large hand in groves and drifts, rather than singly, they do well even in wet, infertile soils. In **P. tremula**, of z2, we have a suckering tree of 50ft, with both fastigiate and weeping forms. **P. tremuloides**, the quaking aspen, is a much bigger tree, of possibly 90ft, so utterly hardy that it braves even the Arctic conditions of z1. The bark is cream or even white and when the leaves turn brilliant yellow in autumn the combined effect is beautiful. A fine mountain tree, superb in the Rockies.

We now turn to a few hybrid poplars.

A big tree that has a special character of its own is the uncommon golden poplar, **P. 'Serotina Aurea'**. Fortunately a male tree, it is late in

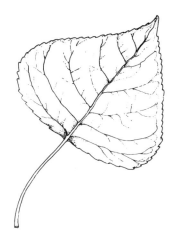

The hybrid "black Italian poplar", P. 'Serotina'.

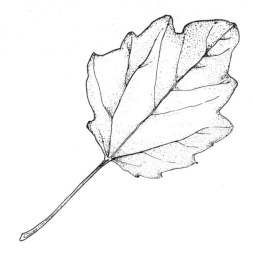

The grey poplar, P. canescens.

coming into leaf, gleams brightly in spring and early summer and turns golden again in autumn. It is resistant to disease, salt and sea spray, but not always of a gracious habit, since its random branches sometimes form an uneven crown. Prune it back every other February to encourage its young foliage and control its size. There is also a columnar form, 'Serotina Erecta'. z4.

A few other hybrids have come to the fore for their good qualities. Perhaps the best is **'Robusta'**, a big, fast, vigorous male, with a fine, straight mast running right up the middle, columnar in habit, aglow with red catkins in April. It is one of the best trees for the regeneration of derelict soils. Another is the very narrow **'Eugenei'**, a child of the Lombardy poplar, reaching 100ft in 30 years. Its other parent, 'Regenerata', is a tough, utility tree, widely used in industrial areas. z4.

Most other poplars, such as the huge, suckering grey poplar (*P. canescens*), must also be considered as utility trees, while others are noted for their rich and pervading aromas in spring, such as the Ontario poplar (*P. × candicans*); the balsam poplar (*P. balsamifera* or *tacamahaca*); and the black cottonwood (*P. trichocarpa*), much plagued by canker. In *candicans* there is an attractive form called 'Aurora', in which the young leaves open cream and pink. Encourage these by occasional hard pruning in February. All are big trees of z4.

PRUNUS

Here we enter upon a large field, of which, within our restricted scope, we can graze only the verges. Rich treasures lie within – cherries, peaches, plums, damsons, nectarines, almonds and sloes – both those that are grown for the bounty of their

fruits and those that we cherish for the splendour of their springtime blossoms. We shall be concerned here only with the latter but even among them the choice is bewildering; hundreds of species and varieties are in cultivation.

So we shall begin by passing by all those that are normally used for hedging and suchlike, and those that are only small shrubs. But, as we have done with crab-apples and hawthorns, we shall allow ourselves some tolerance in the sizes of the tree forms, admitting some that do not reach our 25ft minimum.

Prunuses are easy enough to grow on any reasonably good soil, limy or acid, provided that there is good drainage and no danger of the roots becoming waterlogged. They enjoy sun, particularly for the ripening of next season's buds. The roots grow fairly close to the surface and should not be harried by fork or hoe. Birds can be a sore trial in some areas, pecking off the young buds in winter. Various other pests and diseases also worry the trees. In the peaches and almonds the commonest is peach-leaf curl, in which the leaves are distorted and blistered; this can be avoided by spraying with the same copper-based fungicides as are used for black spot on roses, doing so at leaf-fall and again a little before the leaf buds break in late winter.

Avoid pruning unless essential, when the only right time for major cutting is June or early July, but small twigs can be cut off at other times. As a rule the trees are grafted and trained as standards, but many look splendid when branching naturally just above ground, as may be seen at the Royal Botanic Gardens at Kew. Shoots sprouting from the ground, or near it, should be removed, as they are likely to be from the undesired rootstock.

Except for the autumn-flowering cherries, blossom time extends from February to late May. Many flower on naked branches, others just as the leaf-buds break open, the young leaves often coming out in dresses of chestnut or bronze before maturing to green. The barks, especially of the cherries, add to the beauty of the whole picture. Several have been raised or introduced by that great English expert in this genus, Captain Collingwood Ingram. The group of wild "bird cherries", which are pretty big trees, are not florally as glamorous as the popular small species, but are valuable in the landscape and in larger gardens and are extra hardy.

There is a good deal of confusion and duplication of names, especially in the cherries of Japanese origin. We shall here follow what we consider to be the best authorities. For convenience, we have grouped those known as "Japanese cherries of garden origin" under *P. serrulata*.

P. 'Accolade' Hybrid cherry. Rich pink,

The gean or mazzard, Prunus avium, *a favourite in Britain.*

semi-double, elegant, fringed, pendulous flowers on a broad, low-crowned tree. Early April. To 30ft.

P. × **amygdalo-persica** An almond-peach hybrid. The variety 'Pollardii' is a beauty. Large, single, almond-like flowers of rich pink on naked branches in March. To 25ft. z6. See also *P. dulcis.*

P. avium 'Plena' The big, double-flowered form of the gean or mazzard. A beautiful bird cherry native to Britain and parts of Europe and very hardy. Triangular in profile, the branch structure very neat, regular and open. Clusters of small, dangling, white flowers all along the branches. Leaves drooping slightly. A natural woodlander, a fine amenity tree for landscaping and for avenues and one of the very best for degenerate soils. Introduced to the American colonies in the year of the *Mayflower.* It suckers and can be coppiced. To 60ft. z3.

P. × **blireana** A plum-apricot hybrid. Light pink, double flowers in April with copper foliage. Beautiful small tree to 22ft. z5.

P. cerasifera is the myrobalan or cherry plum much used for hedging, but 'Pissardii', with pink flowers and copper leaves, is handsome on its own. The American 'Thundercloud' is better still, with rich purple foliage. In 'Nigra' the leaves are almost black. 24ft. z4.

P. conradinae 'Semiplena' An elegant, early tree with scented, pale pink, semi-double flowers, sometimes as early as late February. 25ft. z6.

P. dulcis New name for *amygdalus,* the common almond, grown commercially for its nuts, but also in gardens for its beautiful pink flowers, usually appearing on naked twigs. Slender, pointed buds. Varieties include 'Roseoplena' (the double almond), and the drooping 'Pendula'. z6.

P. 'Hally Jolivette', a cherry hybrid. Small, graceful, dense, willowy tree from the Arnold Arboretum. Pink buds, opening to double, white flowers, longest in bloom of all cherries. May. Perhaps 18ft. z5.

P. × **hillieri 'Spire'** Very fine columnar cherry raised by Hilliers of Winchester. Single flowers of soft pink. Fine autumn colours. Ideal street tree. 25ft by 9ft wide. z5.

P. 'Kursar' Hybrid cherry. Vigorous, upright, twiggy tree. Single, deep-pink flowers in profusion as the chestnut leaves unfurl. Early April. 25ft. z5.

P. maackii One of the bird cherries. Useful as being ultra hardy and esteemed for its glossy, honey-coloured bark. White, scented flowers in erect, oval spikes. Known as the Manchurian cherry or Amur chokecherry. 45ft. z2.

P. mume, the Japanese apricot, is one of the most beautiful of prunuses, with pink, almond scented flowers, sometimes flowering in England as early as February (but more often April) and makes a marvellous picture when encased in ice. There are several good variations, especially notable being the scented, double, pink 'Beni-shi-Don'. 25ft. z6.

P. 'Okame' This lovely little hybrid cherry, massed with dangling, single, carmine blossoms through March is ideal for small gardens. 23ft. z6.

P. padus 'Plena' The English bird cherry, fond of Scotland, smaller than the gean. A round-headed tree with slender drooping branches and long, dangling streamers of dense, white florets. Leaves light green, colouring well in autumn. Smooth, dark-grey bark. The single-flowered 'Watereri' is also very handsome. z3.

P. 'Pandora' Small hybrid cherry. Large single, shell-pink blossoms on ascending branches. Young foliage bronze. Excellent for very small gardens. 20ft. z6.

RIGHT *The laburnum alley in the Queen's Garden at Kew.*

P. persica, the peach. In addition to the varieties grown for their luscious fruits, there are several ornamental ones that excel in their blossoms. They are fast-growing but seldom long-lived. The best of them is 'Klara Mayer', charmingly arranged in double, long-lasting blossoms. Others are 'Helen Borchers', with semi-double, rose-pink flowers, 'Iceberg' and two or three "weepers". Beware of peach-leaf curl. All grow to 24ft except for the "weepers". z5.

P. sargentii is a glorious cherry, its bark a lustrous chestnut and its crown massed with single, deep-pink flowers in early spring. As the blossoms fall the foliage breaks out in copper-bronze, maturing to green, before becoming ensanguined in crimson and orange in autumn. It may soar to 70ft, though not in Britain. When on its own roots it forks low above the ground; as a standard it is usually budded on a stem of the gean. z4.

P. serotina, the black or rum cherry, is a big, spreading American bird cherry of 80ft, with dense, lustrous foliage and erect 5in stems of crowded florets, like candles, followed by red cherries turning black. A good landscape tree. z3.

P. serrula, the Tibetan cherry, is particularly distinguished for the brilliant gloss of its red-mahogany bark, which is improved by being stroked. Few trees are so colourful in winter. In spring masses of small white flowers dangle from the branches, but are partly obscured by the willow-like leaves. 30ft. z5.

P. serrulata This is the dominant parent of those sumptuous little trees called the "Japanese Cherries of Garden Origin". The Japanese themselves collectively call them "Sato Zakura". We shall use their Japanese names, which are botanically correct, not their dog-Latin ones. The spellings are phonetic transliterations of the Japanese script and vary according to the author writing them. Except where stated otherwise, all may be reckoned to grow to about 25ft, or less, and to be on the borderline of Zones 5 and 6. The leaves of most are about 6in long, saw-edged and finely pointed. Many open in copper or bronze tints and their thin barks are picturesquely ringed. From among the 40-odd cultivars we have had to prune hard, and choose the following:

'Amanogawa'. Erect, slim, fastigiate, fitting the smallest corner. Unique of its kind. Bears dense clusters of semi-double, pale-pink flowers. Ideal street tree or as an accent note in the private garden.

'Asano'. Dense cluster of deep pink, very double flowers. Good, upright habit.

'Botan Zakura'. Small tree with large, semi-double, pale pink scented flowers.

'Daikoku' (or 'Benifugen'). Purple buds opening lilac-pink, in loose, dangling clusters of double flowers. Strong, ascending branches.

'Fugenzo'. Large, double, pendant, rose-pink. Flat-topped and wide-spreading. Young leaves bronze. Still listed by some nurseries as 'James H. Veitch'.

'Hokusai'. Large, semi-double, pale pink. Vigorous, wide-spreading, well-tried and trusty.

'Ichiyo'. Double, shell-pink, fringed flowers, dangling on long stalks. Very pretty.

'Jo-nioi'. Single, white, scented blossom wreathe the widely flung branches in May.

'Kanzan' (or 'Kwanzan'), often erroneously called 'Sekiyama' or 'Hisakura'. Probably the most popular of all cherries. Strong, upflung branches obliterated in May by massed clusters of very double flowers in brilliant, deep orchid pink, but only for 7–10 days. The high-angle branches make it a good pathside tree.

'Kiku-shidare Sakura'. Loveliest of the weepers and popularly known as Cheal's weeping cherry. Deep-pink, very double flowers make an alluring crinoline, 18ft wide.

'Pink Perfection'. Bright rose-pink buds opening to double, paler flowers on long, dangling stalks. Raised in England, not Japan.

'Shimidsu Sakura' (known also as 'Shogetsu' and *longipes*). One of the loveliest of hybrid cherries. Double, fringed, blush-pink flowers, waning to white, hanging like ballet skirts from long-stalked clusters on a wide-spreading, flattish crown. Superlative.

'Shirofugen'. Purple-pink buds opening to large, double white flowers, flushing again to purple-pink, very long lasting. Very late May. Branches arching and pendulous. Bronze foliage, turning green. A beauty.

'Shirotae', the Mount Fuji cherry. Very striking and distinctive small tree, with branches so horizontal that it looks like the letter T until later they droop at the tips. Very large, semi-double, white, scented flowers in long, drooping clusters. Splendid as a specimen tree. z6.

'Tai Haku'. The superb 'great white cherry'. Very large, single flowers of dazzling white on a stalwart tree, 35ft high and nearly as wide. Leaves 8in long, opening red. Of unforgettable beauty.

'Ukon'. An almost unique cherry with pale, semi-double, yellow flowers, making a rare combination with the bronze young leaves. A robust, spreading tree.

P. subhirtella, the "rosebud" or Higan cherry, is a hardy, early-flowering species marked by small, toothed, faintly hairy leaves of fine texture. z5. Here again there are some superlative variations, the chief of which are:

'Autumnalis', the autumn or winter cherry, a

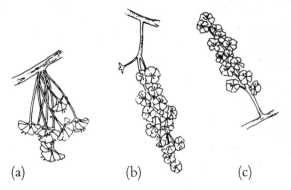

Diverse flowering habits of some bird cherries: (a) *the gean (*Prunus avium*); (b) P. padus; (c) *the American black cherry (*P. serotina*).*

Pruning the fastigiate cherry 'Amanogawa' on arrival from the nursery (and subsequently if needed). Leave the leader alone but prune back all other stems by a quarter or a third to an outward-facing bud.

One of the most beautiful of all flowering cherries, the ballet-skirted 'Shimidsu Sakura' (or 'Longpipes').

PREVIOUS PAGES, LEFT *The Kentucky coffee tree,* Gymnocladus dioicus.
PREVIOUS PAGES, RIGHT Nyssa sylvatica *in autumn.*
LEFT *The London plane,* Platanus × acerifolia.

III

beautiful small tree of 25ft with tiny, white, semi-double flowers, pink in bud, which are clustered all along the boughs and produced from November to March according to the weather, blossoming in mild spells, closing up in cold ones. The chief floral glory of winter. The most favoured form is the deep pink 'Autumnalis Rosea'.

'Fukubana'. Stunning small tree with warm, semi-double, rose-madder flowers in early spring.

Three beautiful weeping forms of *subhirtella* are also offered us in 'Pendula Rubra', wreathed in deep rose-pink, 'Pendula Rosea', in lighter pink, and 'Pendula Plena Rosea', with warm pink, semi-double flowers that last a long time.

P. × yedoensis is the celebrated Yoshino cherry, of large, graceful, arching carriage, profusely decorated in single, blush, almond-scented flowers in March–April (if not robbed by the birds). It can be 45ft high and is an excellent tree for industrial sites and roadsides. In 'Ivensii' it becomes a beautiful "weeper" with long, slender, tortuous branches cascading to the ground in single snow-white blossom. It is better than the usual 'Pendula', which is all too fleeting. z5.

PYRUS
Pear

We shall consider only two of the ornamental, non-fruiting species. The first is **P. salicifolia 'Pendula'**. In good specimens this is a picturesque, semi-weeping tree, densely clothed in small leaves like those of the willow, but beautifully silvered, changing slowly to silver-grey. The habit is upright and it is the branch tips that "weep", so that it does not become, like many other weepers, a broad and spreading crinoline. It is essentially a tree for the private garden. You must pick your specimen at the nursery, for some are of ungainly growth, bushy and matted. In its early years you must accordingly give it careful thinning and training, to induce a main leader to grow tall and erect. It prefers a rich, well-drained soil, but succeeds in chalk. 30ft. z4.

The other species that we choose is **P. calleryana**, the Callery pear. It was of no interest until two very good clones established themselves for their tolerance of bad town conditions, stiff clay soils and resistance to the fire blight disease. These clones are 'Bradford', which has been dramatically successful in America, and the narrowly pyramidal 'Chanticleer', which in Britain has done better than 'Bradford'. Both are wreathed in clouds of pure white flowers in spring and have splendid red or maroon foliage in autumn. z5.

QUERCUS
Oak

The oaks, which so handsomely ornament the three continents of the north temperate zone, vary surprisingly in their forms and features, some being merely stunted shrubs, others lordly and dominant, seeming to claim dominion over all nature. This sense of dominance is felt particularly in the woodlands of the British Isles, where every third tree is an oak. No environment more readily evokes a feeling of serenity and security, none arouses so many pleasant phantasies of antiquity and fairy tale as an old oak forest, carpeted with primroses, wood anemones and bluebells. Your forests of beech, maple, conifer and birch stir quite different evocations.

In all oaks the sign-manual to the ordinary man is the acorn, a word anciently derived from the Old English *ac* meaning oak, and *corn*, meaning seed – an exact description. The nut nestles in a little cup, formed by the fusion of several very small, leaf-like bracts. In most oaks also we see a leaf of wavy, sinuous or lobed outline, but this by no means occurs in every species, some being very deeply indented and sharp pointed, others having no indentation at all in the margins. Several are evergreen.

The flowers of the oak are borne in catkins, usually quite inconspicuous. After ripening, the acorns fall to the ground, where they used to provide the traditional food for pigs. So important was the mast or acorn crop to the economy of England in the old days that, in the Domesday Book of William the Conqueror, a village might be assessed for tax as having "wood for 50 swine".

The small, round "oak apple" often found on some oak trees, and sentimentally associated with Charles II, is not, of course, a fruit of any kind, but is a gall, or swelling, caused by a tiny grub that, having emerged from an egg deposited by its mother, feeds on the tissues of the tree, without doing it any harm at all. Several other galls are formed by various insects that find the oak to be a good maternity home, but they do little damage and in Europe the oak is usually highly resistant to illnesses.

Unfortunately the same cannot be said of oaks in North America, where they are much more susceptible to harassment by various insects and bacteria that are difficult to repel. Nor are the majority of America's species well fitted for limy soils. On the other hand, unlike the Europeans and Asiatics, most of the native American oaks burst out in a blaze of brilliant colour in the autumn.

An enormous range of species and varieties is at the command of the gardener and the builder of landscapes. We have here chosen a selection of those that are the most desirable. It needs hardly to be said that, to display their full splendour, all oaks should be given the maximum elbow room.

Q. acutissima is an Asiatic oak equipped with leaves like those of the sweet chestnut – lustrous, narrowly oblong, with saw-tooth margins. It wears a handsome, shapely crown with far flung branches, but has no fall colour. 50ft by 40ft wide. z6.

Q. alba The great white oak of America is a massive and majestic tree, very long-lived, reaching to 100ft (more in very old specimens, but much less in Britain), with classic, rounded outline when in isolation and a lusty spread of 80ft. In autumn it is splendidly dressed in shades of purple and the withered leaves linger for most of the winter. It develops a strong tap root, so must be planted young, and grows slowly. z4.

Two specimens of the white oak are particularly famous. One is the Mercer Oak at Princeton, beneath which the young General Mercer died of wounds in 1777. The other is the Kilmer Oak at New Brunswick, New Jersey, a venerable tree with a large trunk and a spread of 100ft, which inspired Joyce Kilmer to write his famous poem "Trees".

Q. borealis See *rubra*.

Q. canariensis, the Algerian oak, grows very fast to form a compact dome, sometimes 100ft high. Its characteristic is that it is densely enveloped with dark-green, regularly lobed leaves, which persist right up to Christmas. The acorn sits in a shallow saucer. Safe in chalk soils. z7.

Q. castaneifolia is obviously known as the chestnut-leaved oak from the close resemblance of its leaves to those of the sweet-chestnut (*Castanea*). It is a magnificent, hugely domed, fast-moving tree, looking rather like the Turkey oak, with a massive trunk. Exceeds 100ft. z7.

Q. cerris is the big, easy and distinctive Turkey oak from the Mediterranean. It grows very fast, making some 17ft in the first ten years, finally becoming a fine tree of 120ft in 70 years. Coated with a fissured bark, the Turkey oak is excellent in a maritime situation, enjoys a stiff loam and is less dense and spreading than the English oak. The leaves are narrowly oblong and very variable in pattern, some deeply incised, others with saw-like notches on the margins. Having withered in the autumn, they cling on to form a russet winter jacket to the lower branches. The stalkless acorn cups are coated with soft, mossy hairs. Best planted in spring. Safe in chalk. z6.

Q. coccinea is the splendid scarlet oak, so named from the brilliance of its autumn colour. Of more open and erect habit than most oaks, it

The Japanese "chestnut oak", Quercus acutissima.

The variable Turkey oak, Q. cerris; *some leaves are more deeply incised.*

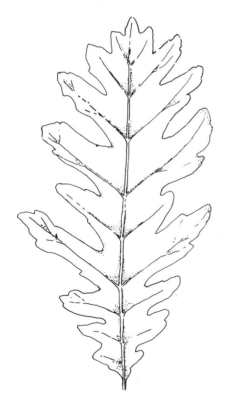

The magnificent Hungarian oak, Q. frainetto.

The scarlet oak, Quercus coccinea.

wears handsome, glossy, dark-green, deeply lobed, bristle-tipped leaves in its summer dress and is a fine tree for landscape use, but unfortunately difficult to transplant and needs extra care after moving. A good example of its use is in the Veterans' Highway outside Boston. The English-raised Knaphill oak, 'Splendens', has big leaves (7in long) and is a fine, richly hued clone, the best for colour. The deep autumnal crimson persists for many weeks, then changes to a warm chestnut, often holding its own all winter. For any good soil.

The scarlet oak grows about 12–15ft in the first 10 years and reaches 80ft in about 70 years. z4.

The Hungarian oak, **Q. frainetto**, is a magnificent tree with which most of us are not nearly as familiar as we ought to be. In good, loamy soil it grows fast, shooting up a stout central mast to 100ft and more, from which the straight branches radiate to form a huge dome, densely draped in large (7 to 8in), dark green, glossy leaves, which are slim at the base and irregularly scalloped into multiple lobes. An impressive and valuable adornment for parks and ample public places. z5.

The name **Q.** × **hispanica**, the so-called Spanish oak, embraces a number of progeny resulting from the marriage of the Turkey and the cork oaks. Because of the exuberance of their seedlings, they have taken widely different forms, to which one might have expected the botanist to attach separate labels. Often evergreen, or partially so, they are lime-tolerant and rated z7.

The best known of the Spanish oaks is called the Lucombe oak, which originated in England in the eighteenth century, but even here we find two totally different forms, lacking precise labels. One is a large, sparsely branched, rather upright tree, with pale-grey bark, slim leaves, 4 to 5in

The holm oak, Q. ilex.

The shingle oak, Q. imbricaria.

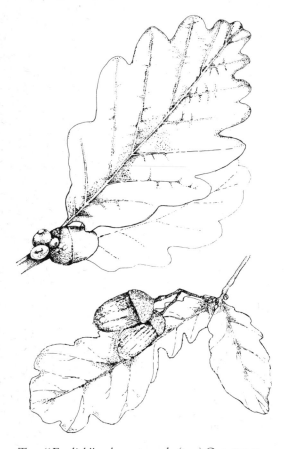

Two "English" oaks compared: (top) Q. petraea, *the sessile oak, with the acorns sitting tightly down on the twigs; (below)* Q. robur, *the pedunculate oak, the acorns having stalks (but not the leaves).*

long, notched on the margin, and evergreen until January. The other form becomes a broad, dense dome, luxuriantly furnished overall with small, oval, similarly notched leaves, which are wholly evergreen in all but the harshest winters.

Another form of the Spanish oaks, quite different from 'Lucombeana', is the Fulham oak. This is a slender tree, with drooping, evergreen branches and inheriting the bark of the cork oak. A corky bark is seen also in 'Diversifolia', a very slim, erect tree, with a narrow leaf almost cleft in two about the middle.

Q. ilex is the big, evergreen holm oak, grandest of all broadleaf evergreens in northerly latitudes. Still known as the holly oak, "holm" being the Old English for the holly and hence the botanical *ilex*, Latin for the holly. An exceptional tree from the Mediterranean, it grows to 80ft in southern England, with a massive, symmetrical, half-moon crown and far-spreading arms and is a magnificent spectacle when grown alone, particularly memorable in earliest summer, when the pale young leaves and the yellow catkins are put forth. The leaves are usually willow-like – narrow, slender, almost entirely without any fretting on the margins, though wide variations are found – and are dark green on the upper surface, paler below. The bark is black and rugged, split into small squares.

The holm oak prospers in any kind of soil, except very cold ones. It is a maritime tree and prefers an open, dry, sunny place. You can cut it back as hard as you like and in the British Isles it is often used as a seaside shelter-hedge. You must plant it when small and expect it to grow 12–15ft in the first 10 years. z8.

Q. imbricaria is the shingle oak, so called from its use for shingles by the early settlers in America. A beautiful oak, but rare in commerce, it is pyramidal in youth, spreading broadly later, and is known by its shining, dark-green, oblong, laurel-like leaves, usually without lobes or notches. These leaves turn russet and often cling to the boughs in winter, like those of the common beech. Also like the beech, it submits to being cut back hard to make a hedge. To 70ft. z5.

Q. libani, the Lebanon oak, is a handsome, small tree, almost evergreen, with glossy, narrow, persistent leaves, their margins saw-edged, like those of *acutissima*, and exceptionally large acorns. It is scarce in commerce and deserves far wider recognition. 50ft. z5.

Q. palustris, the picturesque pin oak, is a great favourite in North America, finely exhibited in Monument Avenue, Richmond, Virginia. It is a free-growing, broadly pyramidal tree with slender boughs, the lowest of which stoop down at their tips to stroke the earth, giving to the whole tree an air of graciousness. From these branches hangs a dense foliage of very small, shining, deeply indented, almost skeletonised, sharply pointed leaves that flush scarlet in the fall. Having a fibrous root system, the pin oak transplants easily and grows quickly, but it does not take to limy soils. It needs elbow room and is unsuitable for streets, except the American clones 'Crown-right' and 'Sovereign' in which all the branches are ascending, without drooping at the tips. To 75ft. z4.

Two impressive European oaks of noble bearing and old renown now come to our notice. They are very much like to one another in general appearance, but have their distinguishing marks. These are **Q. petraea**, known as the sessile or Durmast oak ("sessile" meaning "stalkless"), and **Q. robur**, usually known as the English oak, though in fact it is widely distributed in Europe and Asia. In the timber trade both are called "English". From these were built the wooden ships of old.

Both grow into massive, strapping trees, with wide-flung limbs. In exceptional circumstances they may soar up to 150ft, though rarely to more than 120ft. The biggest in England is the antique specimen of *robur* at Bowthorpe Farm, Lincolnshire, professionally estimated at 650–700 years old, which has a trunk girth of 39ft, but is severely storm-damaged in the crown. The second biggest and "the best", as adjudged by Mr Alan Mitchell, is a superb tree known as "Majesty" at Fredville Park, in Kent. This is 441 years old, has a girth of 38ft, but a modest height of 70ft. One is reminded of the old English saying that an oak "takes 300 years growing, 300 standing still and 300 dying".

These two oaks have leaves of very similar pattern but are distinguished by a few significant points.

In *petraea* the acorn is short, blunt and stalkless ("sessile"), sitting down tightly on the twigs. The crown is more open and its branches the straighter of the two. The leaves are leathery and healthy.

In *robur* the acorns dangle from long stalks ("peduncles") and thus has also been called *Q. pedunculata*. The crown is rather more irregular, often with twisting branches, the leaves are thinner and the tree is much pestered by insects. Another difference is that *robur* is by nature a lowlander, rejoicing heartily in a stiff loam over clay, and its place on higher ground is taken by *petraea*.

The warm, rich brown timber of both is highly prized for its hardiness, durability and beautiful graining, as seen in many a fine piece of antique furniture and many house timbers still in prime conditions after several hundreds of years. From these same timbers were also built the men o'war of old. In ancient times they were objects of much veneration. The early colonists from England took one or other, or both, to North America, where they have become widely distributed. The rating for both is z5.

Each has several variations. Of *robur* we have:

'Fastigiata', the Cypress oak, an imposing columnar tree, far more beautiful than the Lombardy poplar, and the smaller 'Fastigiata Purpurea', robed in purple-flushed foliage. There are several other clones of 'fastigiata', varying considerably in their resistance to mildew.

Winter aspect of a mature English oak, Q. robur.

'Concordia', the "Golden Oak", an unique, small, slow-growing tree with leaves suffused bright yellow and of upright carriage. A very pretty tree, of which there is a beautiful specimen at Wilton House, the home of Lord Pembroke, but in America it gets scorched by hot summers and grows weakly.

Of *Q. petraea* we have:

'Columnaris', narrowly erect, densely branched, of moderate stature.

'Laciniata', with narrow, very deeply indented leaves 6in long.

'Purpurea', looking rather like the purple beech.

After *Q. robur* we have to deal with two other names that their botanical godfathers have made confusingly like to it. The first is **Q. rubra**, the red oak (not to be confused with the scarlet oak), a superlative American which has taken root happily in Britain and other lands, where it often exceeds 100ft. It has been known by the more distinctive name of *Q. borealis*. The red oak is an extremely hardy tree of Zone 3, growing in typical oak form – very broad-spread, with a half-moon crown. The large leaves, which have been aptly described as flame-shaped, are deeply lobed and finely pointed, with three small points at the tip of the leaf, but they are variable; a variety called *maxima* has extra large leaves, more deeply cut and pendulous. When the young

leaves unfurl in April they are bright yellow before they become rich green, then in autumn they blaze out into a bonfire of scarlet, crimson and fawn, especially in an acid soil. The acorn, which is broadly conical, sits on a shallow base which is more a saucer than a cup. The red oak differs from the scarlet in its more horizontal primary branches, in the less deeply cut indentations of the leaf, and in their matt surface. Young trees transplant readily and grow away very fast and vigorously. It is a fine and versatile tree on all counts, whether for the landscape, or for a noble avenue (as seen in The Fenway, Boston), or for industrial atmospheres, where there is room for its ample spread.

The other of these oaks with like names is **Q. suber**, the cork oak, another evergreen familiar to travellers in Spain, Portugal and now becoming familiar in the southern United States. Of much economic value, it is also an ornamental tree and valuable for its adaptability to dry climates, capable of growing to 60ft, with a short, very thick, corky trunk, massive branches and small, evergreen leaves of fine texture. There are good examples at Kew. z7.

Q. virginiana, the magnificent "Live Oak", is evergreen in Britain and in the southern states of its native country, but it becomes deciduous in colder ones. It is remarkable for its enormous spread, often greater than its height, the branches

Bark of the cork oak, Quercus suber.

The red oak, Q. rubra *(or* borealis*).*

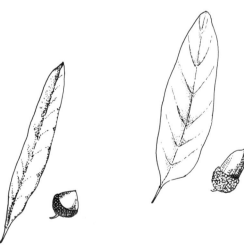

The cork oak, Q. suber.

The willow oak, Q. phellos, *and* Q. virginiana.

growing almost horizontally from a massive trunk. The leaves are somewhat laurel-like, usually without indentations, glossy dark green above, pale below. Its most famous example is the enormous and venerable Middleton Oak in Charleston, South Carolina, which is 900 years old and has a trunk girth of 37ft and a spread of 150ft.

The live oak is a superlative tree for town, if there is room for its lordly limbs. Very drought-resistant, it hangs on grimly in the most inhospitable sites, cramped in by pavements and breathing toxic fumes without harm. It is also first-class at the sea-shore. Only seedlings are available so far, but there is promise of greatly improved selections. z7.

Another "live" or evergreen oak is **Q. agrifolia**, the Californian live oak, which is an 80ft tree, with broad-spread, irregular limbs, thriving on the sea coast and preferring an open, gravelly soil. It has a tap root, so must be planted when quite small. Rather slow. z8.

From these oaks of old tradition, we turn to the distinctive **Q. phellos**, the willow oak. This is characterised by narrow, unindented, willow-like leaves, borne on slender boughs. It might be called the American brother of the English holm oak, but makes an excellent street tree, roundly

conical in outline. It transplants best in spring and can reach 90ft, but will not face lime. z5.

There are not many hybrid oaks, but one that we must especially notice (in addition to the Spanish) is the exceptional Turner's oak, **Q. × turneri**, named after an eighteenth-century nurseryman who arranged an imaginative marriage between the English and the holm oaks. The result is a lovely, broad-shouldered dome of 60ft, richly massed with lustrous, very dark-green leaves, which are slim and only faintly lobed and which persist until Christmas. Kew has a noble specimen. Safe in chalk. z6.

REDBUD See CERCIS

ROBINIA

Our predominant interest is the tall, handsome, scented, very hardy **R. pseudoacacia**, a tree with some highly fanciful and false associations. In America it is popularly known as the locust or black locust, as the early settlers there fondly imagined that its seeds, carried in bean-like pods, might have been the "locusts" on which John the Baptist fed in the wilderness. In fact the robinia

occurs in nature in America only, not Palestine, and the "locust" of John the Baptist was (if not the edible insect) almost certainly the carob (*Ceratonia siliqua*), which is a Palestine native.

A similar sort of perversity occurs in Britain, where the robinia goes by the spurious name of acacia, because of its pair of small thorns at the base of each leaf and because it was erroneously identified with another Biblical tree. The true acacia (which we in turn absurdly call "mimosa") is the totally different tree that we described earlier. Such is the perversity of popular names.

Robinia belongs to the pea family, as seen not only in its delightful flowers, borne in hanging clusters like white wisteria, but also in the grey, swollen, twisted seed-pods, within which are the black bean-seeds. On young trees the bark is a rich, smooth brown, on older ones it is handsomely fissured and ridged. It is an ideal ornamental tree for parks and large gardens, as hardy as you can wish, and is of particular value for poor, dry and derelict soils, for areas of industrial pollution and for the salty sea-shore too. A great all-rounder, therefore, but it must have plenty of sun and its brittle branches may break in fierce winds. In its native America it is sorely afflicted by ravenous insects and did not fulfil itself until it emigrated to Europe, where it has prospered exceedingly. In France and elsewhere it has become naturalised, seeding itself in waste ground and, having been found resistant to the smoke of coal-fired locomotives, is often found close to railways. z3.

There are numerous varieties of *R. pseudoacacia*. The most fashionable one is the bright golden 'Frisia', a Dutch form, now ornamenting many a garden, both large and small. It is too often seen looking like a bush sitting on a pole, due to the manner in which it is usually treated in nurseries for sales purposes. The gardener should therefore order either a young, feathered tree or else one grafted just above ground level, from which a stem can be selected to make a leader. In both cases he should foster a central stem, from which, if he likes, the lower branches can be gradually removed head-high. It is then a beautiful tree of natural form.

Another very pretty variant is 'Rozynskyana', a small tree, with nodding branches, from which the large leaves hang down like curtains.

'Inermis', known in Britain as the "mop-headed acacia", is a small, compact, thornless, round-headed, rather smug tree, much used for suburban street planting, especially in France, but almost flowerless. 'Semperflorens' flowers intermittently through the summer. In 'Erecta' and 'Pyramidalis' we have slender columnar trees.

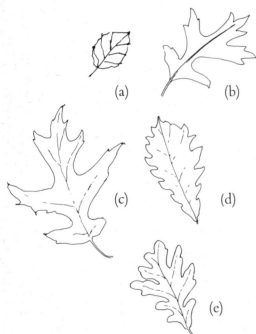

Some oak leaves compared: (a) *the Californian evergreen oak,* Q. agrifolia; (b) *the pin oak,* Q. palustris; (c) *the black oak,* Q. velutina *(leaves often mis-shapen);* (d) Q. robur; (e) *the white oak,* Q. alba.

Leaf and flower of Robinia pseudoacacia.

RIGHT Robinia pseudoacacia *in winter;* *note the boldly ribbed trunk.*

The sap of *pseudoacacia* is carried on in a handsome hybrid known as *R.* × *ambigua* 'Decaisneana'. Often seen as a street tree in France, it is of easy culture, of moderate vigour and displays clusters of rose-pink flowers in June. z3.

ROWAN See SORBUS

SALIX
Willow

Willows often surprise us in their diversity. They may be tiny, ground-hugging shrublets or stalwart, upstanding trees and in between these extremes we find the popular weeping willows, big furry "pussy willow" shrubs and many small trees, both decorative and utilitarian. Usually the leaves are narrow and contrived like lance-blades. Most grow very fast.

In the mind's eye willows are commonly associated with streams and ponds, and they are certainly of particular beauty in such an environment, but most are quite content with any fairly moist, loamy soil. They do not mind lime, but few are happy in chalk. Elegant coloured stems are found in such as *S. alba* 'Vitellina', 'Chermesina' and *daphnoides*, the violet willow, and these, when hard pruned in March to promote new shoots, help create a beautiful winter scene if consorted with silver birches, the snake-bark maples, the Westonbirt dogwood and the white-stemmed brambles.

Willows are essentially trees for a rural environment or for a private garden, not for streets. They are often bothered by diseases and insects, especially in America, but suffer little from attacks by knife and axe, regenerating with enthusiasm after the most savage mutilations. Many indeed, are regularly pollarded or even cut to the ground for commercial purposes. Cricket bats are made from the express-speed, blue-grey hybrid of the white willow, 'Caerulea', in itself a fine, handsome, upright tree when allowed to mature and an excellent screen tree.

Willows are propagated with the greatest ease; any shoot stuck in the ground will take root. They are uni-sexual, the male and female catkins being borne on separate trees.

Let us consider first the weeping willows, since they are far and away the most popular as well as the most picturesque. Here we have a fearful confusion of names, due in part to the lax moral habits of the willows and in part to the diverse opinions of botanists. Two basic species are involved – the Babylon Willow (*S. babylonica*) and the big white willow (*S. alba*).

The Babylon willow is a fine tree in its own right, by no means confined in nature to the realm of Nebuchadnezzar. It was not the tree "by the waters of Babylon" upon which harps were hung (which was probably *Populus euphratica*), but it was the tree under which Napoleon liked to sit on St Helena and under which he was buried. Its branches are yellow-brown, with the typical lance-shaped leaf of a willow, smooth to the touch.

The other basic species was the white willow, not a weeper, which produced a golden-stemmed variety, 'Vitellina'. In due course the marriage of 'Vitellina' to *babylonica* was solemnised and their progeny was a magnificent tree with the weeper habit of the Babylonian and the slim golden branches of 'Vitellina'. This hybrid is now preferably called **S.** × **chrysocoma**. For the reasons that we have given, however, you may find in catalogues a record of aliases for it as long as a burglar's. To identify it properly, you must be aware of these aliases, which are:

alba 'Vitellina Pendula',
alba 'Tristis' (too sad a name),
babylonica 'Ramulis Aureis' ("golden branched"),
'Niobe' (in America, sometimes).

Whichever you choose to call it, the golden weeping willow is one of the most picturesque of trees, immensely popular and extremely hardy, growing fast to 50ft or more and throwing out lax branches which start semi-erect and then swoop down in thin, golden rods, equipped with trim little leaves, to trail along the ground, forming a leafy skirt which, ever growing, will spread 40ft wide. Except in a flat calm it is always in movement and when the wind blows hard the long, slim, whippy wands stream out like a girl's hair, almost horizontally. Whether motionless or in excited movement, it makes a lovely backdrop for the coloured drama of roses, flowering shrubs or hardy perennials. In the second year the young twigs turn light brown, to be followed by new golden ones.

As an adolescent tree in a nursery or a garden centre the golden weeping willow is quite enchanting and the inexperienced owner of a small garden falls for it on sight, only to find that in a few years it has to be cut down. Never plant it in a garden of less than half-an-acre. Better to plant a weeping purple osier instead. On the other hand, *chrysocoma*, like other willows, is not at all afraid of the knife and mature trees can be restrained by cutting back every two or three years, but an experienced hand and a steady head for heights are needed. z2.

A few other weeping willows deserve attention. Two of them are closely related to hybrids,

growing to about 40ft. In *S.* 'Elegantissima' the Thurlow weeping willow, the young branchlets are green and long. In *S.* × *blanda*, the Wisconsin weeping willow, the young growth is short and likewise green, but the leaves are highly polished. Both z4.

When there is no room for these big weepers, a charming volunteer comes forward to take their places. This is the pendulous form of the purple osier, **Salix purpurea 'Pendula'**. It is built up of long and sinuous wands, tinted purple and trimmed with typical willow leaves. A graceful small tree for small gardens, less than 25ft high. z4.

Leaving the pendulous willows, we turn to those of more erect carriage, choosing only four from the several hundred provided by nature and bypassing all the small shrubs.

S. alba, the big, billowing white willow, is far the best of the larger upright willows and among the best of all trees for parks and country areas. Growing extremely fast (23ft in the first 10 years and going on to 80ft) it bears itself with a slender carriage, with silky, lance-point leaves, white on their under-surfaces, and borne in great, shimmering, silvery masses on slender branches, drooping at the tips. A beautiful landscape tree, but primarily a lowlander and a creature of moist meadows and riversides, valuable for preventing erosion of river banks and excelling also by the sea.

Besides the cricket bat willow, several good varieties of the white willow have evolved, of which the following are the most important:

'Sericea' (or 'Argentea'), the silver willow, is a small tree, even more brilliantly silvered than its parent. A lovely landscape tree, but slow for a willow.

'Chermesina', sometimes known as 'Britzensis', is the beautiful scarlet willow, bearing brilliant, orange-scarlet stems, most conspicuous in winter and all the more so if it is hard-pruned every other year to induce the colourful young shoots; otherwise it becomes quite a big tree.

'Vitellina', the golden willow, is a smaller male tree of similar behaviour, but its shoots are deep golden and may be pruned back the same way. It is one of the proud parents of the golden weeping willow.

S. daphnoides, the beautiful violet willow, is a very fast growing tree, yet does not exceed about 30ft, remarkable for its violet stems, which become suffused with a white bloom, creating a beautiful picture in winter and summer. The leaves are lustrous green and silky catkins dangle among them. Prune hard late in March. 'Aglaia' is a male clone with extra large, yellow catkins. z4.

As further evidence of its versatility, the willow has produced what might be taken for an outsize Bonzai. This is **S. matsudana 'Tortuosa'**, known as the corkscrew willow from the queer writhing of its boughs. It is a curiosity rather than a beauty, the twisting stems not being fully revealed until winter, when the leaves have been shed. Only really effective against open sky. To 30ft. z4.

The "pussy willows", with their soft, fluffy catkins, largest and handsome on male trees, sparkling with tiny, golden stamens as they mature, are great favourites, especially among children. Most of them are small shrubs, but the best of them is the big **S. caprea**, the 'goat willow' or great sallow. "Goat" derives from the fact that goats (and other animals) find the leaves very palatable and browse them eagerly, so that they are safe only in soft, boggy ground. Another popular appellation is "Palm", since in Britain they were carried to church on Palm Sunday. A. A. Milne tells us that "People call me Palm they do; They call me Pussy Willow too". And here we go right back to Leviticus – "Ye shall take on the first day the boughs of goodly trees, branches of palm trees, the boughs of thick trees, and willows of the brook".

The goat willow can grow to a good 40ft, the gilded male catkins maturing in March, before the leaves, and the females turning into cottonwool seed tufts in May, but for the rest of the year is of little interest. If cut to the ground every few years, it produces vigorous new wood, with large catkins. The leaves are broad, superficially rather like those of the elm. z4.

SASSAFRAS

Given an acid soil and an open position to display itself properly, the aromatic **Sassafras albidum** makes a fine tree up to 60ft, with a broadly conical, open habit, rather sparsely branched and having twisted twigs. A very useful tree for poor gravelly acid soils. The oval, aromatic leaves are oddly

The diverse leaves of Sassafras albidum.

varied in pattern and size, having one, two or three lobes or none at all. They colour brilliantly in the fall. Inconspicuous yellow flowers are followed by small, blue-black fruits. Not easy to transplant. The early American colonists made an infusion from its bark and roots, and sassafras bark was their first export to the mother country. The name derives from the Spanish *salsafras*. z4.

SERVICEBERRY See AMELANCHIER

SERVICE TREES See at end of SORBUS

SILK TREE See ALBIZIA

SNOWY MESPILUS See AMELANCHIER

Sophora japonica, *first-class among buildings.*

SOPHORA

These are unique and beautiful flowering trees or shrubs, curiously neglected by gardeners, planners and those responsible for the embellishments of towns. They bear themselves very elegantly and their floral displays (in time) are lovely. They prosper in any kind of fertile soil, if well drained and not pronouncedly acid, but they do need plenty of sun and are at times best in a hot, dry summer. Belonging to the pea Family, they have typical pea flowers, followed by dangling pods. The following are the chief tree forms.

The hardiest species is **S. japonica**, rather fatuously called by some the Japanese pagoda tree or

the scholar tree. It builds up into a very handsome, rounded, spreading tree 70 to 80ft high, with twisting, serpentine branches, very "Japanesy" clad in lacy, compound leaves in the manner of the robinia and is a superb town tree. Unfortunately, it takes many years to flower, but is then of rare value for doing so in August, when it breaks out into large, bold, pyramidal clusters of deep cream (flushed violet-rose in the variety 'Violacea'), followed by yellow seed pods that usually hang on all winter.

Though classed as of Zone 4, *Sophora japonica* really needs plenty of sun to promote its flowering, which is seen in great splendour in the comfortable warmth of southern Europe, though it does not fail even in southern Canada. Bring it up on a 7ft trunk, when the branch tips will droop gracefully to the ground. Use it as a specimen tree on a large lawn, or in an open landscape. Use it also in town squares, courtyards and among buildings. A fine example of how to use it is seen in Paris, where it surrounds the Arc de Triomphe in massed depth.

Only a few variants of the Japanese sophora occur. The new clone 'Regent', raised by Princeton, is vastly superior to seedlings, being upright and vigorous, thriving under harsh conditions, growing fast and flowering when fairly young. Other varieties are the attractive 'Pendula' (a mass of twisting branches) and 'Fastigiata', which speak for themselves.

S. tetraptera, the beautiful kowhai of New Zealand, sometimes known as the New Zealand laburnum, is a connoisseur's tree of grace and distinction and gives New Zealand its national flower. There is nothing quite like it, but it is passing tender, needing the conditions of Zone 9. As often grown in England, however, it is amenable to a cooler climate if grown on a large,

south-facing wall or in some sunny nook. In warm climates it is evergreen, in colder ones deciduous, so has a fair chance of survival. It does well in sandy soils.

The kowhai is easily recognisable by its zigzag branches. Its long leaves are divided into up to 40 leaflets (usually less) with drooping clusters of elongated tubular flowers, about 1½in long, which are yellow and unfurl in May. The curious seed pods have quadrangular wings. In the open it may reach 40ft in the best conditions, but rarely more than 25ft in Britain. Does not conform well to pruning.

SORBUS
Whitebeam and Rowan or Mountain Ash

This very diverse regiment is organised in four companies, distinguished mainly by the shapes of their leaves. We need not inspect them in detail, but can usefully note that the captains of the two most important companies are *Sorbus aria*, the whitebeam, with simple, one-piece leaves like those of elms and lindens, and *S. aucuparia*, the rowan or mountain ash, which is the larger company, with boldly pinnate leaves as in the common ash. Both types of leaves may be found in other companies, but to the gardener and the designer the important factor is whether the leaf is pinnate or simple, or more or less so, and we shall here group them accordingly.

Sorbuses in general are easily grown trees of modest dimensions, pretty hardy, satisfied with any reasonable soil, and they grow fast. Very well formed specimens are often found in poor, stony ground on hillsides. In late spring or early summer they put forth conspicuous bunches of massed,

tiny, white or cream flowers, and from these are developed brilliantly coloured clusters of small fruits, like tiny apples, which richly bejewel the trees in autumn, often accompanied by glowing colours in the foliage also. In informal situations it is good to plant specimens forking naturally close to the ground rather than standards. Unless stated otherwise in the following notes the flowers are always white or cream and the fruits always red or orange-scarlet. Unfortunately, the birds often find these brilliant little fruits irresistible and when the cold days set in little is left for the gardener to admire, but as in viburnums, cotoneasters and pyracanthas, the paler "berries" borne on some of the daintiest species are usually ignored.

In North America sorbuses are also sadly harassed, and sometimes killed by insects, especially borers, which can be kept at bay by spraying the trunks with DDT, or an equivalent, just before the eggs are due to hatch (for which you need local knowledge) and again three weeks later.

THE ROWANS

We shall inspect first the sorbuses that have the pinnate, "feathery" type of foliage.

These are headed by **S. aucuparia** itself, the true rowan or mountain ash, which will grow sturdily to 45ft in lowlands as in highlands. The former of the two popular names derives anciently from Scandinavian and the latter more obviously from the resemblance of its foliage to that of the common ash and to its frequency in high places, very often in rocky clefts difficult of access, keeping company with birches, pines and heathers.

The rowan is one of the hardiest of all our trees. It is native in large stretches of far-northern

The New Zealand kowhai, Sophora tetraptera.

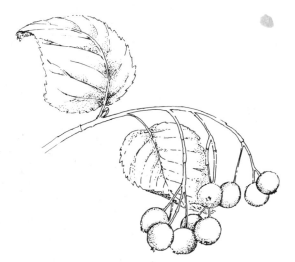

The whitebeam, Sorbus aria.

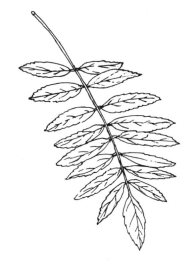

The rowan or mountain ash, Sorbus aucuparia.

Europe, including Iceland, and has become naturalised in Alaska and parts of Canada. It has a rich folk-lore, being revered in ancient days (and even today in some rural areas) as a potent antidote to witchcraft. Its bright red fruitlets were for many centuries a favourite lure for snaring birds, the specific name *aucuparia* being indeed mongrel Latin for "bird trap".

The soil that the rowan prefers, but does not insist upon, is a light, sandy, acid loam (quite the opposite of the lowland whitebeam). It transplants up to as much as 18ft. The decorative leaves have up to 19 leaflets, slightly toothed. z3.

There are some excellent variations of *aucuparia*, to wit:

'Sheerwater Seedling'. Egg-shaped outline, upright, compact, with ascending branches. A first-class street tree.

'Beissneri'. Beautiful upright tree also excellent for streets. Deeply incised, fern-like leaves, golden-green. Bark a warm, waxy, copper-pink.

'Aspleniifolia'. Graceful leaves, deeply incised and toothed, upright posture.

'Edulis'. Strong tree with larger leaves and larger fruits that are sweet and edible (if the birds permit).

'Xanthocarpa' has amber fruits.

There are also the usual weeping and fastigiate forms, the latter liable to breakage.

After these variations of *S. aucuparia* itself, comes another red-fruited contingent of the mountain ash. We choose the following few.

S. americana is ultra-hardy and grows strongly to 30ft, usually in a shrub-like manner, with fine autumn colour. z2.

S. commixta is valuable for its columnar habit, though broadening with age, growing 25ft. The leaves are glossy and brilliant deep-purple in the fall. The fruits are very prominently displayed in large trusses. z5.

S. 'Embley' is very similar, but in the fall is at first pure scarlet in leaf, later dusky crimson. An extremely fine foliage tree, excellent in towns. See under *discolor*. z5.

S. sargentiana is a magnificent tree of 30ft, with luxuriant foliage colouring gloriously in autumn. A conspicuous white down grows on the reverse of the leaf and on the stalks of flower and fruit. Conspicuous also are its large, sticky winter buds, like those of the horse chestnut, but red. z6.

S. scalaris A wide-spreading tree of 30ft, remarkable for its densely packed orange-scarlet fruits, perhaps the most brilliant of all. The fern-like foliage is prettily clustered in rosettes. z6.

Besides these red-fruited rowans, there is a distinguished band bearing pastel-tinted fruits, not eagerly gobbled up by birds, the first three being of particular delicacy and charm.

S. cashmiriana is airy, graceful and full of style. Of recent introduction, it is pyramidal in outline, beautiful in both flower and fruit and may perhaps reach 30ft. Uniquely, the flowers, appearing in May, are blush-pink and the very large fruits are glistening white or flushed with pink on rose-pink stalks, persisting after leaf-fall. z4.

S. vilmorinii is a delightful, very small tree of 20ft, of open, spreading habit with ferny, clustered leaves thronged with innumerable tiny leaflets. The fruits, dangling in loose clusters, start red and wane to blush-pink. A beautiful tree for the small garden. z5.

S. hupehensis has much the same character as Vilmorin's rowan, but is rather larger and easily distinguished from it by the blue tint in its foliage, which colours gloriously in autumn. The fruits are glistening white, sometimes flushed pink, but in the variety *obtusa* definitely pink. In *aperta* we have a tree of particular elegance and distinction, smaller in all its parts. z5.

Another small and charming tree is **S. prattii**,

Sorbus aria '*Majestica*'.

of little more than 20ft. Its small, pearly white fruits are strung out in clusters all along the branch. z6.

S. 'Joseph Rock' is a strapping fellow, a good 30ft high, erect, compact and impressive, its foliage colouring brilliantly in autumn. The unusual fruits start cream and deepen to amber, hanging on long after leaf-fall. It has been introduced recently. Probably z4.

S. discolor, which has creamy fruits, is extremely rare in cultivation. Plants sold under this name are usually either 'Embley' or *commixta*. z5.

THE WHITEBEAMS

Turning now to the whitebeams, led by *S. aria*, we find a small company of trees with "simple", one-piece leaves, grown primarily for their foliage, which is marked by a delightful silvery cast.

S. aria itself is a fine tree of 40ft, with small, oval, bright green, faintly saw-edged leaves, the under-surfaces of which are coated with a white down and give to the whole tree a lively and

sparkling gaiety when tossed by the wind. In the autumn the leaves adopt hues of gold and russet. Unlike the rowan, the whitebeam thrives in chalk (as elsewhere) and is a familiar sight in the chalk downs of England and France, where it is seen with yew, dogwood and juniper. It is impervious to the buffets of wind, sea spray and industrial pollution. It transplants at up to 12ft but is slow at first. z5. The following forms of *S. aria* deserve strong commendation.

In 'Lutescens' the silvery-white shroud is intensified, spreading to the upper surfaces, the whole tree seeming to be shimmering with silver sequins before becoming sea-green towards the end of summer. Beautiful and exciting in a wind. 40ft in 30 years.

In 'Majestica' (also known as 'Decaisneana') the tree becomes larger in all its parts, the leaves 6in long and the deep-red fruitlets more than half an inch in diameter. A splendid, impressive, rather slow tree of 50ft and more, with upswept branches.

In 'Chrysophylla' and 'Aurea' the leaves are clearly flushed yellow and in 'Salicifolia' they are almost willow-like on gracefully lax branches.

Another species of whitebeam of outstanding merit is **S. intermedia**, the Swedish whitebeam. A robust all-rounder, like the London plane and the robinias, it prevails over all sorts of harsh conditions – deprived soils, salty sea gales and the tainted breath of cities. It is a 40ft tree with notched leaf-margins and the general appearance of *aria*. In stony ground it tends to become a large spreading bush, unless the central leader is maintained. z5.

OTHER SORBUSES

Having reviewed the rowans and the whitebeams, we should notice a few sorbuses from other companies of that regiment. The first two belong to the Micromeles ("little apples") company, resembling the whitebeam in leaf.

S. alnifolia is a superlative tree of about 30ft (60ft in the Arnold Arboretum), beginning life with an upright stance, then billowing out exuberantly. The bark is grey and smooth, like a beech's. The small, toothed, deeply veined, shining, single leaves, wear a white felt on the reverse. An ornamental and colourful tree of strength and grace, it has rich autumn colouring. The new clone 'Redbird' is of upright bearing with large leaves and showy red fruits. z4.

S. folgneri A very handsome junior of *alnifolia*, quite remarkable in its unique form 'Lemon Drop', in which the fruits are bright yellow, borne on slender, drooping branches. It grows to 25ft. z5.

The wild service tree, Sorbus torminalis.

S. 'Mitchellii' is a strapping sorbus that surprises us by its big round leaves, 6in in diameter. In late April the opening leaf-buds, brilliantly silvered, look astonishingly like small magnolias. A new tree with a future. It grows 55ft high and wide. Probably z5.

A few sorbuses are known as "Service Trees", the name being adapted from *cervisia*, Latin for beer, the fruits having been used in the brew. The wild service tree (*S. torminalis*) is of strong build with a leaf which is clearly lobed like a maple's at the base and strongly toothed in the upper part. The true service tree (*S. domestica*) has pinnate leaves like a rowan's and is 60ft high, with colourful bark. In the bastard service tree (*S.* × *thuringiaca*) the leaf shows the whitebeam in the upper part and the rowan's leaflets in the lower.

SORREL TREE See OXYDENDRUM

STEWARTIA

The aristocratic stewartias were named in honour of an eighteenth-century Earl of Bute, a patron of botany, whose family name was more usually spelt Stuart, but in those days people were not so fussy about such things as they are now. Fortunate earl to be so gracefully immortalised! For his memorials are beautiful trees and shrubs bearing flowers that resemble white, single-petalled camellias, adorned in the centre by ringlets of deep yellow or orange anthers, like little halos.

Their requirements are a moist, humusy, acid or neutral loam and an open, woodland setting. They must not be crowded by other trees but want shade at their roots; and in a woodland

clearing, with a grass sward sweeping up to them they create an idyllic picture. The flowering time is July, extending in Britain into August, the individual white blossoms, which occur in the leaf axils, being of short duration but borne in continuous succession. The foliage is small and neat, turning to a fine red autumn colour.

Stewartias must be planted when very young, their roots not being adapted to disturbance. Avoid pruning them.

The outstanding species is **S. pseudocamellia**, a name that florally speaks for itself. It can grow to 60ft (rarely so high in Britain) with a pyramidal stance and lovely rufous bark, peeling as the tree begins to mature. The autumn leaf colour is red-purple. z5.

S. koreana is a hardy tree of maybe 45ft, with the same lively, brick-red bark, but with larger flowers and foliage. The autumn colour is orange-red. z5.

S. sinensis is a delightful, smaller, rather shrub-like tree of 30ft, in which all the bark is shed to reveal smoother limbs varying in colour from pink to orange. z6. Other stewartias are large shrubs, very desirable, especially *malacodendron*, studded with large, wide-open, purple-eyed flowers. z7.

STRAWBERRY TREE See ARBUTUS

STYRAX

These small, pretty trees or shrubs, nearly all from China or Japan, but perpetuating their ancient Greek name, are charming for very small gardens that have a moist, loamy, lime-free soil and preferably a warm corner. In America they are often fancifully dubbed "snowbells" by the garden press. From their slender, wide-spread branches hang, in June, small, pure white, somewhat fuchsia-like flowers, with amber stamens, in great abundance when the plant is happy, but not when very young. To appreciate their beauty to the full, plant them on a bank or some raised piece of ground, or else as standards. They all need sun, except in the warmer zones.

The best is **S. japonica**, a tree of dainty beauty to about 25ft or more, the branch tips drooping elegantly. The small, neat leaves stand erect on the upper sides of the branches and the clustered flowers dangle below. It is the source of a fragrant resin, used for incense. z6.

S. hemsleyana has slightly larger leaves and carries its flowers in long, lax clusters. z7. *S. obassia* has still larger leaves, up to 8in long, varying in shape according to age, which often obscure

RIGHT *The Lombardy poplar,* Populus nigra *'Italica'.*

The fuchsia-like flowers and upswept leaves of Styrax japonica.

the long, hanging, fragrant flower clusters at the tips of the branches; its handsome bark is chestnut, curling and flaking. z6.

SWEET BAY See *Magnolia virginiana*

SYCAMORE See *Acer pseudoplatanus* (English) and *Platanus occidentalis* (American)

TILIA
Linden or Lime

The linden is one of the dominant foliage trees, spread widely over the north temperate zone but seen at its best in the European species. Of its two most popular names, the older "Linden" seems far the more desirable, deriving as it does from the Old English *lind* or *linde*, and still perpetuated in several English place-names, such as Lyndhurst, in the New Forest. Apart from the sweet scent of its small flowers, "lime" has no validity, the true lime-tree, the fruit of which provides such a delicious drink, being utterly unlike the Tilia. In North America it is still often called basswood, a survival of the English "bass" or "bast", the fibrous inner bark, which was made into rough ropes as a binding material or woven into mats.

No argument, however, questions the value of the lindens for avenues, city streets and parks, though they have their faults. Most make fairly big, upstanding, towering trees, with a dense foliage of small, heart-shaped, pointed leaves, many with a pale reverse, giving a pretty fluttering effect in the breeze. The creamy flowers are not of much account but give forth a sweetly aromatic and pervading scent in July; a refreshing infusion is made from them, when dried, in France and elsewhere. The paltry fruits are like hard peas.

Lindens live to an enormous age, a specimen of

The heady flowers of the Crimean linden, Tilia × euchlora.

the broad-leaf linden at Upstedt, near Hanover, being more than 1,100 years old. They prosper in all sorts of reasonable soils, rooting well even when their seeds fall among the austere rocks of the Welsh border and Yorkshire, safe from the browsing sheep. The luscious nectar of their rather dull flowers is to the bees as drink or drugs to man, so much so that they fall off in a drunken stupor after feeding on the blossoms of the Crimean and the weeping silver lindens.

The bark of the lindens is smooth and pale grey. The wood also is smooth and is grainless, a quality shown to sculptural perfection in the carvings of Grinling Gibbons in St Paul's Cathedral and other Wren churches. The linden readily submits to being cut back, lopped and trained into artificial forms, as in the beautiful pleached walks of our ancestors and occasionally of ourselves today. All pruning operations should be done in late summer, to avoid bleeding. Cavities often form in the trunks and exposed wood must be given a protective dressing.

The worst foes of the lindens are the aphids, which in some seasons affect them grievously. The aphids not only suck the sap out of the leaves but also coat them with a sticky "honeydew", to which dust and soot adhere and on which a black fungus may spread, so that in a bad year the whole tree becomes a sorry sight.

We choose the following species, with preference for the silver-leaved ones.

The most beautiful of the lindens (when not ravaged by aphis) is the weeping silver linden, **T. petiolaris**. It is not a true "weeper", not cascading like the willows or the weeping ash, but gracefully pendulous, growing from a narrow head, 70ft high. The leaves are silvery white beneath and the tree becomes whipped into a sparkling foam when agitated by the wind. The nectar is an opiate to bees. This weeping silver linden is essentially a specimen tree for the open landscape, the park, or the large garden, and is not suitable for towns, where smoke and dust ruin the beautiful silver patina. z5.

PREVIOUS PAGES, LEFT Robinia pseudoacacia.
PREVIOUS PAGES, RIGHT Stewartia
pseudocamellia *in autumn.*
LEFT *One of the hybrids between a whitebeam and
a mountain ash,* Sorbus 'Meninghe'.

127

Akin to it, but not pendulous, is the silver linden, **T. tomentosa**, a very big tree, broadly pyramidal, that may reach 90ft, with long, strong, upright branches and lopsided leaves undercoated with the same white down. One of the most beautiful and impressive of all trees, it has an outline so trim and well defined as to seem to have been clipped. It grows fast and is a favourite tree everywhere for industrial sites. Seedlings vary greatly and the gardener should choose grafted specimens. z4.

Not quite so big is the Crimean linden, **T. × euchlora**, a tree growing sinuously up to 60ft, the boughs twisting and arching and becoming pendulous in the lower tiers. The reverse of the uneven leaf is sea-green, and the obverse dark green and shining. Very good in a hot, dry environment, rarely affected by aphis, but its flowers intoxicate bees. A greatly favoured tree in Europe, but in the USA gets smitten by spider mite. z4.

T. cordata is the popular small-leaf linden. A broadly pyramidal, towering tree of 90ft, densely matted with leaves about 2½in long, dark green on the obverse, paler below. Growth is rather slow. The flowers come in dense, random bunches. Excellent for cities, especially the following fine varieties. All z3.

'Swedish Upright' is a perfect tree for broad thoroughfares, erect and closely compact. In 60 years it will be 35ft high but only 12ft wide.

'Greenspire' grows with a single, straight trunk, forming a beautiful oval specimen to 90ft. A child of Mr William Flemer III of Princeton.

Contrasting with the small-leaf linden is the big-leaf or broad-leaf, **T. platyphyllos**, a huge, shapely and splendid tree of maybe 120ft, notable for its success in even degenerate soils. The leaves average about 4in in both length and breadth, somewhat coarse of texture. It produces some suckers. Its cultivar 'Rubra', known as the red-twigged linden, is outstanding, clothing its young shoots in chestnut and bearing itself with a firm, semi-erect carriage, which, together with its resistance to pollution, suits it well for city streets. 'Laciniata' has deeply lobed leaves and is a much smaller tree, very distinctive and unusual. 'Fastigiata' is valuable as being much narrower or columnar. z3.

T. × europaea is the "common lime" of Britain, also found elsewhere in Europe, marked by red, zigzag twigs, pale green leaves of soft texture and forming a billowing dome to 120ft. A very long-lived and very hardy tree which, over the centuries, has formed many an imposing avenue to a lordly mansion, château and schloss. At Dunscombe Park, in Yorkshire, it has reached 155ft – the tallest broad-leaf in Britain.

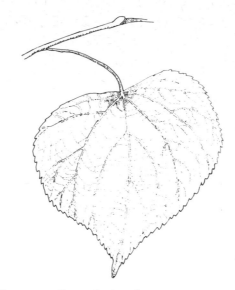

The common lime or linden of Britain, Tilia × europaea.

The Mongolian linden, T. mongolica.

The common lime is less in favour today because of its suckering habit when mature and for the burrs or knobs that mar the trunk; cut the twiggy growths from these burrs right back at the end of summer. The tree is a favoured host for both mistletoe and aphis, the lower branches often blackened by sooty mould. For ornamental use the common lime is not so good as its parents, *cordata* and *platyphyllos*, but is still a good tree elsewhere. z3.

A fine tree that we see also too seldom is the Chinese linden, **T. oliveri**. This is marked by large (5in) leaves, almost round but furnished with a fine point and richly silvered beneath and elegantly poised on long stalks. About 70ft. z5.

T. americana is an open-crowned tree of 120ft in its own country, but it does not thrive in Britain. It is easily recognised by its very large, coarse leaves, anything up to 8in long. Although much subject to aphis, it has value as a stalwart, upstanding, extra-hardy tree, particularly in the clone 'Redmond', from Nebraska, which becomes a dense pyramid and is a great improvement on the parent species. z2.

Likewise superior is its rare hybrid offspring,

T. × moltkei, a handsome, vigorous and large-leaved tree of 75ft.

Very different from these big, traditional lindens is the small Mongolian, **T. mongolica**. This is a graceful, neat, compact, rounded tree of only 30ft. The leaves (which are chestnut-red as they unfold) differ much from others, being broad, jaggedly toothed and often drawn out to a fine-pointed tip. z4.

TOON See CEDRELA

TREE OF HEAVEN See AILANTHUS

TULIP TREE See LIRIODENDRON

ULMUS
Elm

Elms of nearly all sorts are being decimated throughout Europe and North America by the fell Dutch elm disease, a fungus that follows the entry into the wood of the adult of the elm bark beetle in the course of excavating its brood galleries. Trained minds are working actively to produce resistant varieties and meanwhile elms are still being actively planted. Rightly so, for the elm is one of our prime environmental trees and some of our choicest landscapes would entirely lose their character without the long, martial files, the avenues and the hilltop copses of tall elms, where Robert Bridges watched the rooks,

> *settling in ragged parliament,*
> *Some stormy councils hold in the high trees.*

Most elms grow with a roughly fan-shaped silhouette, the lower branches drooping languorously at their tips, the uppermost erect, so that their winter tracery delicately trims the skyline with a selvedge of intricate lace. Some of their weeping forms are exceedingly picturesque. To their value as ornaments of the landscape they add many utilitarian uses. They are very important shelter trees in any exposed place, especially along the borders of the sea, where they seem to shake with laughter as the salt-laden gales batter their rugged limbs in vain.

They do well in almost any soil, including solid chalk, and they transplant easily, but are greedy feeders and their roots, running close to the earth's face, and even on top of it, range far and wide if good food is not close at hand. Many throw up suckers when mature.

The tiny flowers of the elm are nearly always red or purple-red. They break out in the very early spring on naked boughs and if you look

Elm leaves:
(a) *Huntingdon elm,* Ulmus × vegeta;
(b) *wych elm,* U.glabra;
(c) *English elm,* U.procera.

upwards in the wan sun at February's end you will see a dim red glow along the boughs. The pollen, impatient of the still-cloistered bee, entrusts itself to the wind, so that the fruits follow quickly, racing likewise to beat the leaves, and showing their single seeds within a frail papery envelope in the form of a disc.

The leaves of the elms are small, furrowed by veins and saw-edged, but their special characteristic (by which you shall know all elms) is that they are slightly lop-sided ("oblique" in botanese), one half of the leaf blade being further extended at its base than the other. Those of the European elms are all pretty much alike, yet often vary in minor detail even within each species, for in bygone days their morals were promiscuous, so that today their identities may perplex even skilled botanists, who, as we shall see, differ a good deal about their names and classifications.

For the elm disease, of which the first sign is premature wilting and death of the foliage on a few branches, there is no cure except by the axe and by fire. Usually the whole tree must be felled, but occasionally it is sufficient to lop one or more branches if the disease is detected early enough. Burn all fallen twigs and bark. Strip off and burn the bark of tree stumps. Where the disease is very bad, a very good alternative to the elm is *Zelkova serrata,* described later.

The elms, especially the English elm, are often accused of being dangerous to man, beast and property from their propensity, once in a way, to drop whole branches without warning, usually in the evening after a hot day. They behave in this manner, however, only if in poor health or else very antique. Bad culture, particularly disturbance of their hungry roots such as the serious disturbance caused in the construction of new roads, factories and housing estates, will undermine the tree's virility. Another weakening factor is the practice, hitherto considered the right thing to do, of excessive lopping of the limbs. Do not lop elms unless really necessary. And if you think 100 years ahead, do not plant wide-ranging species where the branches will overhang roads.

We shall look first at the European elms, which constitute the majority.

No doubt the most generally popular is the wych elm or Scotch elm, **Ulmus glabra.** The antique name wych derives from the Old English *wice,* a word that had nothing to do with witches, but meant "supple", and in former times it was often used for any elm. Its leaves (which are almost stalkless) are fairly large, averaging 5in, very lop-sided and rough to the touch. In Britain they are a pointed oval, but in continental Europe they are often high-shouldered and coarsely toothed.

Winter outline of the wych elm, U.glabra, *forming a high dome.*

The wych has many virtues. It throws up no suckers. It branches low down, giving rise to strong, ascending limbs, the tips of which tumble down in twiggy masses to present to the beholder a dome-like outline, 120ft high and nearly as wide. In Scotland it is the only common elm, thriving in both the Highland glens and the towns. Besides being a noble parkland specimen, it is a coastal tree *par excellence,* withstanding the salty buffets of Atlantic gales with no more than a dance and a muted song of its supple twigs.

Several forms of the wych have been named. The most distinctive is the Camperdown elm, one of the finest weeping trees, a wide-flung, rustling crinoline with twisting stems, making a delightful bower. It is often confused with 'Pendula', a tree with branches that grow outwards and then droop at their terminals. Both are seen at their best as lawn specimens. Quite the opposite form is shown in 'Exoniensis', erect and narrowly columnar until aged, with smaller, wrinkled, deeply cut leaves; an excellent street tree.

Yet another form of the versatile wych is 'Lutescens', a particularly fine, big tree, decked with shining, pale-gold leaves. All z4.

U. procera is the traditional English elm, inseparably associated with its native landscape and nostalgically represented in Constable's paintings. The Duke of Montague of the early eighteenth century, known as "Planter John", planted 72 miles of them as avenues in Northamptonshire. It very rarely sets fertile seed, and is known in the wild only in England. In contrast to the broad domes of the wych, it is a relatively narrow, upright tree with a single, powerful, erect mast to 140ft, terminating in a narrow dome. The leaf is

RIGHT *Winter aspect of the wych elm,* Ulmus glabra.

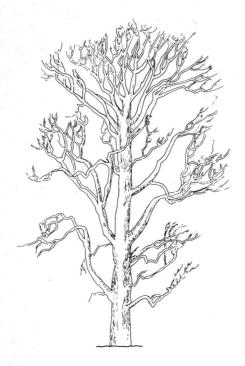

Winter aspect of the English elm, U. procera.

rough to the touch, but it is very variable, having local forms. Tiny red flowers are borne in profusion and suckers from old trees are likewise profuse. z5.

The English elm has been severely afflicted by the elm disease, but many trees have proved resistant and planting has been resumed. Among its several colour forms are 'Louis van Houtte', beautifully golden all summer, differing from *glabra* 'Lutescens' by having smaller leaves and a

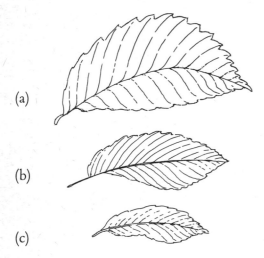

More elm leaves:
(a) *the white elm,* Ulmus americana;
(b) *the smooth-leaf elm,* U. carpinifolia, *very "oblique" at base;* (c) *the Chinese elm,* U. parvifolia.

narrow outline. 'Argenteovariegata' and 'Silvery Gem' are conspicuous with their silvery-grey stripes and mottlings and 'Viminalis' is slender in outline and in leaf.

U. carpinifolia is the smooth-leaf elm. Again variable, but in its best form it is a graceful tree of up to 90ft, usually composed of a single trunk and slender, ascending branches, cascading at their terminals to form a mushroom crown and bearing shining, dark green leaves. When it is thrashed by sea winds (which it resists with equanimity) the head spreads out fanwise. z4.

We find even greater diversity of form when we come to **U. × hollandica**, which is rather a group name than a fixed species, puzzling to botanists. In its various shapes and forms it is the predominant elm of Germany, France and the Low Countries, but is widespread also in the eastern counties of England. They are all very vigorous trees, hardy in z4. Among these forms are *hollandica* 'Major', the suckering Dutch elm (which is what in England and America is understood by *U. × hollandica*), and *hollandica* 'Belgica', the Belgian elm, which is what *U. × hollandica* appears to mean in Holland and Belgium! Two of the best forms, however, are the erect and compact 'Dampieri' and 'Wredei', of similar bearing, the latter gold-leaved.

Other varieties sometimes listed under *carpinifolia* have been found resistant to the elm disease, though by no means immune. Perhaps best are 'Groenveldt', rapid and upright, and the elegant 'Commelin'. In Europe (not America) 'Bea Schwartz' and 'Christine Buisman' are satisfactory but of little ornamental value. z4.

Also often regarded as a variety of *hollandica*

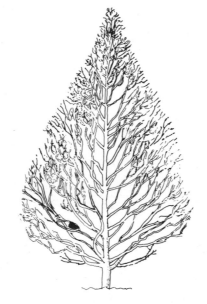

Winter aspect of the Wheatley elm, U. × sarniensis.

(and of other species also), is a much better one now enjoying the more elevated status of a species. This is the splendid Huntingdon elm, **U. × vegeta** is distinguishable by the long stalk (half an inch or more) of its elliptical leaf. Having a single, straight bole and the outline and drooping branch tips of the smooth-leaf, it billows out like a great leafy lozenge or ellipse, 115ft high, and makes a perfect tree for a lordly avenue. z4.

Also very well suited by its habit as a street or avenue tree is the very distinctive **U. × sarniensis**, known variously as the Jersey, Guernsey or Wheatley elm, and sometimes classed as a variety of the smooth-leaf. Its carriage is elegant, forming a symmetrical pyramid in outline, rounded at the base and reaching 120ft. Renowned for its resistance to sea gales, it is also very good for cold, exposed places and for industrial sites. Its variety 'Purpurea' however, is wide-spreading and looks rather like a copper beech. In 'Dicksonii' the foliage is bright golden. z4.

The Cornish elm, long familiar as a variety of **U. stricta**, but now called by some *U. angustifolia cornubiensis*, has little merit as an ornamental tree, but is a very sturdy barrier against sea gales. The single trunk breaks out into a narrow, umbrella-like crown, with a lot of whiskery growths beneath.

Here we leave the European elms and turn to those of other origins. America is weak in good native elms, but **U. americana**, the white elm, so called from its ashen bole, challenges comparison with any. Quite the most popular shade tree in North America and exceptionally hardy, it develops boldly arching branches when mature, that shape the whole tree into a king-size vase, 120ft high, though often of lax and open habit and liable to storm damage. Much revered in the eastern states for its local association, it is of sub-Arctic hardiness, but terribly scourged by the elm disease. The leaves are slender, but in the choice variety 'Princeton' are large, leathery and resistant to insects. All z2.

In general, Japan and China have little to contribute here, but **U. parvifolia**, the Chinese elm, is a gracefully poised, very ornamental tree of moderate size, rapid growth to 50ft and resistant to elm disease. Its tiny, glossy, rich-green leaves, evergreen in mild climates, form a dense dome in maturity, enhanced when mature by its mottled, peeling bark. z5. Its weeping variety, 'Pendula', is most picturesque. z7.

Akin in style is the Siberian elm, **U. pumila**, a fine 60ft tree which is nearly evergreen. This also is small-leaved, developing a high-domed head from a grey trunk engraved with multiple cracks. The American clone 'Hansen' is said to be resistant to the elm disease. z4.

RIGHT Zelkova acuminata.

WALNUT See JUGLANS

WASHINGTON THORN
See *Crataegus phaenopyrum*

WATTLE See ACACIA

WILLOW See SALIX

YELLOW WOOD See CLADRASTIS

YOSHINO CHERRY
See *Prunus × yedoensis*

YULAN See *Magnolia denudata*

ZELKOVA

The ravages of the Dutch elm disease are beginning to bring into prominence the elm's oriental

Zelkova serrata.

cousin, *Zelkova*, which has most of the attributes of the elm, but not its susceptibility to the dreaded beetle so far. The zelkova's requirement is a deep, moist loam. Growth is often slow at first but soon accelerates.

The usual species is the Japanese **Z. serrata**, a very ornamental tree which towers up to more than 100ft in Japan, but less in the West. From a smooth, mottled bole it forms a broad, spreading dome of toothed, pendant leaves. Sometimes apt to have a crooked trunk and a ragged top, but these faults appear to be corrected in the shapely 'Village Green', raised in America from Korean seed, and now being grown at Exbury. z4.

The Caucasian **Z. carpinifolia**, which has leaves toothed like a hornbeam's, is an unique tree, growing like a tall, slender goblet or sometimes a billowing dome, with quantities of aspiring stems from just above the ground. More elegant and distinctive than the Japanese, it exceeds 100ft in England and is a striking accent note in the landscape or large garden. z6.

Z. cretica is a small, elegant, light and airy tree, with many slender, ascending branches, drooping at their tips, arising from a low-forking base. The slim, 2in leaves have rounded teeth. z6.

Z. sinica is a very attractive newcomer from China, with an orange-tinted bark, zigzag shoots and leaves smoother margined than the others.

The Conifers

IN THE EVOLUTION OF OUR GLOBE conifers, or softwoods, flourished long before the appearance of any of the broadleaf or hardwood trees. They were and are to be found in both the Northern and the Southern Hemispheres, growing in areas of poor soil and harsh conditions, yet the largest of them still out-top the tallest broadleaf, soaring up maybe to 350ft. They also give us some of the smallest and most alluring dwarfs and crawlers (with which we shall not be concerned here).

Because of their strong and distinctive forms, conifers, used with taste and discretion, are exceedingly important elements of the landscape and the private garden. The majority that we cultivate for adornment bear themselves with an elegant carriage – erect, more or less slender and pointed at the tip like a spearhead. These forms have a statuesque quality that stamps itself upon the scene and their placement needs careful thought. If room allows, clusters are usually better than single specimens, each cluster according to its kind in spacing and numbers, though a single Italian cypress, shrewdly sited to pierce the sky like a spear raised aloft in triumph, may make a marvellous accent note or point of focus. So can a single, broad-topped umbrella pine. The narrowly columnar forms make marvellous avenues.

Nor are their lineaments, whether lance-like or bushy or towering castles, their only asset in the environment. The aromatic breath of the pines, the spruces and the cedars under a noonday sun, the wash of gold that floods over many of the smaller cypresses, the silvery-blue gleam of the spruces, the sense of awe evoked by the giant redwoods and of mystery by antique yews all lend their flavours and their influence to the composition of the countryside and the garden alike.

One must be careful, however, not to create oppressive "Black Forests", wherein no other life exists and no bird sings, unless one's taste lies that way. Such are the merely utilitarian uses of the conifer, grown to be sold for gain, not to ameliorate man's lot and stimulate his spirit. No doubt there is a kind of austere charm in the massed forests as they grew in millennia long past, but they speak darkly of a silent world closed against the presence of man and beast.

Other utilitarian uses of the conifer are shown more endurably when they are employed to provide shelter against storms and sometimes against salt-laden gales

OPPOSITE *The Scotch pine,* Pinus sylvestris, *flanked by larches, in the Lake District of England.*

from the sea. Here several conifers are very much the friends of man, particularly the pines, the Monterey cypress and many of the neo-cypresses. A phalanx of Corsican or Austrian pines will resist the buffets of the rudest gales. Only a few conifers, however, can resist the poisons of smoky town atmospheres, notable among them being the ginkgo, the yew and the newly re-born metasequoia. Likewise, only a few succeed in chalk, the chief being pines, yews, junipers and thujas.

Most conifers are evergreens and sometimes, particularly in North America, they are known collectively as "evergreens"; but this is an ambiguous term, for many broadleaf plants are evergreen and several conifers – notably ginkgo, larch, taxodium and metasequoia – are not.

All except the various yews, the podocarps, the pseudo-nutmeg (*Torreya*), the ginkgo and the juniper, which bear small soft-fleshed fruits, reproduce themselves from naked seed that fructifies within a hard, woody cone. Such flowers as they have are tight aggregations of very rudimentary flowers which are assembled in catkin-like structures known as strobili. The female strobilus becomes fertilised by the wind-borne pollen of the male and thus develops into the typical hard cone. Male and female strobili are always separate but are often borne on the same tree. They are often quite colourful and decorative to the observant eye. Some trees do not develop their strobili and cones for several years.

Understanding of conifers begins with recognition of their diverse leaf forms. Broadly speaking (apart from the ginkgo and the monkey puzzle) these fall into the following three groups.

1 Needle-like, as in pines, cedars, larches, etc. The needles may be short, stiff and sharp, as in spruces, or long, lax and brush-like as in pines. They may be deployed in little clusters or rosettes, as in cedars and larches, in larger tufts or plumes, as in the pines, or ranked mainly on the upper side of the twig or encircling it. Occasionally the needles adopt special attitudes, as in the neglected beauty, the sciadopitys.

2 Scale-like, in fishy manner, having tiny, compressed, soft, overlapping leaves, so closely hugging the twig as to obscure it, and borne on fanned-out branches that resemble the fronds of a fern. We find this mainly in the cypress, the neo-cypresses, the thujas and some junipers (see section on *Chamaecyparis*).

A peculiarity of some conifers is that, like the eucalypts and some other plants, they have two types of foliage – the juvenile foliage, which is needle-like and is the dress of the young tree or sometimes the young shoots of older trees, and the adult foliage, which is scaly. We find this in the cypress, the neo-cypresses, the junipers and the cryptomeria. The juvenile foliage is often the daintier and it is perpetuated on many of the dwarf forms.

3 Linear, a botanist's term for a narrow leaf with parallel margins. To the lay eye this is much more obviously a "leaf" than the needle or the scale, and in conifers these broader leaves are deployed on either side of a thin, central midrib, in the

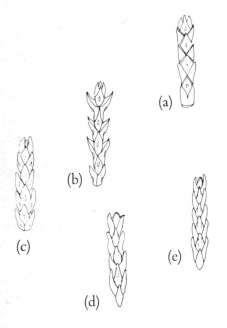

ABOVE *Types of conifer leaf-scales:*
(a) Juniperus virginiana;
(b) Juniperus thurifera;
(c) Lawson's cypress;
(d) *and* (e) *two sorts of Leyland's cypress.*

OPPOSITE *The Norway spruce,*
or Christmas tree of Europe
(*Picea abies*), *appropriately clad.*

manner of a double-sided comb ("pectinate" to botanists). This form of foliage we associate particularly with the yew, the tsugas or "hemlocks", torreyas, firs, redwoods and podocarps. In these pages we shall usually designate this type of foliage simply as "yew-like".

Another feature of conifer leaves is that their undersurfaces are often marked with white or off-white streaks. These show where the leaf's stomata, or breathing pores, are located and are called stomatic streaks. Sometimes the under-surface is all-white, giving the tree a silvery touch.

Within their degree of hardiness and soil tolerance conifers are generally of easy culture, taking kindly to a wide range of soils and environments. By and large, however, most of those that succeed in our temperate climes like rather moist conditions, some delighting in mist and a watery atmosphere. A few, indeed, grow naturally in very wet or even boggy ground, such as *Taxodium distichum*, *Pinus contorta* and *Larix laricina*. In districts warmer than Zone 7 those that originate from more northerly climates, such as many of the firs, spruces and hemlocks, are apt to languish.

Fierce winds and heavy falls of snow can grievously harm many conifers, even the stalwart boughs of the cedar. Some forms of Lawson's cypress can be split down the middle by snow; wherever this is liable to happen take precautionary measures before the onset of winter by firmly tying up all trees of slender form, until they get too big.

Whereas some conifers, such as the Douglas fir, grow with great speed, others adopt the pace of the tortoise. If one is extravagant one can grow several close together and thin them out afterwards, or if a single specimen gets too big for its boots one can simply hew it down. These, however, are essentially trees for the large panorama. A few species, such as the cunninghamia and the redwood, throw out thickets of new shoots from the base when felled.

In general terms the cultivation of conifers is much the same as for the broad-leaves. Select the site with care and prepare the soil conscientiously. Be sure that the nursery supplies them with a good ball of soil in either a loosely woven material or in a firm container. In the milder districts plant any time from October to April, in other areas, or when in doubt, do so in late April. Plant firmly and provide a stake for any tree of columnar habit until it is well established. In areas of high wind provide some form of lateral screening on the sensitive quarter.

The prime necessity, however, is to make sure that your conifer never lacks water in its first year, particularly its first spring and summer. Its dense, evergreen foliage transpires freely and you will find great profit from syringing the foliage liberally as well as applying water to the roots when the firmament does not do so for you. Young conifers die more from lack of water than from any other cause.

Pruning Most conifers respond surprisingly well to the knife, but, unless you want to indulge in topiary work with the yew, it is best to leave them alone except for amputating dead or decadent wood, keeping a good shape (which may include clearing the bole to a desired height, as in Chapter 5) or training as a hedge. All trees of a closely perpendicular build, with a central mast running straight up through the foliage, must be watched from the first moment for the appearance of any rival to that mast ("a rival leader"). Cut them out clean at the point of junction (see page 46). Do the same for any overmighty lateral that might shoot out sideways from the central trunk. Some light trimming of leaf terminals of bushy types is often necessary to improve shape or thicken growth. This can be done at any time, but do all major pruning towards the end of April; never in winter. Hedges, however, are best trimmed in early August. As stated in Part 1, always prune to some joint or junction. A few observations in special cases are made in the following notes.

The Conifers

ABIES
Silver Fir

The true or silver firs (from the Old English *fyre*) are not easy trees for the designer. Though neatly pyramidal, their bearing is stiff and the right place for them is in mountain scenery. They can, however, fulfil themselves as austere foils to softer trees in a mixed plantation, provided that they are planted with a niggard hand in a cool, moist soil. Heat distresses them, and Zone 7 is their southerly limit, where their place is taken by keteleerias. They shoot up to enormous heights with a single, straight trunk, from which their branches radiate in horizontal tiers.

Their cones are handsome, standing erect like slender barrels usually dyed purple when young, turning brown as they age, but in most species do not appear until the tree is some years old. These cones disintegrate after a few weeks, but leave behind their central spike or axis. The leaves are narrowly linear and yew-like, often crowded, and exude an aromatic resin of economic value, especially the Canadian balsam (*Abies balsamea*), known as the Balm of Gilead.

Silver firs are generally fairly free of pests and diseases, though in Britain *A. alba*, of Central Europe, is an easy prey to aphids.

Perhaps the most generally useful of the silvers is the Colorado white fir, **A. concolor**, for it does withstand a fairly dry and warm situation. It grows quite fast to 120ft, arrayed in uniformly blue-grey leaves displayed in two upswept sets, with a wash of yellow on young shoots and a grey, smooth bark. The large, handsome cones are plum-coloured when young. In *violacea* the leaves are deeper blue, in 'Candicans' silvery and in 'Wattezii' pale yellow turning silver.

The natural variety *lowiana* is a variable tree, intermediate between the silver and the grand firs. The northern form has a black bark and green leaves lying flat; the southern has usually a brown bark, sea-green, upswept leaves and a broad crown. Low's fir excels in Scotland, where one specimen exceeds 150ft and several others 120ft or more. z4.

A. delavayi forrestii A handsome and much sought-after fir, rarely exceeding 60ft, this is a variety that is known by its bristly cones of vivid blue, standing erect on brush-like shoots densely crowded all round with yew-form leaves, silvery beneath. z7.

A. grandis, the grand or giant fir, is the largest fir in the world, reaching nearly 300ft on Vancouver Island. In areas of high rainfall it grows prodigiously fast and several in Britain have reached 170ft in less than 100 years. The tallest, now over 180ft, are at Strone in Scotland and at Leighton Hall in Wales. The orange-scented leaves, of variable length, lie in a flat plane, resembling a double-sided comb. The cones are bright green. z6.

A. homolepis, the Nikko fir from Japan, is a very good ornamental tree where there is room for its widespread branches. The leaves are marked with conspicuous, chalk-white, stomatic streaks and the cones are purple before ageing. A tough and adaptable tree to 100ft and useful near towns. z4.

Very like the Nikko fir and easy to grow, but rare in cultivation, is the Manchurian fir, **A. holophylla**. The thin, stiff, bright green leaves are carried nearly erect, the stomatic streaks faint. The bark is tinted pink, mauve or orange. z5.

The Korean fir, **A. koreana**, is of special value and popular on account of its modest size, its decorative character, its coloured strobili and its handsome deep-purple cones, which are borne when the tree is only about 3ft high. The leaves are very short, crowded and erect, showing their chalk-white reverse. It can reach 60ft, but in the West is seldom to be seen yet at anything like that height. z5.

The red fir, **A. magnifica**, is another big American, slim and symmetrical, with a thick, corky bark becoming dark red when mature, rust-red shoots, longish, curled leaves and big, barrel-like cones. z5.

A. numidica, the Algerian fir, is rare but very valuable for its sturdiness, density and luxuriance of foliage and fast growth. The bark is prettily tinted pink or purple. It is useful also for its restrained growth, seldom more than 80ft. z6.

A. pinsapo, the Spanish fir, is a rare instance of a fir that attains its ultimate in regions of moderate rainfall and several specimens in southern England run to about the 100ft mark. Very distinctive are its short, rigid leaves radiating all round the branchlets, as prickly as a hedgehog. The slender cones are purplish-brown. This is a good fir for limey soils, though rather slow. Its form *glauca* is a striking blue-grey. z6.

A. procera, the huge noble fir, towering up to 270ft in Washington, has some very distinctive

Cone of the noble fir, Abies procera *(or* nobilis).

features. The inch-long, blue-green leaves stand erect on the twigs, as dense as the bristles of a hairbrush. Among these stand ranks of delightful purple strobili, followed by huge green cones, maybe a foot long, with the bracts from the primitive flowers within protruding and so dense as almost to hide the scales of the cone. z5.

Another fir with brightly silvered leaves on the reverse is **A. veitchii**, a handsome Japanese tree of up to 70ft, and the hardiest of all. The lower branches are upswept and the short, truncated leaves are upcurved and point forward, a very distinctive feature. Growth is fast but life is short. z3.

There are many more silver firs, but few of them make satisfactory ornamentals when mature outside their native mountain regions, such as *alba*, of the central European mountains, *balsamea*, the Canadian balsam, and *fraseri*, the Southern balsam.

ARAUCARIA
Monkey Puzzle

Beloved of the Victorians but considered by most people today as curious rather than beautiful, *A. araucana* suffers from being grown too often in areas of low rainfall, when, with its large, heavily armour-plated and sharp-pointed scales, it is apt to look gaunt and reptilian. In moist areas and deep soil, however, it becomes a dense and massy specimen, broadly conical or columnar. Specimens in the famous avenue at Bicton, Devonshire, are nearly 80ft high and others in Ireland are almost as tall. However, the monkey puzzle, or Chile pine, is best planted in isolation, away from plants of softer texture. z7.

The Norfolk Island pine, *A. heterophylla* (or *excelsa*) and the Australian bunya-bunya, *A. bidwillii*, are tender trees for z10.

ARBOR-VITAE See THUJA

CALOCEDRUS See LIBOCEDRUS

CEDRUS
Cedar

The true cedars give us some of the most magnificent of trees, tall, distinguished and of princely bearing. Their stance is overpowering in the small garden but in ampler scenes, whether of public or private use, they arrest the beholder by the stateliness of their forms and the elegant strength of their horizontal limbs. To boot, they are easy to grow in a deep loamy, well-watered but well-drained soil. They differ from all other evergreen conifers in the arrangement of their needles. On the new season's twigs they are sprinkled singly, but on older growths they become clustered in tight rosettes or "whorls". The needles vary in length, those of the deodar being the longest.

Plant them when not more than about 3ft high, unless the roots are balled. Plant them in isolation or in loose groups not less than 90ft apart and well away from other trees, and in full sun. As they increase in height the lower branches may at one's pleasure be removed a few at a time, flush to the trunk, up to 10ft or more from the ground in late April. This enables one not only to promenade beneath them but also, if one is so inclined, to grow shrubs right underneath them, for their roots go deep.

Cedrus atlantica, the Atlas cedar from the mountains of that name in North Africa, is a superb creation of nature, especially in its beauti-

The deodar, showing single needles on new shoots and rosettes of long needles on the older.

ful blue-rinsed form *glauca*. From its single, powerful trunk the tree builds up into a widely based pyramid, more than 120ft high, the lower branches sweeping out afar. The branches and branchlets are very numerous and irregular in length, densely covered with rosettes of needles less than half-an-inch long, the upright cones, which appear only after several years, nestling among them. A young *glauca* in the nursery, gleaming in silvery blue, is quite bewitching, but its lure must be resisted by people with gardens of less than three-quarters of an acre.

Cones and rosette needles of the Atlas cedar.

If the steel-blue *glauca* is not what is wanted, equally fine architectural effects are given by the straight, darker-hued *C. atlantica*, but, as these are always grown from seed, slightly different colour effects result. There are various other selections of the Atlas cedar, including a rare and handsome fastigiate one and a freakish weeping one. The golden-leaved 'Aurea' is very enticing as a young plant, but seldom satisfactory afterwards, though sometimes grown successfully in continental Europe. z6.

C. deodara is the deodar from Northern India, a noble giant of 130ft or more, and probably the best of the big conifers to grow in the warmer localities. Pyramidal and blue-grey when young, it later becomes a dark-green, very widespread tree of strong, horizontal limbs with the tips of their branches drooping in a manner that gives the whole tree a languorously graceful aspect and serves to distinguish it from other cedars. Specimens do vary, however, as they are usually grown from seed. The needles are deployed as in *atlantica*, but are longer and finer, well over an inch long. Some of the best have olive-green needles arranged in half-open bunches pointing forward. z7.

C. libani is the historic cedar of Lebanon. Conical when young, it then grows rather slowly to 120ft or more (averaging a foot a year) and spreading majestically with regular tiered and rigidly horizontal arms to at least 60ft wide in course of time, with its top absolutely flat or slightly domed. The dark-green needles are disposed as in *atlantica*, and are a trifle more than an inch long. It will do well in any good soil but is at its best in a neutral valley loam. Bean declares: "Irrespective of its sacred and historical associations, no tree ever introduced into our island has

The cedar of Lebanon.

Cones and foliage of the cedar of Lebanon.

added more to the charm of gardens than the cedar of Lebanon."

Its pronounced tabulation gives the cedar of Lebanon a firm architectural quality, very appropriate for associating with large buildings as well as the open country. In England it is often seen in the grounds of castles and mansions and in old churchyards. An historic specimen at Childrey Rectory near Wantage, planted in 1646, is only 50ft high but 25ft in girth of trunk. The Lebanon cedar is very sensitive to atmospheric pollution; nor, rated as z7, is it the hardiest of the true cedars, except in the natural variety *stenocoma*, the seed of which was collected for the Arnold Arboretum in the heights of Anatolia.

This has a broadly pyramidal or columnar form and is hardy in z5.

Of less renown than these classic trees is the smaller Cyprus cedar, **C. brevifolia**. The outline is pyramidal and the rosette leaves only half an inch long. z7.

CEPHALOTAXUS
Plum Yew

The botanist's Graeco-Roman mouthful means "head yew" and refers merely to the shape of the male flower, so "plum yew" is an apter and easier name. For the cephalotaxus can be described simply as a yew bearing fruits like a small plum or a large olive. Like the yew, it prospers in chalky soils (as in others) and in complete shade or sun. It has longer leaves, however, with prominent off-white streaks underneath. It can make a 30ft tree but is more often seen as a large, widespread, languorous shrub with several stems. It responds readily to cutting back. All z6. Refer also to its cousin the Torreya.

C. fortunei, the Chinese plum yew, has the longest leaves (averaging about 3in), scimitar shaped, curving downwards. By contrast, the Japanese *C. harringtonia drupacea*, can be spotted by its shorter leaves sweeping upwards from the twigs like a bird's wings. Known also as the "cow's tail pine".

There is also a fastigiate form of *harringtonia*, somewhat like the Irish yew, but less compact.

CHAMAECYPARIS
"False" or Neo-Cypress

The Greek *chamae* (kamy) means "on the ground", so we would assume that this recent botanical name means "dwarf cypress". But nothing of the sort, for several species are anything but dwarf. So "dwarf cypress" is invalid and we equally dislike "false cypress", for it is anything but false and has a true identity of its own. "Meta cypress" would be just right, but awkward (and generally not understood), so we prefer to call it, in English, neo-cypress. "Cyparis" derives from Cyparissus, the youth who, overcome with grief at having killed Apollo's favourite stag, was consoled by being transformed by the gods into a cypress.

No genus of conifer has given us so broad and varied a range of varieties or cultivars for the embellishment of gardens of all sizes. Their appeal is wide, their uses many. A great many are

decidedly dwarf and very alluring, but these we shall have to pass by.

Visually, chamaecyparis differs from the true cypress (*Cupressus*) in minor detail only. As seedlings, the foliage of both is needle-like. Both then replace their needles with minute, scaly, twig-hugging leaves, clothing splayed branches of many branchlets; but in chamaecyparis the foliage becomes compressed and flattened and is carried in sprays that resemble the fronds of a fern, while the cones become very small and irregularly round. Also unlike cupressus, the neo-cypress does not resent disturbance and can be transplanted when a fair size.

For the rest, the neo-cypresses need a moist, well-drained soil, preferably a place in the sun and fairly high atmospheric moisture. They are remarkably free from pests and diseases. The variants are considerable and the buyer should be particularly careful that he is getting a form neither too large nor too small for his needs. In the nursery rows they can be very deceptive. We shall deal here only with the tree forms.

The most widely known of all and the most versatile is Lawson's cypress, **C. lawsoniana**. In cultivation its bearing is slender and spear-like in the best forms, broadening with age, and in favourable situations where the atmosphere is moist it reaches 120ft and sometimes more, clothed to the very ground with dense, dark-green foliage. It originated in the fog belt of California and Oregon but takes its name from Lawson's Edinburgh nursery, who introduced it in 1854. It is now the most popular of all conifers in one or other of its forms and colours, which may be golden, silvery or many shades of green many of them unknown in America. In groups of three, five or more it strikes a decisive note in the garden or landscape, particularly if consorted

Lawson's cypress.

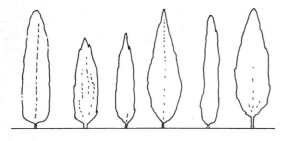

Variations on the theme of Lawson's cypress:
Left to right 'Columnaris'; 'Fletcheri';
'Ellwoodii'; 'Allumii'; 'Pottenii'; 'Erecta'.

with plants of contrasted hues and habits. It is lovely with heathers, small rhododendrons, pernettyas and the variegated pieris. Given proper treatment by the nursery, it will transplant safely at 12ft. It makes one of the most elegant of screens and an excellent hedge even in exposed positions and in shade; but normally it should be in full sun, especially the sparkling golden varieties. It is often confused with *Cupressus macrocarpa*, which is less hardy but a tougher sea-coast tree. We must confine ourselves to the taller variants. z5.

The sovereign of them all is 'Columnaris', a tree of very distinguished bearing. A positive blue wash is sprayed over the dark green and the tree is very slim, beautifully compact and like a lance held on high. Its ultimate height is not yet known; 25ft so far.

'Pembury Blue' resembles 'Columnaris' in colour, but is conical, plump at the base. To 30ft or more.

'Kilmacurragh'. Slenderly columnar or elliptical and rich green. Looks like an Italian cypress. 40ft.

'Allumii'. Soft blue-grey foliage, plump at the base but fine-tipped. 60ft.

'Fletcheri'. Grey-green, feathery, slenderly oval, getting plump and more columnar with age. Easy and popular. To 35ft.

'Fraseri'. Like 'Allumii' but grey-green, 40ft.

'Pottenii'. Slenderly oval, sea-green, soft and feathery, 40ft.

'Erecta'. Ovoid, with slim tip. Several stems. Bright deep-green. 80ft.

'Ellwoodii'. Grey-green. Very slim, tightly compact and elegant. Can occasionally reach 25ft.

'Triompf van Boskoop'. Large, broadly conical, loose and open. Good blue-grey. Needs trimming to thicken it. 75ft.

'Youngii'. Dark-green, slim, with up-curled sprays of frond-like foliage. Beautiful but rare. 60ft.

Lawson's cypress has also produced some splendid golden or gold-tinted cultivars, which consort particularly well with the blue-rinsed ones. All are broadly conical and grow to about 40ft or

more in time. They must have full all-day sun to bring out their sparkle. The brightest in colour is 'Lanei'. Near to it is 'Lutea'. More widely grown, however, is 'Stewartii', which may exceed 50ft and in which the gold usually changes to green in the interior by winter time. 'Smithii' is less well known but attractive with its drooping sprays (like 'Lutea'). Note, however, the new golden forms of Leyland's cypress and of *Cupressus macrocarpa*.

C. nootkatensis, the Nootka cypress, is a big, fairly fast-growing tree of broadly conical structure, its upcurved branches densely draped with long drooping curtains. In the landscape it stands out as a picture of melancholy elegance, but on close approach the foliage is seen to be coarser, duller and more prickly than those of its brethren. It also has a disagreeable odour. Its many variations include the yellow-green 'Lutea', the sea-green 'Glauca', and the dreary 'Pendula'. z4.

C. obtusa is the Hinoki cypress, sacred to the followers of the Shinto faith in Japan. You will know it by its broadly pyramidal outline and its horizontal, spreading branches terminating in beautiful, flat, fern-like sprays, in which the tips of the tiny leaves are blunt (*obtusa*). In time, and in damp soils, it can become a great pyramid of emerald green perhaps 100ft high ultimately with its lower branches tip-tilted. z4.

The Hinoki cypress has given us another rich assemblage of diverse forms and colours, most of them dwarfs, beloved of Bonzai fanciers, but over many years some become gaunt or awkward specimens of 30ft and more, as in 'Filicoides', 'Lycopodioides' and 'Tetragona Aurea'.

Outstanding among the larger variants is the golden 'Crippsii', loosely pyramidal, showing contrasting zones of light and shade in an elegant *chiaroscuro*, its broadly spreading, horizontal branches dipping at their tips in frond-like sprays. It is one of the loveliest of conifers for private gardens, wearing its golden dress all winter. It grows about 9ft in 10 years, later 50ft perhaps. It must have all-day sun. Prune the tips rather lightly in April to increase its bushiness.

C. pisifera, the very hardy Sawara cypress (z3), is not a very attractive tree, but some of its progeny certainly are. Its loose and open branches terminate in sprays in which the tiny leaves come to a fine point, distinguishing it from both the Hinoki cypress and Lawson's. The cones are the size of a pea (hence *pisifera*).

The offspring of the Sawara cypress constitute four distinct groups. In the Filifera group the foliage becomes thread-like, in Plumosa it is juvenile in feathery tufts, in Squarrosa even more juvenile with the points of the leaflets tilted up, not frond-like, and finally there is a group in

which the offspring differ from the parent only in colour or habit. Again, many of these variants are exceedingly attractive dwarfs or alleged dwarfs.

If we were to choose one only from among this galaxy for picturesque garden effect, it would be 'Squarrosa'. This is a beautiful, broadly pyramidal tree, not often seen above 30ft, though there are examples of 60ft and more. The foliage is a silvery grey-green, very dense, very soft, almost fluffy, inviting one to stroke it. In some situations one can with profit remove the lower branches, when its attractive chestnut bole is revealed. When aged it tends to get thin. Trim the extremities lightly from time to time. There are yellow-tinted forms in 'Aurea' and 'Sulphurea'. From 'Squarrosa' also came its popular little sport 'Boulevard'.

In 'Plumosa' the branches are ascending, with pale-green, feathery, frond-like terminal sprays, to 60ft in places. There are yellow and silvery forms.

In 'Filifera' the structure is broader than tall, with thread-like foliage. A poor thing, except in its glittering offspring 'Filifera Aurea', which will grow slowly to a mound of gold wire of 35ft.

One other species of the neo-cypress is of landscape value. This is **C. thyoides**, the very hardy "White Cedar" from North America, usually occurring in swamps. Rarely taller than 50ft, it adopts a slender, columnar form with short branches and a good-looking chestnut trunk. The leaves are grey-green or grey-blue, white beneath. Vast quantities of trunks, submerged for hundreds of years, have been found in the swamps of New Jersey. z3.

We may note also a relative of *pisifera* in the rare **C. formosensis**, a very distinctive tree with U-shaped lower branches. A giant in Formosa, with a mast of fantastic girth, it is doing well so far in the West in places where the climate is moist and the soil acid. z3 (Rehder).

CRYPTOMERIA

Cryptomeria japonica, occasionally and ambiguously called Japanese "Cedar", is a huge forest pyramid. Its twigs look like rough cordage, close-set with needles like little curved daggers pointing forwards. Its reddish brown bark peels off in strips. It needs an abundant rainfall. The Japanese form is usually of dense foliage, the Chinese more open and lax.

The cultivar usually recommended is 'Elegans', in which the softer, fuzzy juvenile foliage is perpetuated, the tips drooping, the general aspect loosely bushy. In winter the foliage turns a rusty

RIGHT Chamaecyparis lawsoniana *'Erecta' in Lord Aberconway's garden at Bodnant.*
OVERLEAF *The Nootka cypress,* Chamaecyparis nootkatensis.

Foliage and cones of Cryptomeria japonica.

bronze. Attractive when young, apt later to become top-heavy and fall over on reaching about 20ft, but without breaking the supple trunk. It can be much improved by pruning and by heading back when top-heavy.

Another cultivar often grown is 'Lobbii', which is a slim, sparsely-branched pyramid, with erect tufts of leaves at its branch-tips. All z6.

CUNNINGHAMIA

Of more interest to conifer specialists than to the gardeners and designers, Cunningham's firs are columnar survivors from the birth of the world. The one usually grown (and that not often) is *C. lanceolata.*

It develops a mast-like trunk, with irregular, horizontal branches, densely covered with leaves like those of the yew, but sharp-pointed and sprouting out at all angles. The lower branches

Cunninghamia lanceolata.

fall off. Growth is rapid and in nature the tree grows to 150ft, in Britain to 105ft. Watch for rival leaders. It submits to pruning. z7.

C. konishii, occasionally grown, is smaller in all its parts and less hardy.

CUPRESSOCYPARIS
Leyland's Cypress

This polysyllabic botanese covers the issues of marriages between the Nootka cypress (or other neo-cypresses) and the true cypresses. They are new stars in the conifer firmament, of which we are certain to see new offspring in the future. The most recent, and the most spectacular, is the glittering, golden 'Castlewellan' which we describe at the end of this entry.

The story starts with the **C. leylandii**, born of the Nootka cypress and the Monterey cypress (*Cupressus macrocarpa*). Clothed in bright green, soft, lacy, sinuous sprays, it grows as straight as a lance three feet a year once it is established and then slows down a bit until it nears 100ft in about 60 years. In Ireland and California it is much plumper and can be quite a broad specimen.

The Leyland cypress is a superb screening plant and resistant to salt winds, although it does not quite stand up to the worst Atlantic gales if exposed to their first fury. It also rapidly makes a very fine hedge up to any feasible height (40ft at Buckland Monachorum, not far from Plymouth), for it answers willingly to the shears. For a screen you plant it about 5ft apart, for a hedge 3ft.

You must, however, plant it when very young and whippy, never more than 30in high, with a well developed root system, and you must stake it. Those that have had their roots forced downwards by constriction in small containers are easily blown out of the ground by rude winds.

Though both its parents are natives of America, Leyland's cypress was a foundling born at Leighton Hall in Wales. Six seedlings from Nootka cones were taken by Mr C.J. Leyland in 1892 to Haggerston Castle, Northumberland, where they remained in quiet seclusion for some 40 years before being investigated by specialists and published to the world. Five of the old trees, all about 80ft high, still flourish in what is now a camping ground, their limbs festooned with TV aerials and clothes lines.

Some more cones arose, some using the Monterey cypress as the seed parent; they include 'Leighton Green', 'Haggerston Grey', 'Green Spire', 'Naylor's Blue'. The Nootka cypress has fairly recently been paired with other mates, two of the most promising results being *notabilis*, dark

grey-green, sinuous, sparingly branched, and *ovensii*, which bears a strong resemblance to its Nootka parent. All z6.

More exciting than any of these green spires is the glittering new star from Northern Ireland, **'Castlewellan'** (formally × *Cupressocyparis leylandii* 'Castlewellan'). This is a real beauty and almost sensational in being all-gold. According to the certificate lodged with the registration authority, it is the issue of a marriage between one of the golden forms of the Monterey cypress (*Cupressus macrocarpa* 'Lutea') and of the Nootka cypress (*Chamaecyparis nootkatensis* 'Aurea'). Its growth rate is terrific, outstripping that of the original Leyland, yet it is compact and needs no tailoring. Mr Alan Mitchell, of the Forestry Commission (who now own the Castlewellan estate), tells us "I am confident that, we now have, for the first time, a golden conifer that will exceed 100ft at least". Though the colour is most vivid in summer, it is brilliant in winter also, when its gleaming spires will cheerfully "warm the cold bosom of the hoary year".

One always needs to be wary about new introductions, but 'Castlewellan' is certainly one of the most promising conifers ever introduced and is destined to make a very significant impress on the landscape and on private gardens. Indeed, the danger is that, like many other good things, it may be overplanted and in time become commonplace. It should make a stunning hedge.

CUPRESSUS
True Cypress

The true cypresses have been overtaken in popular favour by the neo-cypresses, but many splendid species still hold their own in the landscape and the larger garden. They differ from *Chamaecyparis* in that their twigs branch radially, not in flat, frond-like sprays, their cones are larger, their constitution rather less hardy, their dislike of wet soils and their objection to being moved except as small plants. They are celebrated for their aromatic timber. Several prosper in chalk.

In **C. arizonica** the busy botanists have again led the gardener into confusion. What we have long known and admired as the Arizona cypress some botanists (not all) have divided into two species, one of which retains the name *arizonica* and the other is classified as *glabra*.

The latter group is the more decorative, the foliage being a dark blue-grey and the bark flushed purple with cream patches after a few years. All take the form of a fairly slender pinnacle and have poor root systems, especially in

LEFT *The "chiaroscuro" of* Chamaecyparis obtusa *'Crippsii' in Brigadier Lucas Phillips's garden.*
PREVIOUS PAGE LEFT *'Castlewellan', a young plant of the new golden Leyland cypress (* × Cupressocyparis leylandii *'Castlewellan'), at the Slieve Donard Nursery, Northern Ireland.*

151

ABOVE *Foliage and cones of* Cupressus bakeri.

LEFT *Foliage of the Arizona cypress, showing also the small, round strobili.*

C. macrocarpa, the Monterey cypress of California, is one of the best known of all conifers, not for reasons of beauty but because of its fast growth, its adaptability for screening and for its sturdy resistance to salt-laden gales. It begins life as a pyramid but when aged usually becomes a big beehive or a flat-topped, widespreading, dark-leaved tree. In Ireland it is hugely broad and multi-stemmed. The foliage is dense and scented of verbena.

In the British Isles the Monterey cypress has surpassed its performance in its native country in a very short time, growing to a 120ft with huge trunks. A tree at Powerscourt, Ireland, though only 70 years old, measured 90ft high, with 47 stems from the base and a trunk-girth of 37ft 6in. In the Melbourne Gardens, in Australia, it has developed broad, massive domes.

Macrocarpa is often recommended for hedging, but it is seldom satisfactory. For general use it has now largely given place to its hardier offspring, the Leyland cypress, though probably still better as a first line of defence against ocean gales. z7. Compare it also with the Lawson cypress.

Though the Monterey cypress is not usually considered to be an attractive garden plant, its gold-leaved varieties are fine indeed, as in 'Goldcrest', 'Donard Gold' and 'Lutea'. Beautiful and shapely, they grow up to, say, 30ft, if in all-day sun.

To these established varieties of *macrocarpa* can be added three new ones which seem to be of greater promise. 'Golden Pillar' is a good strong golden colour, very, very slim, tight and com-

heavy soils, needing to be well staked. Light, warm soils are best. Drought and lime are both tolerated.

Whichever specific name you prefer, the prime selection for most people is the blue-grey 'Conica', a fine tree to 75ft with a handsome bark, very good in an architectural setting. Apparently syn-onymous with it, though variously listed, are *bonita* and 'Pyramidalis'. z7.

Hardiest of all the true cypresses is **C. bakeri**, the Modoc cypress, a tree of loosely conical outline and resinous leaves. Worthy of wider use and seldom more than 30ft. z5. Rather taller is its sub-species *matthewsii*, the Siskiyou cypress.

pact, in the manner of the Irish yew. The second is 'Golden Spire', a bright clean, gleaming gold, of looser and broader build. The third, fresh from the mint, is 'Golden Cone', which, so far, looks very like the second. It is too early to make a final assessment of these, though some good specimens of 'Golden Spire' can already be seen at Warnham Court, near Horsham, Sussex, and 'Golden Pillar' has been growing successfully for some years in the pinetum at Wisley, where it is now about 9ft high.

The king of all cypresses, however, is **C. sempervirens**, the famous dark-green Italian cypress, which so picturesquely stipples the landscapes of Italy and Greece, shooting up like a spear as though aspiring to penetrate the sky, and standing sentinel at many a cemetery.

This was the original *Cupressus* of the Romans. In southern Europe it was as full of legend and as closely associated with life beyond the grave as the yew was in the north. No other tree grows so tall yet keeps so slim and wand-like a silhouette, even when a hundred feet high and hundreds of years old. The avenue in the Boboli Gardens at Florence is 300 years old but still in "incontaminate vigour".

The Italian cypress, however, is very variable in its behaviour and in the form *horizontalis*, which is the wild state, you get a widespread tree. If you want the spear-like one you should ask for *stricta*, though this is what good nurseries normally supply unasked. Of the same shape is the elegant, dense New Zealander 'Gracilis' and in 'Swane's Golden' from Australia, there is a golden tint.

Except in the warmest climates young plants of *sempervirens* should have some protection for the first year or two. It is liable to damage from severe gales and heavy snow. z7.

"CYPRESS" For the true cypress see CUPRESSUS above; for the neo-cypress see CHAMAECYPARIS; the like for Lawson's cypress; for Leyland's cypress, see CUPRESSOCYPARIS

DAWN REDWOOD See METASEQUOIA

DOUGLAS FIR See PSEUDOTSUGA

GINKGO
Maidenhair Tree

To new eyes this antediluvian tree, surviving from many million years ago, seems to bear no relation to one's conception of a conifer. For not only is it deciduous but also its leaves are shaped like little fans, resembling the pinnules of the maidenhair fern, and it bears no cones, its fruit looking like a small pale-green plum, the flesh evil-smelling but enclosing a sweet and edible little nut.

"Ginkgo" is the Japanese version of the Chinese *yin-kuo* ("duck's foot") and it was from China that the tree came back to us in the West, having found a refuge there from the last Ice Age, which had swept it away from vast areas of the world elsewhere. The full name is *Ginkgo biloba*, the leaf being formed in two lobes. It came back to Holland about 1734, to Britain in 1754 and a little later worked its way back to America, where it has been of priceless value as a street tree, brushing off with contempt the most poisonous of city vapours. Perhaps its most celebrated appearance is along the Roosevelt Boulevard in Philadelphia.

The ginkgo is thus an easy-going tree, hardy and suitable for most soils, acid or alkaline. As a juvenile it is usually eccentric rather than handsome, shooting out jagged branches of differing lengths at all sorts of angles. After about 20 years, having by then reached some 25ft, it begins to settle down to become a splendid, dense, widespreading specimen free of disease and pests and finally 100ft high. In autumn the leaves turn to a canary yellow, but soon drop. Because of the smell of the fruit on the female, it is usually best to plant a male tree (the ginkgo being unisexual). Where its great bulk cannot be accommodated, as in narrow streets, the erect variety 'Fastigiata', known best as the Sentry Ginkgo, should be planted. There are also a pendulous form and a conical one called 'Tremonia'.

In Europe the maidenhair tree is not planted on such a wide scale as in the States, but it is often seen in the larger private gardens. A giant specimen is reported in Milan. The tallest known in England is 92ft. The Duke of Argyll's historic original tree, transferred to Kew in 1762, stopped growing 20 years ago at 72ft. z4.

HEMLOCK See TSUGA

INCENSE CEDAR See LIBOCEDRUS

JUNIPERUS

The juniper is another conifer that bears small, fleshy berry-like fruits, but its needles declare its family resemblance. Versatile and rugged, it prospers in any reasonable soil, if not too wet or shady, and is among the best of plants for chalk. It transplants easily when young. The majority are small shrubs or ground creepers, of immense

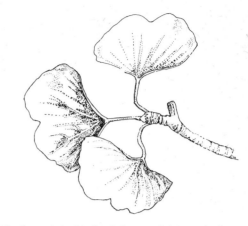

The fan or "duck's foot" leaves of the maidenhair tree, Ginkgo biloba.

The maidenhair tree in snow.

value in many a situation, but our concern will be only for the taller brethren, which are mostly narrow and dense, often having an outline similar to that of the cypresses. Pictorially they perform much the same kind of service, usually not quite so well, though *virginiana* and *chinensis*, which are the best two, are extremely hardy, and others will perform better in very dry conditions.

The leaves of junipers are variable. In juvenility all have sharp needles in whorls of three, or in pairs. Some species, such as *communis*, retain this juvenile foliage throughout life. Others, after first youth, develop minute scaly leaves closely pressed to the twigs, as in *virginiana* and *chinensis*.

The Chinese juniper.

The range of even the tree forms of junipers is large and our selection must be limited.

J. chinensis, the Chinese juniper, is a pyramidal or ovoid tree to 60ft, bearing both types of foliage, in light green. Very fine when at its best but usually seen in one of its smaller varieties. After a fairly quick start, growth becomes slow. z4.

Of its varieties, we choose:

'Keteleeri'. Small, elegantly conical tree to 25ft, of vivid green, adult foliage. Very good indeed.

'Mountbatten'. Narrowly columnar, very dense and compact, grey-green, slow, small, hardy. Raised in Canada.

'Aurea'. A particularly fine golden (male) form, known as Young's Golden Juniper. Tall, dense and slender but slow. Has both juvenile and adult foliage. To 40ft.

'Kaizuka' is used with great success in "landscaping" around private houses in California.

J. communis is the vital spark in the original and genuine gin. The tree forms have no garden merit except for shady boggy or chalk places, where the slim 'Suecica' would be valuable, reaching perhaps to 35ft. z2.

J. drupacea is the Syrian juniper of perhaps 60ft, slim and spire-like. A very handsome tree of a fresh light green, it bears generous quantities of large fruits, an inch wide, covered with a blue bloom. z7.

J. deppeana pachyphlaea is the alligator juniper, the thick bark of which cracks up into squares. A broad, sprawling, pyramid to 60ft, useful for dry, warm soils. z8.

J. recurva coxii is the best variety of this species. Imagine a single, spire-like trunk from which long, soft, sage-green sprays cascade in loose and open draperies, with small needles lying close to the twigs and imagine a tree perhaps 60ft tall. All the recurvas have this pendulous character. z7.

J. scopulorum, known in North America as the Rocky Mountains juniper, is an extremely variable species in size, shape and colour, seldom a success outside its own territories and extremely rare in Britain. Its great virtue is its resistance to drought, even in Mexico. Probably the most popular variety is the silver-tinted 'Pathfinder', a showy tree. Several others are very slow indeed to reach tree size, as in 'Columnaris'. z5.

The extra-hardy **J. virginiana** flourishes in almost any soil, including gravel and chalk, but is very slow. It is the most widely grown tree juniper in America where it is colloquially known as the pencil "cedar" or, more often, as the eastern red "cedar", complementing its western brother. Female trees bear abundant crops of handsome, blue berries. It prospers in the wild from eastern

Canada right down to the gentle air of Florida, so that its provenance is important to gardeners; those from the south tend to make broad pyramids, up to 90ft high after many years (50ft in Britain) and those from the north became more elegantly slim and not so tall. Only selected cultivars should be planted. These are numerous, the following being usually the best. z2.

'Canaertii'. Conical, very compact, rich green, profuse in purple fruit. 30ft. The best.

'Glauca'. Silvery sea-green, beautifully upswept. 20ft.

KETELEERIA

These are big trees that strongly resemble the silver firs, *Abies*, and are the natural substitutes for them where conditions are dry and warm. They need a hot summer and are not much known in Britain but thrive in Italy.

The usual one is *K. fortunei*, a pyramid when young becoming flat-topped in age and sometimes developing like a cedar of Lebanon, ultimately maybe 90ft high. The green, yew-like but pointed leaves are streaked beneath with white stomatic lines and the handsome cylindrical cones, borne erect and purple when young, average 5in in length. Unlike those of the firs, they do not break up on the tree but fall complete. z7.

K. davidiana is a trifle hardier, with larger cones still, which are flushed with red in youth.

LARIX
Larch

Larches are deciduous. Primarily, they are forester's trees, grown for commercial ends, growing very fast and making tall masts in crowded phalanxes. Their use in gardens is only as well-spaced specimens in large estates, where their naturally fine figure, with downswept pagoda-like branches, can be well displayed. They are also of value as copses in a hilly landscape, for they are mountaineers by nature and like nothing so much as a steep hillside. They will grow in the poorest soils and are especially to be praised for bringing fertility to thin and degenerate soils by their heavy leaf fall, very marked in the Japanese species. Though enjoying a high rainfall and snowfall, they must be kept away from wet valley bottoms, except for the American species. They are bothered a good deal everywhere by insects and diseases.

The European larch, Larix decidua, *showing rosettes of needles on adult shoots and single needles on the new.*

The foliage of the larch is a fine needle. Except on the new season's extension shoots, these needles are grouped in little clusters or rosettes, as in the cedar, mounted on tiny woody stubs. The tree bursts into leaf in spring and there is then nothing else of so tender a green. In summer the colour becomes leaden, but in autumn it turns pale gold before at last falling to earth to provide in time a rich humus.

The larch owes its world-wide reputation to successive dukes of Argyll, who have planted many millions of them in Scotland over a span of 250 years. The vogue was begun by the second duke, naturally using the European larch, *L. decidua*. Thereafter it spread to nearly all parts of the temperate world. In Scotland 300-year-old specimens (planted in 1675) are still in good health at 80ft. Plenty of others exceed 100ft.

In 1885 a later duke brought in the Japanese larch, *L. kaempferi* (or *leptolepis*), rather more decorative, denser and of stockier build, its leaves a dark grey-green, turning orange in autumn. Finally (or perhaps not finally) the European and the Japanese came together in a clandestine marriage on the Argyll estate about 1900, so that we now have *L.* × *eurolepis*, a variable, vigorous hybrid of great commercial value. All z4.

The hardiest of larches (and one of the hardiest trees in the world) is the North American *L. laricina*, the "Tamarack", which grows to 60ft in the Arctic regions of Zone 1 in Canada, usually in very wet ground, unlike others.

For convenience we may consider here a closely related but more handsome tree than the larch

and another victim of the botanists' unhappy choice of name, to wit –

Pseudolarix amabilis. There is nothing pseudo about it. Sometimes known as the golden larch, it can grow pyramidally to 120ft (60ft in Britain), with an enormous lateral spread, and is suitable only for very large gardens or as a landscape tree. In the autumn it puts on a beautiful all-gold dress before assuming the nudity of winter.

Compared with the larch, the leaves are laxer and not so needle-fine, the rosettes in which they are grouped are looser and the little stubs on which they sit are longer and curved. The young, erect cones, in the words of Hillier's *Manual*, resemble "small pale-green artichokes", before maturing to a warm russet. The neo-larch is intolerant of alkaline salts. z5.

LIBOCEDRUS
Incense Cedar

This small, but distinguished clan includes the celebrated incense cedar, which some botanists tell us should now be called a *Calocedrus*, but we are sticking to the old and familiar name **Libocedrus decurrens**. Others of the tribe have also been expelled by the botanist and sentenced to dwell in strange new tents.

At its best, the incense cedar is perhaps the finest tree of its kind in the world. Of all the fastigiate, slender trees, this is the most slender, forming, in cultivation, a slim minaret, of sumptuous, tightly packed green from base to apex and in time reaching well over 100ft (in its best specimens). So regularly is it moulded that you might suppose it to be a triumphal column erected for some hero. In the richness of its colour and in its statuesque bearing it excels the Italian cypress, from which it differs also in terminating not in a pointed finial but a blunt one, thus emphasising its likeness to an architectural column. The leaves are of the close-pressed, scaly type, borne on very short, upswept branches.

The incense cedar, however, is another tree that changes its character according to its environment. In Ireland, in California–Oregon and sometimes in Italy it becomes a much broader, plumper tree, occasionally forking, compared with those seen in England and elsewhere. The term 'Columnaris' is occasionally used to specify the very slim form, but this is not quite botanically valid, as it is not a fixed, unchangeable variety or cultivar. In any form, however, the incense cedar is an ideal tree to plant in association with large buildings or in bold colonies in the landscape. Both wood and leaves are impregnated with an aromatic resin and it is pest-free. The best specimens are seen in a deep, moist, well-drained loam in a moist climate free from impurities. z5.

The only other libocedrus grown to any extent, and that all too rarely, is the smaller **L. chilensis** from South America. It is a slow but beautiful tree with fern-like, almost mossy, laterally spreading sprays in an informal pyramid or cone. Specimens in southern England and Ireland grow to 50ft. z8.

Other species of the libocedrus occasionally grown, but not really hardy enough for us, are *plumosa* (the Kawaka of New Zealand), the similar *bidwillii*, the South American *uvifera* and the definitely tender *formosana*.

MAIDENHAIR TREE See GINKGO

METASEQUOIA

Known colloquially as the "dawn redwood" by those who cannot face botanical names, the metasequoia has an almost romantic story. Known until very recently only by fossil remains from bygone millennia, it was discovered still alive and thriving in a remote Chinese village in 1941. Eagerly and easily propagated, it spread rapidly, via the Arnold Arboretum, throughout the world and its hard-hearted botanical godfathers branded it with the jaw-cracking name *Metasequoia glyptostroboides*. The specific part of the name implies its likeness to another deciduous conifer, the Chinese *Glyptostrobus*.

All the same, the metasequoia has proved to be a very nice, fast-growing, deciduous conifer with light-green foliage, the leaves yew-like but curved and lax, the whole forming a neat but usually rather open tree of oval outline (a very narrow spire in the clone 'National') and bearing small cones dangling on long stalks, like cherries. The leaves flush to tones of rich pink, red or russet before falling in late autumn. As the tree ages the trunk becomes deeply fissured in a honeycomb design, mahogany coloured.

The metasequoia is a lover of moist, but not waterlogged soil; in others it progresses slowly. In the wild it grows 115ft high and specimens in Britain, America and Russia already exceed 50ft, after little more than 20 years (62ft in the Savill Gardens, Windsor, and at Princeton University). An impressive avenue, 150 yards long and 25ft high so far, is to be seen on the island of Mainau, in Lake Constance, Germany.

Young trees are liable to damage by late spring frosts. Treat it as a specimen tree and do not amputate its lower limbs. z5.

ABOVE *The "dawn redwood",* Metasequoia glyptostroboides.

PICEA
Spruce

The word "spruce" comes from *Pruce*, once the English name for Prussia, whence, we suppose, England obtained her first examples of what we today call the Norway spruce, in about 1500.

The spruces are a mixed bag. Some, particularly the Americans, are stiff and rigid, excellent when that effect is desired and when the tree is young, but they degenerate after some 20 years into gaunt creatures deprived of their lower limbs. Those from Europe and Asia are better furnished. Only a few make really good garden trees, the majority being primarily commercial commodities, grown for their timber in massed army corps. Their needs are for a damp soil, not waterlogged, and a moist, cool atmosphere and not warmer than z7. Heat distresses them. For gardens and parks the most ornamental is the Serbian *Picea omorika*.

In general, spruces form themselves into pyramids, slender or plump. The needles are usually

BELOW *The hanging curtains of Brewer's spruce.*

RIGHT *The Serbian spruce,* Picea omorika.

The broad needles of the blue spruce,
Picea pungens glauca.

The Serbian spruce, Picea omorika.

Foliage and cone of the Serbian spruce.

sharp, tough and stiff and are set on tiny pegs, a clue to recognition. The bark is roughish and the cones, some very handsome, hang down when ripening. Identification within the species is often difficult.

The Norway spruce, **P. abies** (*excelsa*) is a stalwart and very hardy, slimly conical tree of up to 150ft, but too stiff for the garden or other aesthetic setting. This is the usual Christmas tree of Europe, though not of America. It is a mountaineer and is grown in vast, shoulder-to-shoulder masses for its timber. Excellent as a shelter belt. z2.

P. brewerana is very distinctive. From its stiff, curiously curved branches hang heavy, dark-green drapes of close-set, whippy branchlets, like curtains. You may call it "graceful", "mournful" or just "odd", according to your reaction. It certainly has a dominant character, very effective as a lone specimen. z5.

P. engelmannii has sharp, glaucous, pungent leaves, with silvery and blue-washed varieties as in *glauca*. Elegant when young, it is best suited to moist, acid soils. 130ft. z2.

P. glauca, the white spruce, is exceptionally hardy (growing in Alaska and Labrador) yet endures heat and drought also. It can grow 75ft high, but is attractive only when young. 'Coerulea' is a silvery grey-blue and *albertiana* 'Conica' is a favourite dwarf. z2.

The Chinese **P. likiangenis**, though a variable species, is one of the most ornamental of all spruces. In spring (when mature) it arrays itself in a splendour of coloured strobili – the males

brilliant crimson, the females bright red – followed by empurpled cones. The habit of the tree is broadly conical, the branches usually tip-tilted. The leaves are yew-like, mostly forward pointing, their reverses boldly marked with white stripes. Growth is a foot or more a year. In the variety *purpurea* the cones are a rich plum-purple, the leaves lack the white stripes and the branch habit is more upright. To 100ft. z5.

P. omorika, the Serbian spruce, is quite the handsomest for gardens, landscapes and community neighbourhoods and, indeed, one of the finest of all conifers. It flourishes almost anywhere, excelling in chalky soils as in acid ones and is proof against city fumes. It shapes itself into the likeness of a church steeple, finely pointed at its apex, spreading slightly at ground level. From its central mast, which may reach 90ft, growing fast, its short branches stoop a little and then curve

upwards. The foliage is a beautiful, glossy, bluish green, the needles broad and flat. Plant it singly or in well-spaced clusters, not crowded. z4.

P. orientalis is a very big tree of up to 150ft and of neat, slender, pyramidal structure, densely furred with very small, blunt, glossy needles and clothed to the ground. Growth is slow for five years, and then rapid. In the favoured 'Aurea' the new shoots are gilt-tipped. z4.

P. pungens, the Colorado spruce, is a handsome fellow till about 20 years old, when it degenerates. Stiff, rigid, broadly pyramidal, with sharp, bristly needles and having its branches built in horizontal tiers, it is very variable in colour but is most favoured in its blue forms, especially the natural variety *glauca* and its forms 'Moerheimii' and 'Koster'. z2.

P. sitchensis is the well known Sitka spruce, a forester's commercial tree rather than a gardener's. Grows very fast in a cool, moist climate. Is the coastal equivalent of the Norway spruce. z6.

PINUS
Pine

Unlike the spruces, the pines offer us not only timber trees of commercial importance but also many ornamental ones of beauty and distinction for our gardens, public places and large landscapes. Their versatility of form, feature and behaviour is enormous. In nature they range from sub-Arctic zones to sub-tropical ones and there is a pine for almost any situation – ice, rock, sand, drought, gales, bogs, all except smoky towns. In places where almost nothing else will grow the jack pine and the northern pitch pine (*P. banksiana* and *rigida*) will flourish. Few trees perform better in sandy soils, so well that the pinaster and the lodgepole pines are used to reclaim sand dunes and convert them to fertility. The pines, indeed, have in general a close affinity with the sea and certain of the them have no superior in standing firm against the salty breath of ocean gales or as inland shelter belts for less rugged plants.

You will know the pines by a few distinctive features. While they usually begin life in the semblance of a pyramid, most of them subsequently swell into wide-spreading trees, like oaks and chestnuts. You will often know them also by the beauty of their coloured bark and no sight in nature excels the beauty of a slanting sun caressing the rose-red trunk of a tall Scotch pine. On closer inspection you will know them even more conclusively by the assemblage of their needles, which are in bunches of two, three or five wrapped at their base in a papery sheath. The

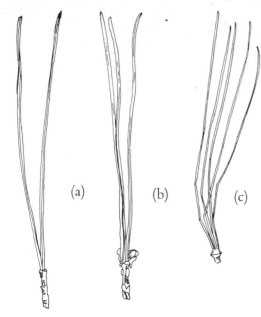

Pine needles are assembled in bunches of two, three or five, according to species, sprouting from a papery sheath at their base: (a) Pinus pinaster; (b) Pinus coulteri; (c) Pinus ayacahuite.

leaves may be anything up to a foot long, as in the longleaf pine (*palustris*). Those that go in fives are subject to a rust disease, but a few are immune. In most species the cones cling on for many years.

Most pines are quite unsuitable for gardens unless they be lordly ones. They are essentially adornments for the landscape and when not used as shelter belts the designer will use them to create an atmosphere of open, sunwashed or windswept or snow-clad countryside. He will site them with restraint, either singly (as for the umbrella or stone and the Scotch pines), or in scattered groups. The forester, of course, will do otherwise, in solid chunks shoulder to shoulder, to sell them for gain.

From the 125 or so species and varieties available in commerce we have chosen the following few for their beauty or other special merits for the gardener and designer. We omit the purely utilitarian and the weird *P. aristata*, still living in the American drought-lands after 4,000 years.

P. ayacahuite, the Mexican white pine, is a very elegant tree of 120ft for mild climates, of pyramidal form, with long, thin, glistening needles in shaggy, brushlike, pendulous tufts of five, and long, tapering, resinous, drooping cones, the whole graceful and rather languorous. z8.

P. bungeana, the lacebark pine, is a beauty for the patient gardener. A broad, bushy tree, it often thrusts out several trunks, from which the old bark peels off to reveal the new bark patterned in varied pastel colours. Your heirs will find it grows to 75ft. z4.

P. canariensis, the Canary pine, is useful for

dry or rocky situations in a warm climate. A slender but round-topped tree to 80ft, it bears very long, drooping needles, which are intensely glossy on young plants. Fairly fast. z8.

P. cembra, the Swiss stone pine or "Arolla". Very hardy, slow, tightly columnar, with needles in fives, and blue cones, it grows about 20ft in 20 years, then to 80ft. z2.

P. contorta, from western North America, is found from Alaska to Mexico in two main natural varieties. One, known to botanists as *Pinus contorta contorta* and to others as the shore or beach pine, ranges along the coast and a little inland in lime-free soil. Rampant, tough and vigorous, with short needles, it bushes out broadly and then shoots up at 3, 4 or 5ft a year. A tree of strong character with a rich brown bark.

The other variety is *P. c. latifolia*, known as the lodgepole pine, from its use by the American Indians for their wigwams or "lodges". This is a slimmer, inland variety, with longer leaves, not bushing out and with level branches regularly arranged. Not a very attractive garden plant. z6.

The big and picturesque Japanese red pine **P. densiflora** grows fairly fast to 100ft (50ft only in Britain), with a handsome orange bark, a flat-topped head and dense clusters of cones. At its best it resembles the Scotch pine. A yellow-streaked variety is called "Dragon's Eye". z4.

The beautiful Himalayan or Bhutan pine, formerly called *griffithii* or *excelsa* but now **wallichiana**, is another fast-growing giant, with widespread arms. The long, lax, blue-green needles in bundles of five, resistant to rust disease and falling curtain-like, give fluidity to its great bulk. In the milder parts of Britain it exceeds 100ft. z5.

P. koraiensis, the Korean pine, is loosely columnar, with rich green foliage of slow growth. A good tree for small gardens when young, but it can reach 100ft. z3.

P. lambertiana is the sugar pine, largest of all pines, reaching well over 200ft sometimes and bearing also the largest cones, up to 20in long. The needles are in fives, twisted and subject to rust. It exudes a sweet resin. The largest in the world grows in the Siskiyou Mountains. Usually unsuccessful in Europe. z5.

The Bosnian pine, **P. leucodermis**, is a delightful, distinctive and unusual conifer, being of oval outline, neat, compact, tough, amenable and decorated with small cones of brilliant cobalt, holding that colour for 15 months. The bark is pale grey-green, the needles very dark, in twos, on upswept shoots. One of the most serviceable trees, it succeeds in dry soils, damp ones, shallow ones and over solid chalk and in acid ones. Its neatness fits it well for fairly small gardens. Rather a slow starter – 30ft in 20 years, ultimately 80ft (60ft in Britain so far). z5.

P. monticola, the western white pine. Very handsome, very fast, averaging 2ft a year to easily 100ft and occasionally far more. It is slim, symmetrical, cypress-like in outline, and makes a beautiful garden tree when there is room. Needles come in fives, straight and stiff, liable to rust. Needs lime-free soil. z5.

P. muricata, the Bishop pine of California, is extremely fast and vigorous, highly resistant to sea gales and an invaluable shelter tree, with plume-like clusters of needles. Those from South California are pale-green and broad domed; those from the north are narrower. Both seem to prefer Britain to their homeland, often growing 30ft in 10 years and reaching 100ft. z7.

P. nigra offers us three variants of outstanding worth as shelter trees, on sea coasts or elsewhere, but of limited ornamental value. The original *nigra*, the Austrian pine, is ungainly, shaggy, sooty and coarse, but densely branched, fast-growing, very wind-firm and tough.

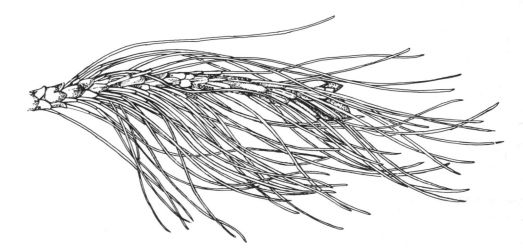

The Corsican pine, Pinus nigra *var.* maritima.

Its Corsican brother, *P. n. maritima*, is a better tree all round, forming a regular, narrow pyramid or column, with short, level but sparse branches. It likes a low elevation near the sea and a low rainfall. It grows right down to the high-water mark and withstands sea gales better than any other conifer. But, having sparse roots, it is difficult to establish if planted when taller than about one foot, after which it will make 20ft in 10 years and go on to perhaps 140ft, with a pointed crown.

Inland, an equally good bet, but much rarer than either of the others, is the Crimean pine, *P. n. caramanica*, an excellent tree with tip-tilted branches and, in older trees, quantities of erect stems ("like organ pipes", says Mr Alan Mitchell), close to the bole. It can reach 120ft. All do well in almost any soil. All z4.

P. peuce, the handsome Macedonian pine, is a dense column of blue-green needles, white beneath, which you may see mantling the lean and rocky flanks of Mount Olympus. The leaves are in fives, but disease-free and of virile health. The picturesque bark is mauve-grey, broken up into small plates. A fine landscape tree to 80ft. z4.

P. pinaster is a familiar sight to all who travel the Atlantic coast of France or the southern shores of England, where it has been growing for nearly 400 years and where it is known as the Bournemouth pine from its prevalence in that resin-scented resort. It is famed for its skill in reclaiming sandy maritime wastes. When aged it makes an 80ft tree with a bare, chestnut trunk, topped, in the manner of a palm, with a broad crown, often leaning, looking just right for the seaside. A fast mover. The sap of the pinaster provides turpentine. z7.

P. pinea is also a seaside tree but of greater distinction, beloved of the Old Masters, especially Claude, Poussin, and Richard Wilson, and of the modern snap-shot artist. This is the umbrella or stone pine. Happy the landscape designer who is given a spur or ridge with nothing to be seen beyond it but the sky, for it is upon the crest of such a spur that he will surely place a single stone pine in "excellent solitude". The sea will help him too but is not essential. It stands like an open umbrella, with its bare chestnut trunk for the handle and its branches for spokes, but is often quite flat-topped, when it resembles an inverted pyramid. Beneath its canopy the scene beyond is clearly visible and low-growing plants may carpet its floor. Happily, it grows quite fast, maybe to 80ft. The long needles are safely in twos. It grows well in lean, sandy or rocky soils. z9.

Rivalling the Scotch pine in the beauty of its bark but outstripping it in stature is **P. ponderosa**, from western North America. When past first youth the bark is deeply cleft with ornamen-

tal fissures and tinted in cinnamon or pale chestnut. The foliage is densely bushy. Essentially a tree for the larger landscape, it grows fast to 150ft. z5. Its variety *scopulorum* is a little hardier and smaller.

P. radiata, the celebrated Monterey pine, is another tree of great value on sea coasts. When in isolation and not gnarled and battered by gales, it becomes a sumptuous, high-domed, dense mass of strong, lustrous green with powerful, wide-flung lower limbs. When beset with other plants it becomes a big beehive set on a long bole, with the lowest branches naked. It grows very fast indeed to 120ft, but to 202ft in 51 years in New Zealand. z7.

P. strobus is known in Britain as the Weymouth pine, having been introduced by Lord Weymouth early in the eighteenth century but, being prone to disease, seldom a great success (though in France and Germany it is). In America, where vast forests of it existed before "men grew rich by destroying it" (to quote H.J. Elwes), it is the eastern white pine. Though an important timber tree, it is also ornamental when in isolation, but unless restrained by careful pruning, is far too big for any but baronial gardens, growing to 150ft or more (25ft in the first 20 years), first as a pyramid then gradually becoming flat-topped. The foliage is dark-green, soft in texture. It transplants easily. There are fastigiate and pendulous varieties. z3.

P. sylvestris, the very hardy Scotch pine, in its right setting, is perhaps the most picturesque and evocative of all. That means heathland, lakeside, hillside or clearings in woodland. It breathes of open air and free spaces gilded by a mild sun or washed with soft mists or carpeted with snow away from the haunts of men but acquainted with the wandering deer and the browsing sheep; and acquainted also with its close friend for many millions of years, the silver birch. Characteristically, you will see the Scotch pine as a tall bare mast, not always straight, topped with an irregular, blue-green crown. The poise is delightful but the feature that most catches the eye is the bark. As a seedling it is grey-green, quickly changing to a charming rose-pink tinted with orange. As the tree ages this colour is held on the boughs but the bole becomes variable, sometimes dark brown but more often pinkish-grey with a random pattern of fissures.

The Scotch pine begins life as a little pyramid, then grows fairly fast, putting out its branches laterally, growing a good 15ft in the first 10 years, then going on normally to 80ft, but sometimes 120ft. It will prosper in any reasonable soil that is acid and briskly drained, enjoying both pure peat and pure sand and is found in good health in sand dunes close to the high-water mark.

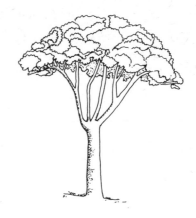

The stone or Italian umbrella pine, Pinus pinea.

The Scotch pine, Pinus sylvestris.

The male strobilus is flushed with gold and the female with crimson, developing into a pointed, drooping cone. The needles are in pairs. There are several garden forms, of which the choicest is the small and rare 'Fastigiata', as slim as a ship's mast and delightful with heathers. A specimen at Wisley is about 24ft. All z2.

PODOCARPUS

The podocarps are an interesting and very diverse genus with some resemblance to the yew or some-

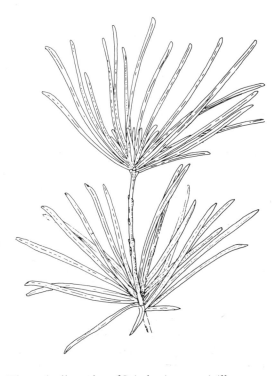

Podocarpus salignus, *the leaves sprouting all round the shoots.*

times the willow, but with leaves of a softer, glistening green. Also like the yew, they bear fleshy, red or purple fruits instead of hard cones. As a rule, they are elliptical and many-stemmed. They grow, slowly, in any reasonable soil and a moist atmosphere. Where winds are cold they will be grateful for a protective screen of pines or such like. All z7.

The one usually recommended is the oriental **P. macrophyllus** with slim, glossy, dark-green leaves, 3–4in long, spiralling round the twig; but after 20 years it is still little more than a large, many-stemmed shrub, though it can reach 60ft. Very effectively used in the USA and Japan as a hedge. Unlike other podocarps, it needs acid soil.

P. andinus, the "plum-fruited yew" from the Andes, is rather quicker off the mark, growing as a slender ellipse to 70ft. It looks very like a yew with soft, one-inch leaves. The yellow male strobili are held up prominently in branched clusters and the fruit resembles a damson. It thrives in south-west England and Ireland.

P. salignus is perhaps the best and is a rich pile of glossy green, willow-like leaves, 2 to 5in long, borne in lush profusion from sinuous, drooping branchlets in a slender pyramid. It grows about a foot a year and reaches 65ft in the British Isles.

PSEUDOLARIX Included under LARIX

PSEUDOTSUGA
Douglas Fir

Here we have a pretty glaring example of ill-considered christening, for this great and stately tree is neither a bogus tsuga (hemlock) nor a fir, though visually much more like a fir than a tsuga. It has its own particular personality and very impressive it is.

What we might call the original one is **P. menziesii**, discovered in 1791 by Archibald Menzies, a surgeon in the Royal Navy, in western North America but left in the silence of the great forests until re-found and introduced to the world by that intrepid Scot, David Douglas, on his hazardous exploration for the London (now Royal) Horticultural Society in 1827. It grows along nearly the whole length of the western flank of the North American continent and in places towers up to 300ft.

When not crowded the Douglas fir is an immense, slender spire, looking rather like a pagoda with its tip-tilted branches. It is often of irregular outline, which should not be interfered with. On close inspection it can be recognised by its pendulous masses of soft, aromatic needles, its thick, corky, deeply furrowed bark, its plump, chestnut-coloured buds at the tips of its twigs and by its egg-shaped, pendulous cones with little, pointed bracts peering between the scales. It grows very fast, sometimes reaching 100ft in less than 30 years. It likes a moist, acid, well-drained soil, with ample rainfall and shelter from high winds, as afforded by the lower slopes of hills. z6.

The Douglas fir delights the heart of the forester but obviously a tree of anything like 300ft (180ft so far in Britain) is of very limited use to anyone else. Fortunately in the form *glauca*, the blue Douglas fir, we have a fine tree restricted to about 100ft, with blue-washed foliage, rather slow but hardy enough for z4.

The Douglas "fir".

A few other forms and cultivars are also to be had, such as *caesia*, the extra-hardy Fraser River Douglas Fir.

Another species altogether, *P. macrocarpa*, is the large-coned Douglas fir, of S. California, with hard, sharp needles, very like a fir.

REDWOOD See SEQUOIA

SAXEGOTHAEA
Prince Albert's Yew

Named after Queen Victoria's consort (who was of the house of Saxe-Coburg-Gotha), *S. conspicua* is a bushy tree of up to 40ft from South America. It has a loose and open construction with lax, spreading branches deployed in circular tiers and hanging, weeper-like laterals. The linear leaves are hard, sharp, irregular, with gleaming white undersides. Grows slowly at the rate of 15ft in 20 years. z7.

SCIADOPITYS
Japanese Umbrella "Pine"

Quite unlike the umbrella or stone "pine" of Italy (a true pine), this beautiful, very distinctive, but much neglected conifer is usually a trim,

The umbrella spokes of Sciadopitys verticillata.

RIGHT *The incense cedar,* Libocedrus (*or* Calocedrus) decurrens.

slim, dense pyramid and the sobriquet "umbrella" comes from the manner in which the clustered needles are grouped round the circumference of their stems, like umbrella spokes. The foliage is lush and glossy, the leaves being in clusters of 20 to 30, one above the other, the needles about 5in long; what appear to be single leaves are in fact conjoined pairs. The whole tree, neat and symmetrical, glistens in garden or landscape rising to 120ft in its native country (75ft in England) at about a foot a year. Trees in the Arnold Arboretum are only 25ft after 50 years but it is still well worth growing. The full name is *S. verticillata*. It must have acid, moist, rather cool soil. Watch out for rival leaders and over-lusty laterals. z5.

SEQUOIA
Redwood

The celebrated *Sequoia sempervirens* is a Goliath among trees, the tallest in the world, towering up to 367ft in the Howard Libbey specimen in the Humboldt State Redwood Park, and often lives for more than 2,000 years. It might thus be thought of little use to gardeners and landscapers, but it grows phenomenally fast, reaching 50ft in 20 years in good conditions, and is therefore a fit tree for those who look beyond today.

Giving immortality to Sequoya, the Red Indian half-breed who invented the Cherokee alphabet, the redwood, or coast redwood, is another of the trees discovered by Archibald Menzies in 1794. It is native chiefly of the foggy coastal flank of California, where it grows in dense, crowded phalanxes, the huge trunks, 20ft in diameter and bare in their lower reaches, soaring up through the mists like Gothic columns in a vast cathedral, no sunlight reaching the deep, russet pile of fallen leaves that carpet the floor, except where a splinter of light streaks through to illumine the rich, chestnut-red bark, soft, spongy and a foot thick.

The redwood begins as a slender pyramid which later usually becomes a column with sparse branches sweeping down and out. The leaves resemble those of the yew, borne in double ranks. Felled trees break out into dense coppices from new basal shoots.

To fulfil itself properly the sequoia needs the shelter of hills taller than itself and a rich, deep, moist soil, preferably acid and preferably in a moist atmosphere. Before the Ice Age it was fairly well spread over the world and has now returned successfully to some of its ancient haunts, including Britain, where many fine young specimens grow up to 138ft so far. z7.

ABOVE *The yew-like leaves, with some scale-type, of the coast redwood,* Sequoia sempervirens. BELOW *The cord-like foliage of the wellingtonia.*

SEQUOIADENDRON
Wellingtonia or "Big Tree"

Another enormous tree, this is the inland version of the coastal redwood, and was formerly called by the easy and sensible name *Wellingtonia*, after the duke, until meddling botanists inflicted upon it a whole series of aliases before submerging it under the polysyllabic waves of *Sequoiadendron giganteum*. The foliage is totally unlike that of the sequoia and, when measured in height, the wellingtonia is not so gigantic, not such a "big tree" as the sequoia, the Douglas fir, or *Abies grandis*, but the girth of its trunk is fantastic. The biggest living specimens are the "General Sherman", 273ft high by 79ft in girth, and the "General Grant", 267 by 79ft. They are estimated to be nearly 4,000 years old.

In habit the wellingtonia is a narrow pinnacle, its point pricking the sky, with widely spread, relatively short branches, showing daylight between them, and sweeping out from the mast in downward and outward curves. The bark resembles that of the sequoia, but the leaves, instead

LEFT *Foliage of the blue spruce,* Picea pungens glauca, *from the form* 'Procumbens' *in Brigadier Lucas Phillips's garden.*

The wellingtonia, Sequoiadendron giganteum, *at Alice Holt Lodge.*

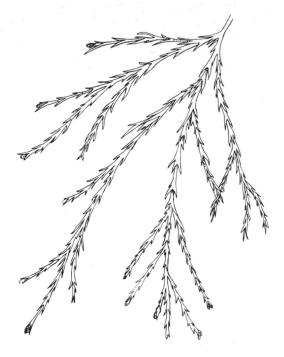

A closer view of the wellingtonia foliage.

TAXODIUM
Swamp or Bald "Cypress"

Taxodium distichum is a decorative, easygoing, very healthy conifer which is not in the least like a cypress and much more like a big, light-green yew. Its foliage is neither scale-like nor needle-like, but comb-like, with flat, linear leaves. It is deciduous, its leaves falling in showers of golden-bronze in late autumn; and in very late spring it comes to life again with a burst of soft, tender green after the fashion of the larch.

In nature, as in the Everglades of Florida, it grows in swamps or shallow water, whence its roots throw up knobbly "knees" at intervals, supposedly to seek oxygen. It does not by any means need a swampy soil, however, and grows magnificently in relatively dry ones, where it does not usually throw up any knees; but it is certainly at its most picturesque by the waterside where, like Narcissus, it can admire its own image below, as in the inspired example in Major Edmund de Rothschild's garden at Exbury, where Japanese maples and azaleas enamel its feet.

In favourable conditions the swamp cypress can grow to 150ft, forming usually a great, soft green pyramid, but sometimes adopting other shapes. In Britain, where it arrived in 1640, several examples easily exceed 100ft and no dead or diseased tree is known. The base of the trunk is radially buttressed in a way that suggests the fluted vaults

of being yew-like, are of the scaly type, but hard, rough, prickly and cord-like and scented of aniseed. The tree tolerates lime if not in the form of chalk.

The wellingtonia has been a great success as a colonist in Europe. A tree in Northern Italy has grown 73ft in only 17 years. In Britain it has been planted in most large estates and in Devonshire has already reached 165ft. It makes a most impressive avenue tree, as shown in the Duke of Wellington's seat at Strathfield Saye. Designers should use the wellingtonia in loose and open groves, blending it with other plants. z6.

There is such a thing as a weeping wellingtonia, but (except to conifer fanatics and lovers of the weird) it is a hideous deformity.

RIGHT *The memorable* Taxodium distichum *beside the lake at Exbury.*

Winter aspect of the swamp "cypress",
Taxodium distichum showing its "knees".

of a Gothic cathedral ceiling. It grows to a great age, but in senility has a haggard look. z4.

Not nearly so well known, but just as good, is **T. ascendens**, sometimes known as the pond "cypress", to distinguish it from *distichum*. This is a smaller tree of some 80ft, of more columnar shape and ascending branchlets dressed in bright green, the leaves falling in gorgeous chestnut showers late in the year. In very wet places the base of the trunk develops a pronounced middle-age spread. The best form is *nutans*, a dense column of pale foliage, drooping at the tips. z5.

A third taxodium is the Mexican *mucronatum*, which is evergreen in warm areas. z8.

TAXUS
Yew

As ancient as the very hills and the heaths, wreathed in legend, its English name certainly more than a thousand years old, the yew has an unfortunate association with the grave.

> *Old Yew, which graspest at the stones*
> *That name the underlying dead,*
> *Thy fibres net the dreamless head,*
> *Thy roots are wrapt about the bones.*

So Tennyson, mourning at the graveside of a lost friend and going on in a famous line to observe how the church clock

> *Beats out the little lives of men.*

Not only were yews planted in English churchyards but also their boughs were placed on graves or even on the buried corpse. "My shroud of white, all stuck with Ew", quoth Shakespeare. And Matthew Arnold:

> *Strew on her roses, roses*
> *And never a spray of Yew.*

Yet the yew was a symbol not so much of sorrow as of immortality, being one of the very few evergreens then available. Moreover, it grows to a great age and several in Britain are believed by the Forestry Commission to be more than a thousand years old. One in Perthshire is expertly assessed as not less than 1,500 years old. Many are older than the churchyards over which they keep watch.

Yews are relatively small trees or else scrambling shrubs of much value as ground cover. Their growth is slow, but can be expedited by a nitrogenous or a general-purpose fertiliser. Their foliage is of the double-sided comb pattern ("pectinate"), not needles but small, narrow flat leaves, a fresh mid-green when young, turning dark above. The foliage is dense, so that the general assemblage is of a very dark-green, almost black tree, which to some beholders appears sombre. There are, however, several varieties glittering with gold tints. The trunk becomes very rugged, picturesque and rust-red when aged, telling of what Tennyson called its "stubborn hardihood".

Yews are nearly always unisexual. The flowers or strobili on the female tree are very small, green, inconspicuous, those of the male larger and quite a bright yellow, throwing out clouds of yellow pollen when ready to mate. Thus if you want a yew to bear its ornamental fruits you must have one gentleman to about five ladies. These fruits are bright red, fleshy, cup-shaped "berries", enclosing a small seed. The seed and the leaves are very poisonous, but not the flesh of the fruits. On no account plant yew where domestic animals may browse; nor where young children might have access to the berries of female trees. Birds eat the flesh but discard or pass the seeds.

Yews grow well in any tolerable soil, if not waterlogged, and they relish chalk. They have also the very great merit of prospering in shade, even the deep shade of overhanging trees. Nothing submits to the knife so willingly, so that they make magnificent, fortress-like hedges and are a favourite medium for the art of topiary.

Only three species of yew are to be recommended: the English (*Taxus baccata*), the Japanese

Leaves and fruit of the English yew,
Taxus baccata.

(*T. cuspidata*) and one resulting from a marriage of these two contrived by an American.

T. baccata in fact flourished over a wide expanse from Britain to the Bosphorus and is the dominant species (z6). In Britain it is most often found in chalky formations. It makes a dense, widely based pyramid up to 50ft, with specimens in Sussex of more than 80ft. The rate of growth is 8 to 10in a year, but this rate slows down as the tree ages. As in other cases mentioned here, it is more honoured in other countries than its own and has found a specially friendly welcome in the United States as far north as New York (no further). A great many varieties and forms have been evolved, among which are some beautiful and lively golden forms.

The outstanding one is the Irish yew *T. b.* 'Fastigiata' (alias 'Stricta'). This departs from the natural pyramid and takes the shape of a perfect, close-knit pillar, or, when many-stemmed, expanded into a broad, sturdy, square-shouldered, blunt-topped mass. A purely chance foundling, it is a female clone spotted by a farmer named Willis in Ireland in 1779, looking dark-green and handsome. Its gold-flecked form is much more lively, but a little slower. This is "Fastigiata Aureomarginata", a male. These two can be planted singly, in small groups or in avenues with great effect.

Of other cultivars of the English yew we pick the following as the most desirable.

*The upswept leaves of the
Japanese yew,* Taxus cuspidata.

'Dovastoniana', the Westfelton yew, found by John Dovaston, of Westfelton, Shropshire, in 1777. Very distinctive, graceful, lusty, wide-spreading, with foliage hanging curtain-like from the long, horizontal branches. Usually female. 'Dovastoniana Aurea' is a beautiful glowing, golden male variant. If either of these lose their leaders, by accident or design, they become widespreading, shrubby thickets, very decorative in the golden form.

'Elegantissima'. Young leaves yellow, fading to straw, but retaining yellow on the margin. Vigorous, widespreading, popular.

'Adpressa'. Ultimately a big, wide-spreading, blunt-headed bush-like tree, with small leaves on elegantly pendulous twigs. Female.

'Adpressa Aurea' is a smaller, beautiful, male, golden variant.

'Erecta'. Female. Seedling of the Irish yew. A broad column, opening out at the summit in time. Quite a big tree.

'Aurea' takes the normal pyramidal form but the foliage is golden in its first year, turning green next season.

'Lutea' has yellow fruits, often spectacular.

T. cuspidata, the Japanese yew is much smaller and broadly bushy, with leaflets upswept from the twigs, yellow on their under-surfaces. z4.

The hybrid between the English and Japanese, raised in Massachusetts by Mr T.D. Hatfield, is **T. × media**, a trifle coarser in foliage than the English but hardier and growing somewhat faster to 40ft. It is often seen in its cultivar 'Hicksii', which has the columnar habit of the Irish yew, but broader, with large, very abundant fruits. z4.

THUJA

In the thuja (often misspelt "thuya" but correctly so pronounced) we return to those conifers that have tiny, scale-like leaves, close-pressed to the twig, very like the cypress and the neo-cypress. The botanic name is the ancient Greek for an unidentified species. In books, both ancient and modern, it is often called the "arbor vitae", a term

originating in France in the sixteenth century, but almost never used in common speech.

The thujas are among the most valuable of all conifers, but dislike dry soils, some requiring a moist atmosphere. The best of them make magnificent screens or hedges. Several are prettily tinted with gold and others are attractive dwarfs.

Easily the best all-rounder is **T. plicata**, from western North America, which quickly forms a dense column or slender pyramid of rich, lush green. In old trees the lower branches stoop to the ground but tilt up their tips. It transplants easily up to 8ft or so and grows 2 to 3ft a year up to 180ft in its native place, with a pointed tip. It closely resembles Lawson's cypress in its flat, fan-like sprays, but its crushed leaves have a rich, resinous aroma and its small cones are elongated, not round.

Magnificent in British Columbia, Washington and adjacent territories, where it is known as the western red "cedar", *T. plicata* has prospered in Europe also. In Britain, though not arriving until 1853, several specimens now reach well up to 130ft. It must have sun, but dislikes dry, sandy soils, revels in lime, but readily accepts acidity if not too pronounced. It is a good town tree if the atmosphere is not polluted. It is also superb as a screen tree (when it may be planted 5ft apart in one or two rows), keenly rivalling Leyland's cypress and the Lombardy poplar. It rivals the yew also as a hedge, submitting to the shears. The designer will use it liberally for such purposes, as well as in private gardens or parks for the same purposes as the slower cypresses.

The gold-flecked variety of *plicata* called 'Zebrina' is the finest of all gold-tinted conifers of large size so far. It will certainly grow to 100ft, but is slower than its parent. Of other varieties of tree size, 'Fastigiata' is very slender and 'Semper-aurescens' has mossy leaves flushed with yellow – a rare beauty. z5.

T. occidentalis, despite its name, is called the white "cedar" in America. Extremely hardy, but of slow growth and more columnar than *plicata*, it would be a fine tree but for its shabbiness in winter. This frailty is most marked in the coloured forms, except in the splendid, gold-leafed cultivar 'Lutea' (formerly known as the "George Peabody arbor-vitae"), which is far superior to its parent.

Another cultivar of outstanding merit but smaller is 'Spiralis', a narrow column furnished with short, tip-tilted branches, often listed as 'Pyramidalis', 'Douglasii pyramidalis' or 'Fastigiata'.

All need a moist atmosphere if they are to thrive. z2.

T. orientalis, from China, is distinguished from other thujas by its scentless foliage and by

the hooks on its cones. When at its best, which is infrequent, it makes a graceful 50ft pyramid, but usually it is gaunt and sparse. Best appreciated in some of its small cultivars, such as 'Elegantissima' and 'Conspicua'. z6.

T. standishii, from Japan, grows up to about 70ft, with long, tip-tilted branches which make it a plump pyramid, with a nodding apex, grey-green, lemon-scented leaves and a lovely deep-red bark. z5.

THUJOPSIS

Thujopis dolabrata, from Japan, is a very slow first cousin of the thujas, distinguished from them by its larger, silver-backed leaves and its rich, chestnut bark marked by cat scratches. It frequently has several stems and creeps up to some 70ft at about 10in a year. Given good soil and plenty of moisture, it makes a handsome, shining tree. z6.

TORREYA

Torreyas might be described as yews of a loose and open habit, with longish leaves, which are stiff and hard and have spiny points. Like the yews, they are at home in chalk (as elsewhere) and in the shade of trees. Their fruits are fleshy, too, resembling small plums. The name honours Dr John Torrey, a distinguished American botanist. Compare with *Cephalotaxus*.

The usual one grown is the Japanese **T. nucifera**, normally a small, narrow, slender, rather gaunt tree, but in favourably moist conditions it can grow to 70ft. The leaves are about 1¼in long, of a deep, glossy green, down-curved. The seeds are edible. z5.

T. californica is the less hardy Californian

The yew-like leaves and plum-like fruits of Torreya nucifera.

"nutmeg" which is usually a slender pyramid of 50ft, occasionally more, with slender branches and a languorous air. The leaves are more irregularly arranged, with a slight outward curve nearly 2in long, the side shoots drooping. It does not grow too slowly. Ensure a straight trunk with a central lead. It does well in Britain. z7.

TSUGA

Apart from the similarity of the smell of their leaves when crushed, we have not discovered why these great and beautiful trees are nicknamed "hemlocks" in North America; for the hemlock properly so called is a poisonous biennial weed of ancient notoriety (*Conium maculatum*), said to have caused the death of Socrates.

My heart aches, and a drowsy numbness pains
My sense, as though of hemlock I had drunk . . .

Thus Keats, overcome with ecstasy by the song of the nightingale.

The vernacular English "hemlock" for this and weeds of similar appearance is of extreme antiquity. Be that as it may, the tsuga, which is not itself in the least poisonous, has now got stuck with the poisonous name. We used to call it "hemlock spruce", which was a trifle less disparaging. The word "tsuga" is the vernacular Japanese name for the tree.

Contrasted with the firs, pines and spruces, the tsugas wear an overall air of softness, though physically as tough as you please. They come from widely separated homelands and, in general, are tall, broadly conical trees with spreading, elegantly pendulous branches. The leaves are yew-like, nearly always with prominent white stomatic streaks underneath. Their barks are a beautiful cinnamon or dark-orange. They like a moist, loamy soil, with plenty of rain, but good drainage. Masculine and feminine strobili are on the same plant. The cones are small and pendant.

The western "hemlock", Tsuga heterophylla.

Tsugas submit willingly to shears, making splendid hedges, formal or informal, and are virtually disease-free. They are not as a rule very good in cities.

T. canadensis. From an elegant infancy, with slender, arching stems and delicate leaves, the Canadian hemlock usually develops into a broad tree, forking widely near ground level and often forming an irregular and sprawling crown, possibly 100ft high. The best conditions for it are a moist, cool atmosphere and moist, open loam. Of its many cultivars, mostly dwarfs or shrubs, 'Albospica' stands out with its white-tipped leaves. In America 'Bradshaw' and 'Pomfret' make dense pyramids. z3 and not further south than z7.

T. caroliniana proclaims its origin (in part) and is more desirable, though of stiffer carriage, with a central trunk and strong limbs thrusting out horizontally and upswept at their tips. It builds up into a broad pyramid or a plump oval. Growth is rather slow, except in moist climates. The leaves are sprinkled more or less all round the chestnut-coloured twigs. The tree can

reach 75ft in the best conditions, but in Britain is rarely more than 40ft so far. z4.

The Japanese **T. diversifolia** is a very neat, shining, dark-green tree, usually small, but known to reach 90ft. Though basically pyramidal, it usually throws up a number of straight stems from the base, forming a broad, dense crown. Growth is very slow and lime is not tolerated. z5.

T. heterophylla, the western hemlock, another of David Douglas's happy discoveries, is a magnificent giant, soaring up to 200ft, rejoicing in mist and a moist foothold on highland slopes. Mr Alan Mitchell found one of 272ft. In such conditions it becomes a huge, densely leafy pyramid, nodding at the slender tip of its straight central mast, its leaves small and delicate, its long, well-spaced, horizontal branches tilted upwards at their tips but its lateral twigs and its small, stalkless cones drooping. Altogether a proud and stately tree, superb in the isolation of a park or big lawn. Growth is very fast, often exceeding 4ft a year in young trees. Specimens in Britain already reach up to 160ft after little more than a century. It makes a superlative hedge and at Wisley is being trained as an arcade. Dislikes lime. z6.

T. mertensiana is another handsome but much smaller mountaineer, though very successful in lowlands also if the conditions are damp and cool and the soil rich; indeed, in Britain the best trees are in lowlands. The mountain hemlock is a very slender steeple, nodding at its tip, as in *heterophylla*, and is notable for its usually blue-grey leaves springing all round the twig and pointing well forward. Blue and silvery forms are found in 'Glauca' and 'Argentea'. Growth is slow at first, then rapid to 110ft or more. z5.

T. sieboldii usually has an oval or elliptical head, multiple stems, an acutely pointed summit and glossy, dark-green leaves. It grows rather slowly to 100ft in its native Japan, but seldom more than half that elsewhere. z5.

WELLINGTONIA See SEQUOIADENDRON

Some Palms

"GOD" WROTE RUDYARD KIPLING in one of his loveliest poems "gave all men all earth to love"; so that some men yearned for Baltic pines and others sighed for "the palm-tree's droned lament".

Palms certainly have their ardent fanciers, who will tell you that palms create "an exotic effect", ignoring the fact that a snowdrop in the Sahara would also be "exotic". Translate "exotic" into "alien" and you come nearer to the testing point. What is of high importance before planting any palm (indeed any plant at all) is to consult "the genius of the place", as Alexander Pope exhorts us. Does the genius rule over burning sands and brazen skies and a peacock sea? Or is his kingdom one of delphiniums and lupins and hollyhocks?

So, quite apart from their degrees of hardiness, one must first be sure that one's palms will not be hopelessly at discord with the environment. Of course, palms are not by any means confined to lands of sunburnt mirth and crocodiles and grass-skirted girls; indeed, one species of date palm (*Phoenix sylvestris*) may be found among Himalayan pines at 5,000ft. But any attempt to create an exotic effect will fail if the palm is forced into company quite out of sympathy with it. The true acacias, the eucalypts, cassias, bauhinias, the jacaranda and such shrubs as the abutilons, yuccas, pampas grass, *Calceolaria integrifolia*, *Fremontia californica*, the corokias of New Zealand, the Australian bottle-brushes and grevilleas, the lemon-scented verbena, the aromatic myrtles and many others are all good company when some accompaniment is needed.

The statuesque pose of the palms, their rigidity, their bare boles, their very limited lateral spread, their lack of shade, the rustle and clatter of the "droned lament" of their large leaves in a high wind really set them apart, unless among the vegetation of their native places, which are many and various. They are not seen at their best as pavement plants on Mediterranean sea-front promenades, but some of them, notably the royal palm, make noble avenues, as may be seen in the Royal Botanic Gardens at Peradeniya, Sri Lanka, the Lancetilla Experimental Garden at Tela, Honduras, and the Botanic Gardens in Rio de Janeiro.

It seems to be a fixed idea, indeed, that palms should always be planted in straight

OPPOSITE *One of the simplest palms,* Trachycarpus fortunei.

Palm leaves:
(a) palmate or fan-like;
(b) arched "costapalmate";
(c) and (d) pinnate or feather-form.

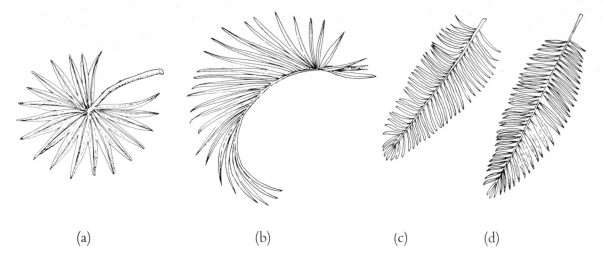

(a)   (b)   (c)   (d)

formal designs, whether as avenues, on sea fronts or as street trees. Their convenience for such uses is that they are content with a restricted root-run, but their weakness, as hot-weather plants, is that they give no shade. Their qualities are much better appreciated if they are planted in groves, copses or little groups rather isolated, as is done, for example, in Dade County, Florida, and in the Huntington Botanic Garden. This is their natural way of life. We may well, indeed, think of them as complementing the conifers of northern latitudes. Like the pines in particular, some are sturdily resistant to salt-laden ocean gales.

Palms have designed themselves to a formula all their own. Except for a few bush types, they develop a single, pole-like trunk, without any branches. Their trunk is a woody cylinder filled, not with heart-wood, but with pith. On top of this pole is a mop of very large, rustling leaves and as the pole extends itself new leaves are thrust up at the summit and the lower leaves decay, usually looking very dreary. In time the dead leaves, if not chopped off by man, fall away on their own, leaving a rather rough stub. Later the stub also goes.

The leaves of palms, emerging from large sheaths or envelopes, have glossy surfaces with a thick cuticle to resist loss of water in their hot climates. They take various shapes. They may be fan-like or almost completely circular and deeply cleft, like a giant hand with many, sharply pointed fingers ("palmate"). These are usually the hardiest species. Almost as hardy are those that develop elongated fans, from a central midrib. These are called Costapalmate leaves and are very handsome when arched. A third type of leaf is pinnate and very long (up to 40ft), the multitudinous leaflets ranged along both sides of the central midrib like a coarse feather or a double-sided comb, each leaflet being pleated along its axis or almost tubular. In others these leaflets, or "pinnae", become very fine and slender, so that the whole leaf looks like a huge green feather, which is exactly what "pinnate" means. (See the illustrations above.) Other types will not concern us.

The flowers of palms usually sprout from among the crown of leaves in large clusters of small florets, dangling on very long stalks, turning into bunches of fruit of one sort or another, only a few being edible, as in the coconut and date.

174

SOME PALMS

The culture of palms is simple enough. They must, of course, have all the sun possible, and the larger ones are gross feeders. In nature some are exceedingly slow starters, remaining little more than a tuft of leaves at ground level for several years, but, if obtained from a reliable nursery, they should get away well. They can be transplanted with a surprisingly small ball of soil, because of their habit of producing new roots directly from the subterranean portion of the trunk and sometimes even from above ground level. Large palms should have most of the foliage removed when planting, unless they be container-grown. This defoliation is a safeguard against excessive transpiration until a new root system has been developed.

Thereafter, the gardener must see that his palms are well nourished, especially where they are in porous, sandy soil, as they so often are. Mr William Flemer III (to whom we are indebted for much in these notes) recommends at least three dressings a year of a 6-6-6 fertiliser, two to four pounds per tree when well established. In soils suffering from mineral deficiencies a little manganese and magnesium may be necessary; or one may use instead a good brand of all-purpose fertiliser, such as fish or seaweed manure, both of which are organic and very acid.

The following is a selection of the most garden-worthy palms for our regions. The most splendid is the royal palm, challenged by the Canary date-palm; the hardiest is the Chinese windmill palm. We omit the coconuts, as they are dangerous to passers-by and traffic.

Some Palms

Alphabetically, we meet first the tall, slender "Queen Palm", formerly known botanically by the easy name *Cocos plumosa*, but now by the fiercely deterrent **Arecastrum romanzoffianum**. A native of Brazil and a slow starter, it picks up quickly into a handsome tree of some 40ft, with a smooth, ringed bole and an open crown of very long, gracefully arching, feather-like leaves. The hanging clusters of bright yellow flowers are followed by small, sweet, edible, plum-like fruits. z9.

Butia capitata is the South American jelly palm, formerly called *Cocos australis*, which bears clusters of golden, acid fruits sometimes used for jellies. Another slow starter, but one of the hardiest, it develops a stout, rather short trunk, with prominent knobs that mark the basal portions of the old leaves. The leaves are 6 to 9ft long and pinnate, with densely crowded leaflets of an unusual glaucous or silvery grey colour. It succeeds in z8, surviving temperatures down to 12°F.

The silver palm, **Coccothrinax argentea**, scarcely qualifies for our Register. Native of Florida and the Bahamas, small, elegant and slender, it reaches no more than 20ft, with fan leaves, drooping at their tips, bright green on the obverse, silvery white beneath. It must be transplanted when small and growth is slow, but it is valuable for its resistance to drought, its tolerance of poor, sandy soils and its defiance of sea winds "heavy charged with brine". It is sometimes called the brown palm or silver thatch. z10.

Coccothrinax crinita, from Cuba, grows stoutly to 30ft, with similar leaves and a trunk clothed with shaggy brown fibre. z10.

The talipot palm, from Sri Lanka and India, **Corypha umbraculifera**, is a striking ornamental for warm places. It is crowned with enormous, dark-green leaves, forming almost completely circular fans, maybe 15ft wide, growing from the top of a thick, sturdy trunk, which is marked with a basket-work texture from the interlacing bases of the old leaves. In the East the big leaves are used as fans and umbrellas. The leaf-stalks have small thorns.

After about 50 years, when it may have grown 90ft, the talipot throws up a huge terminal cluster of flowers, matures its fruits and then dies. z10.

Livistona australis, the Australian fountain palm, is one of the handsomest, reaching up sometimes to 60ft or more. Its stout, smooth, dark, grey-brown trunk is surmounted by a broad dome of large, dark-green elongated fans, deeply cleft, their tips finely drawn·out, their stalks spiny, their bases wrapped in beautifully wrought chestnut bandages. Unless removed, the old leaves hang on, soon looking forlorn. z9.

Phoenix is the ancient Greek name for a person from Phoenicea and applies to the date palm, which, it is inferred, the Phoenicians brought to Greece. The common date of commerce today is *P. dactylifera*, a big tree just growable on the extreme fringes of our regions, having a rough trunk with persistent leaf bases. The species most appropriate to our gardens and public places are the following.

Phoenix canariensis, the Canary Island date-palm, is a first choice for either an avenue or as an isolated specimen. Its massive, stocky trunk, reaching to 80ft, is topped by a huge crown of leaves up to 30ft in width. The leaves are pinnate, glossy green, pleated longitudinally and each up to 18ft. Orange fruits are borne on 6ft, drooping stalks. Too large for small gardens or narrow streets, *canariensis* has few rivals for the adornment of parks or for the creation of noble avenues. z9.

P. reclinata is the Senegal date palm, a tree of 25ft, with a rounded head of leaves arching gracefully. It is much used as a street tree in southern California. z10.

P. rupicola, from northern India, is a more refined and graceful tree, favoured in Britain, rarely more than 20ft high. Its 10ft leaves are bright green and rather lax. There is a variegated form. z9.

Roystonea regia (named for General Roy Stone) is the celebrated "Royal Palm". If given a moist, rich soil, it is one of the speediest of palms, running up to a majestic 90ft and breaking out at its summit in a huge fountain of long, arching, feathery-pinnate, plume-like leaves carrying four ranks of leaflets, the lower leaves drooping, the uppermost erect. The trunk is smooth and pale grey, often with bulges at the base and high up, and has a texture curiously like concrete. Small, purple fruits are borne in enormous bunches. It is a noble avenue tree.

The royal palm is a native of Cuba. Some botanists separate it from *R. elata*, a Florida native, others think that both are merely forms of the same species. z10.

Not quite so regal but much hardier and very popular, is the palmetto or cabbage palm, **Sabal palmetto**, a native of the southern United States. It will defy impoverished coastal sites, growing in sand and exposed to the lash of ocean gales, but will not grow much more than 20ft; transfer it to rich soil inland and it will reach 90ft. In vigorous specimens the leaves are elongated fans, maybe 10ft long, curving out and down and forming a perfectly rounded globe of foliage at the top of a smooth, fairly slender trunk. Bunches of small, black fruits dangle in vast numbers from 3ft stalks. Excellent for an avenue, but better still in groves. It is a first choice for planting in zones too cold for other palms and for exposed maritime counties.

The palmetto is the tree of the Seminole Indians of the Florida Everglades, for whom it provided timber for housing, leaves for thatching and fibre for ropes. Its tough, springy trunk also made excellent palisades, resistant to cannon balls. z8.

The chusan or Chinese windmill·palm, now rechristened **Trachycarpus fortunei**, is the least handsome but the hardiest of all, resisting a freeze of 5°F (and looking rather odd in a snowscape), and succeeding in many parts of Britain and Europe generally. It grows slowly to 40ft. The old leaf-bases linger, covering the bole in time with a shaggy mat of coarse, rust-brown fibres (from which ropes are made), but in very old specimens the hairiness goes, leaving a smooth stem. The leaves are dark-green fans, their stalks armed with sharp teeth. Clusters of small, yellow flowers are produced, followed by small, blue-black fruits. The tree is useful not only for its hardiness, but also for its indifference to neglect, poor soil and atmospheric pollution. Formerly the name was *Chamaerops excelsa*. z8.

Washingtonia filifera is the Washington fan palm, a native of the scorching desert country of southern California. In such conditions it is normally short-trunked, but in good, rich soil will reach 80ft. The fan-like leaves are orbicular, deeply cleft and carried on very long stalks (up to 12ft), which are armed with hooked spines. Unless removed, the withered leaves hang on for a long time, looking like an Amazonian grass skirt. The flowers are white. z9.

Washingtonia robusta comes from Mexico. It grows much faster than its Californian brother, reaching an elegant 90ft. The growth is more slender, the leaves smaller, and of a brilliant green, forming a smaller more compact crown. The leaves drop off neatly at maturity. z10.

PART III

Selected Trees
for Special Conditions

THESE LISTS are intended to provide readers with short cuts to choosing the appropriate trees for diverse circumstances. They do not mean, except as in List 4, that a tree will grow well only in the circumstances named and some trees will be found in several lists. Notice, for example, how often the sycamore, hawthorn, Judaea tree, whitebeam, live oak and koelreuteria occur. The notes in the Register should be consulted at the same time for each tree's suitability on general grounds, but one or two trees specially included in these lists are not in the Register.

1 For Small Gardens

"Small" here means anything of less than half an acre. Readers will apply their judgement with the aid of the Register.

All crab-apples (*Malus*).
Most rowans (*Sorbus aucuparia*) and whitebeams (*S. aria*), especially *S. vilmorinii*, which fits into quite small plots. *S.* 'Joseph Rock' and *S. intermedia*, the Swedish whitebeam are rather too big.
All laburnums.
All hawthorns (*Crataegus*).
All dogwoods (*Cornus*).
Nearly all eucalypts, especially if coppiced.
Nearly all flowering cherries, almonds, etc. (*Prunus*), especially 'Amanogawa', *hillieri* 'Spire', 'Okame' and the like.
Most magnolias, but remember these are usually rather wide-spread. *M. grandiflora*, though a fairly big tree, can be accommodated in a quarter-acre if given pride of place, or even in a smaller garden against a wall not too much cut up by windows.
Maples (*Acer*): *griseum, negundo, japonicum, circinatum, opalus, campestre*, any of the snakebarks and all varieties of *A. palmatum* (shrub).

Catalpa bignonioides.
Koelreuteria paniculata.
Acacia dealbata and *baileyana* (in warm places).
Halesias.
Hoherias.
Judaea tree (*Cercis siliquastrum*).
Pyrus salicifolia 'Pendula' (weeping silver pear).
All mulberries.

CONIFERS

Any of the slim or tower-form ones can be accommodated, except the very tall sequoias, the Douglas fir and their likes. Good choices would be the many neo-cypresses (*Chamaecyparis*), especially the varieties of Lawson's cypress ('Columnaris', 'Fletcheri', 'Ellwoodii', etc.) and *C. obtusa* 'Crippsii'.
Any juniper.
The Irish yew (*Taxus baccata* 'Fastigiata').
Torreyas, yew-like.
Japanese arbor-vitae (*Thuja standishii*).
Thujopsis dolabrata.

2 For Towns

The perils to which trees are exposed in cities, large towns and heavily industrialised areas have been discussed. The following lists, however, show a considerable wealth of safe choices. For sheer resistance to chemical pollution, those marked with an * are the best. Very few evergreens, whether broadleaves or conifers, stand up to these conditions.

Those trees most suitable for narrower streets and small gardens are marked †.

The London plane (*Platanus acerifolia*), best street tree by far where there is room.
†Mountain ashes, particularly *Sorbus aucuparia* 'Sheerwater Seedling' and 'Beissneri'.
Maples (*Acer*): †*A. lobelii*; for wider streets: *pseudoplatanus* (sycamore), *platanoides* (Norway M.), *campestre* (Field M.) and *negundo*.
†Tree of heaven (*Ailanthus altissima*), for streets and squares.
†*All hawthorns.
**Magnolia grandiflora*, a gift from the gods.
*†Mulberries (*Morus*), the white perhaps better than the black.
*The Amur cork (*Phellodendron amurense*), easy and quick, but wide-spreading.
**Robinia pseudoacacia* ("false acacia" or "locust").
*All hackberries (*Celtis*).
**Sophora japonica*, a neglected beauty.
**Pyrus calleryana* 'Bradford' and 'Chanticleer', the thornless Callery pears.

*Lindens or limes: *Tilia cordata, euchlora* and *tomentosa*.

All horse chestnuts.

Ashes: *Fraxinus excelsior, ornus, americana** and *pensylvanica subintegerrima*.

Catalpa bignonioides, for gardens and squares rather than streets.

Gleditsia triacanthos ("honey locust").

Koelreuteria paniculata and its fastigiate form.

†Chinese toon (*Cedrela sinensis*).

†Chinaberry (*Melia azedarach*).

†Most flowering cherries, especially the erect ones.

†All crab-apples (*Malus*), especially the narrow *M. tschonoskii*.

Zelkova serrata.

Poplars: *Populus alba, P. nigra* 'Italica' (Lombardy p.) and *P.* 'Eugenei'.

Elms: **Ulmus* × *hollandica*.

U. americana, procera and *pumila*.

Oaks: †*Quercus virginiana*.

Q. rubra (or *borealis*).

Broussonetia papyrifera, useful in difficult, gravelly spots.

Albizia julibrissin, for similar spots, but wide-spreading.

*Maidenhair tree (*Ginkgo biloba*).

Algerian fir (*Abies numidica*).

3 For the Seaside

The hazards of fierce, salt-laden gales have been discussed. The nearer the shore the greater the hazard. To these are likely to be added severe shortcomings in the soil, which may be excessively sandy, pebbly or chalky, though good loams are sometimes found. All soils of low fertility must be thoroughly prepared with an abundance of bulky organic matter.

Sycamore (*Acer pseudoplatanus*).

Norway maple (*Acer platanoides*).

Elms: Cornish (*Ulmus stricta*), wych (*U. glabra*), Jersey or Wheatly (*U.* × *sarniensis*), Chinese (*U. parvifolia*).

Poplars: black Italian (*Populus nigra*), *P.* 'Robusta' (fast) and *P. alba*.

Hawthorns: *Crataegus oxyacantha* and *phaenopyrum*.

Willows: *Salix alba* and *S. caprea*.

Oaks: holm O. (*Quercus ilex*) and live O. (*Q. virginiana*).

Swedish whitebeam (*Sorbus intermedia*).

Black tupelo (*Nyssa sylvatica*).

Ash, especially the green (*Fraxinus pensylvanica subintegerrima*); also *F. excelsior*.

Tree of heaven (*Ailanthus altissima*).

Gleditsia triacanthos ("honey locust").

Sophora japonica.

CONIFERS

Pines: *Pinus nigra* (Austrian p. especially its Corsican variety *maritima*), *radiata* (Monterey p.), *muricata* (Bishop p.), *sylvestris* (Scotch p., for decorative effect), *pinaster* (especially in sand dunes), *mugo* (usually a large shrub).

Monterey cypress (*Cupressus macrocarpa*).

Colorado spruce (*Picea pungens*).

Most junipers.

Leyland's cypress (× *Cupressocyparis leylandii*), but can be blown down by extra fierce winds if posted in the front line.

Palms (in warmer zones):

Coccothrinax argentea (silver palm).

Sabal palmetto.

Trachycarpus fortunei (Chinese windmill palm).

4 For Acid Soils

Nearly all trees do well in an acid soil, but for the following it is essential.

Magnolias: *campbellii* and its natural variety *mollicomata, denudata* (the yulan), *liliiflora* and its cultivar 'Nigra', *obovata, salicifolia,* × *veitchii, virginiana* and the huge leaved *macrophylla*. Several other magnolias are safe in lime.

Arbutus menziesii, the Madrona.

Nyssa sylvatica (black tupelo).

Halesias.

Styrax.

Oxydendrum arboreum.

All nothofagus (southern beech), or neutral soil.

Stewartias.

Sassafras albidum.

Liquidambar styraciflua, or neutral soil.

Oaks: *Quercus palustris* (pin o.), *rubra* (red o.), *coccinea* (scarlet o.), *phellos* (willow o.) and *shumardii*.

Dogwoods (*Cornus*):

florida, nuttallii and *kousa*.

Tsuga: *T. heterophylla* (western hemlock) and *T. diversifolia* (Japanese hemlock).

5 For Damp Soils

The following trees are good choices for a moist soil, but do not all insist upon it, provided conditions are not excessively dry. Those marked * will grow in swamp conditions.

Acer rubrum, the red or swamp maple.

*Alders (*Alnus*), all.

Carya aquatica, the swamp hickory.

Amelanchiers.

Hawthorns (*Crataegus*).

Magnolia virginiana.

All willows.

Nyssa sylvatica; must be moist.

Birches: *Betula pendula* (silver b., also in dry soils!), *B. pubescens* (very similar) and *B. nigra**.

Sorbus aucuparia (the rowan).

All poplars.

CONIFERS

*Taxodiums (swamp and pond "cypresses").

Larix laricina (the tamarack or eastern larch), also stands extremely cold and swamp conditions.

Pinus contorta.

Libocedrus decurrens (incense cedar).

Thuja occidentalis (American arbor-vitae).

Picea sitchensis (Sitka spruce).

Metasequoia glyptostroboides ("dawn redwood").

6 For Dry Soils

The following do well, but dryness is not essential to all, provided the drainage is very good. Trees of this sort are also useful in areas of good rainfall if the soil is very sandy and thus liable to lose moisture quickly.

Live oak (*Quercus virginiana*).

All acacias (true species).

All eucalypts.

All birches (*Betula*).

All sweet chestnuts (*Castanea*).

Albizia julibrissin (silk tree).

Acer negundo.

Robinias (very good indeed).

Gleditsia triacanthos ("honey locust").

Judaea tree (*Cercis siliquastrum*).

Tree of heaven (*Ailanthus altissima*).

Carob tree (*Ceratonia siliqua*).

Chinese elm (*Ulmus parvifolia*).

Poplars: *Populus alba, canescens* and *tremula* (aspen).

Hackberries (*Celtis*).

Ashes: *Fraxinus pennsylvanica* and *velutina*.

Koelreuteria paniculata.

CONIFERS

All pines (*Pinus*), some in nearly pure sand, especially *P. pinaster*.

All junipers.

Cupressus arizonica (or *glabra*).

All palms (in warmer zones).

7 For Chalky Soils

Maples (*Acer*): sycamore (*A. pseudoplatanus*); Norway maple (*A. platanoides*); field maple (*A. campestre*); *A. negundo*.
All horse chestnuts (*Aesculus*).
The common hornbeam (*Carpinus betulus*) and its varieties.
Judaea tree (*Cercis siliquastrum*).
The common ash (*Fraxinus excelsior*) and varieties.
The manna ash (*F. ornus*).
Hawthorns (*Crataegus oxyacantha*).
The common beech (*Fagus sylvatica*) and varieties.
All crab apples.
Black mulberry.
All flowering cherries (*Prunus*).
All elms (*Ulmus*).
Whitebeams: *Sorbus aria* and *S. intermedia*.
Poplars: *Populus alba* (white poplar) and *P. canescens*.

CONIFERS
Junipers, nearly all.
Nearly all yews.
Pinus leucodermis, *P. nigra* and *P. mugo* (a shrub).
Thujas: *plicata* and *occidentalis*.

Many other trees will grow over chalk if overlaid with a deep belt of loam.

8 For Degenerate Soils and Derelict Sites

Each tree must, of course, be given the best possible start with some good, fertile soil. Ensure no water-logging of roots.

Sycamore (*Acer pseudoplatanus*).
Norway maple (*Acer platanoides*).
Italian alder (*Alnus cordata*).
Hawthorns (*Crataegus oxyacantha*).
Populus 'Robusta'.
The gean (*Prunus avium*).
Robinia pseudoacacia.
Crack willow (*Salix fragilis*).
Swedish whitebeam (*Sorbus intermedia*).
Tilia platyphyllos (broad-leaved linden).
Common ash (*Fraxinus excelsior*).
Broussonetia papyrifera ("paper mulberry").
Melia azedarach (chinaberry).

9 Trees to Grow in Shade

As a rule shrubs give the best promise of enlivening shady places, but there is often a need for trees, such as in the heavy shade of large buildings.

Maples (*Acer*): *circinatum* ("vine maple"), *spicatum* (mountain maple, extra-hardy, small), the snake-bark maples (partial shade) and *pseudoplatanus* (sycamore).
Amelanchiers.
Cornus florida, very good and very decorative.
All yews.
Podocarps, yew-like.
Most junipers.
Hollies.
Thuja occidentalis.
Western hemlock (*Tsuga heterophylla*).

10 For Quick Screens

The following will very quickly create shelter belts or screens against undesirable objects. See also list 3.

Poplars: *Populus* 'Robusta', *P. nigra* 'Italica' (Lombardy poplar) and *P. trichocarpa* (black cottonwood).
Willows: *Salix* 'Caerulea' (cricket-bat willow) and *S. fragilis* (the crack willow, a riverside native, very fast).
All eucalypts, where the climate is warm enough; very fast.
Leyland's cypress (× *Cupressocyparis leylandii*), fastest of all, but must be planted small.
Thuja plicata, almost as fast.
Monterey cypress (*Cupressus macrocarpa*).
Monterey pine (*Pinus radiata*).

The Botanical Jungle

LIKE MOST HUMAN BEINGS, all plants have two names. Many have three and some have more. The first is the name of the GENUS, which is, as it were, the surname of the family, although botanically the term "Family" has a special meaning.

Most genera have several variants, each variant being known as a SPECIES. Each species may itself have several variants, which are known as SUBSPECIES, VARIETIES or CULTIVARS.

Taking the maple as an example, the generic name is *Acer*, which is the old Latin name. One of its species (among a great many others) is *Acer palmatum*, the maple with deeply cut leaves like the palm and fingers of a hand. A variation of this species has leaves which are very finely shredded or dissected and this is called *Acer palmatum* 'Dissectum'. This beautiful shrub has green leaves but it happens to have a brother with leaves of a deep bronzy purple, so this is called, in abbreviated form, *A. p.* 'Dissectum Atropurpureum'.

Observe that the names of the genus and the species are in italic type, while that of its variants in these two instances are in Roman type and enclosed in single inverted commas. This is to show that 'Dissectum' and 'Dissectum Atropurpureum' are not natural variants occurring in the wild but in cultivation and each therefore qualifies for the term "cultivar".

Had they been natural wild plants their names would have been printed wholly in italic and they would qualify for the term "variety" or "subspecies".

The botanist who wants to be thought well of by his brethren differentiates between a cultivar and a variety, but, as we have said at the end of Chapter 1, while not eschewing "cultivar" altogether, we make full use of the liberty given by the International Code to use the simpler "variety" at will. To the user of plants the differentiation is not of the slightest importance. "Cultivar" undoubtedly sounds somewhat stiff and pedantic and, indeed, only the professional botanist or the dedicated amateur has the means of tracing the origins of a plant to determine its classification; nor do botanists always agree.

Besides these classifications by names, there are two classifications by symbols, which are likewise of no particular importance to the gardener or designer (unless he attempts propagation by seed). The most usual one is the multiplication sign ×, which signifies a hybrid plant, as in *Crataegus × lavallei*, the hybrid hawthorn raised by the French nurseryman Lavalle, and *Platanus × acerifolia* (or *hispanica*), the hybrid plane with leaves like an acer's. Both of these are crosses between two species of their own genera, the *Crataegus* and the *Platanus* respectively. Less frequently one meets a cross between two genera and then the name is given as in × *Cupressocyparis leylandii*, the Leyland cypress, a cross between a true cypress (*Cupressus*) and a neo-cypress (*Chamaecyparis*). There are other methods of indicating hybrids of one sort or another, but they need not concern us here.

The maddening effect of all these matters to the simple man who takes the trouble to study them is to discover that precious few nurseries always use the "correct" name. A nursery may produce first-class plants but be all at sea in its nomenclature. Most of them just don't bother, and quite understandably. For the lamentable fact is that certain botanists nowadays are constantly altering the names of plants, to the vast irritation of the gardener and designer, in whom few botanists have any interest whatever. Names familiar to us for generations are swept under the carpet overnight and others are changed and re-changed every few years. In consequence the better sorts of horticultural literature and catalogues are plagued with an itching leprosy of bracketed synonyms.

The most troublesome people in this matter are the pedantic American botanists who specialize in the subject of plant names. Most British and other nomenclature botanists, and even more so the horticultural ones, have been trying for years to get the names of species conserved sensibly, but the Americans – or many of them – are hell-bent on making sweeping changes, thinking that the laws of plant-naming are God-given and not man-made and, having usually no interest whatever in gardening, are imbued with that spirit of which we have complained earlier – transmogrifying what should be a simple human pleasure into an esoteric science. They typify Walter Scott's Mr Dryasdust. The British and others are trying again to hold their own at the Botanical Congress at Leningrad in May, 1975, but the American empire-builders have too many votes. Thus may the gap between botany and gardening become wider and wider. No doubt we shall arrive in time at that situation satirically expounded some years ago in the *Journal* of the Royal Horticultural Society in which it was shown that the correct name for "chair" was "table".

Take heart, however. As Christopher Smart, the eighteenth-century poet, wrote: "The true names of plants are yet in heaven". The main function of these notes is that you should understand the usages of this book and others of its kind and the catalogues of the rare nurseries that pursue orthodoxy. At other nurseries probably the really important thing is to quote the *varietal* name; it is quite sufficient, for example, to order simply "Gleditsia Sunburst" or "Robinia Frisia", instead of the whole thing.

Very often it is fairly safe to use an accepted "popular" or vernacular name, such as "Lombardy poplar", or "Douglas fir" or "holm oak", but there is often danger in these vernacular names, for there is great confusion among them. The "bluebells of Scotland" are not the bluebells of England, and the huckleberries and Christmas trees of Britain are not those of America. Nor would a Frenchman or German understand English vernacular names.

You get into more troubled waters still if you want a robinia but order it by its bogus name of "acacia" or if you want a philadelphus and call it by its equally bogus name "syringa". This is like calling Mr Brown "Mister Smith". Other examples are quoted in our register. "Popular" fancy names are thus serious pitfalls. They are fearfully overdone in America, where garden journalists, on the supposition that their readers have no intelligence, encourage and even invent them. There is no reason on earth or in heaven to invent pet-names for such easy and melodious words as laburnum, liquidambar, nyssa, robinia, sophora, catalpa and many others which deserve to be accepted as nationalized English names in the same way as magnolia, camellia, delphinium, hydrangea and many another have been.

Vernacular English names of ancient lineage, deeply embedded in the language, such as oak, maple, yew, linden and a great many more, are a different matter, of course. These are not invented, fancy names but, as we have shown in several instances, have evolved since the earliest times, long before there were any other names. These are entirely valid, as are old vernacular names in other languages.

The term "clone" will often be encountered. This is a modern word which implies a selected individual plant propagated vegetatively (by cuttings, grafting, etc.) not by seed, so that all its offspring so propagated are (subject to cultivation) exactly like one another. Thus 'Briotii' is a selected clone of the red horse chestnut (*Aesculus* × *carnea*). To all intents and purposes "clone" is synonymous with "cultivar", at any rate in trees, shrubs and herbaceous plants. Any name in Roman type between single inverted commas denotes a clone.

Most generic names are in Greek or Latin, sometimes pure Greek or Latin, as used by the Ancients themselves, or else mongrel ones, conceived by the botanists, which would cause both Homer and Horace to shudder with horror. A few other names are in Arabic, Japanese and other languages, including pure Red Indian. The names of species are also of varied origins, but usually of botanist's dog-Latin. Varietal names may be anything, but in future should be in the vernacular, whether English, French, Polish, etc. A great many names, of both genera and species, commemorate some individual in Latinised form in one way or another, as in *Davidia*, *sargentiana*, *henryi*, and so on. When the commemorative name is for a woman, the termination is *ae*, as in *wilsonae*.

Because of their polyglot origins, all botanical names are pronounced by English-speaking people as though they were English.

Glossary

THE FOLLOWING LIST of botanic and garden terms is very far from being extensive, but covers most of the plants described in this work. By giving the more common suffixes and affixes we cover a fairly wide field. Those whose meanings are quite obvious, such as *japonicus*, *purpureus*, *chinensis*, are omitted. A good many other meanings are explained in the text of the Register. Specific ones, if in Latin or pseudo-Latin, are used adjectivally and must agree in gender with that of the genus. We give here only the masculine forms. Thus *albus* (white) is *alba* in the feminine and *album* in the neuter; *spectabilis* (showy) is both masculine and feminine but *spectabile* is the neuter.

English terms are in Roman type, those of other origins in italics; as we have usually avoided horticultural jargon, the former are few.

acaulis   Stemless
aceri-   Maple-like, as in *acerifolia*, with maple-like leaves
acid   Soil with a low lime content
acuminatus   Sharp-pointed
albus   White
alkaline   Soil with a high lime content
alternate*   Of leaves and stalks, deployed alternatively and singly on either side of the stem. See "opposite"
altissimus   Very high
amygdalus   Greek name for the almond
angusti-   Narrow, as in *angustifolius*, narrow-leaved
anther   Pollen-bearing member of a flower

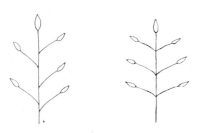

"Alternate" and "opposite" leaves.

-anthus   Relating to a flower, as in polyanthus, many-flowered
arboreus and *arborescens*   Tree-like
argenteus   Silvery
argutus   Sharply notched
atro-   Deep or dark, as in *atro-rubra*, dark red
aucuparia   From Latin *aucupor*, to catch birds
australis   Southern
ayacahuite   Mexican name for the local pine
azedarach   Derived from Persian for the chinaberry

baccatus   Berry-like
baileyana   After Frederick Bailey, Australian botanist
Baumannia   After E.N. Baumann, of Bolivia
bignonioides   Like the bignonia, a climber named after the Abbé Bignon
bi-   Two, as in *biloba*, two-lobed
borealis   Northern
bract   A modified leaf just below the flower, usually small, occasionally very conspicuous, as in the dogwoods and the poinsettia. The whole cluster of bracts forms an involucre
brevi-   Short

brewerana   After Wm. Brewer, American botanist
Briotii   After Pierre Briot, French horticulturist
bud   May be either a flower bud or a growth bud, showing the start of a new branch or twig

caeruleus (or *coe-*)   Sky-blue
campestris   Of the fields
candicans   Shining white
capillipes   Slender-stalked
capitatus   With a prominent head
carneus   Flesh-coloured
carpel   A single pistil or one unit in a many-celled pistil
-carpus   Relating to the carpel or fruit, as in *macrocarpus*, large fruited
carpinifolius   Leaves like those of the hornbeam (*Carpinus*)
-cephalus   Of the head, as in *macro-cephalus*, large-headed
cerasiferus   Bearing cherries
cerasus   Latin for the cherry
chamae-   On the ground
chryso-   Golden, as in *chrysolepis*, with golden scales

cinereus Ashen

clone See "Botanical Jungle"

coccineus Red. Also abbreviated as in *coccifera*, bearing red fruits

compound Of leaves, composed of two or more usually similar leaflets forming one common whole, as in the horse chestnut ("digitate") and the ash ("pinnate")

concolor Of all one colour

confertus Crowded

cordi- and *cordatus* Heart-shaped

cornutus Horned or spurred

crus-galli Shaped like a cock's leg

cultivar A variant of a species arising in cultivation by man or a selected form from the wild

cuspidatus Coming to a sharp point

davidii After the Abbé A. David

dealbatus Dusted with white powder

decurrens Having a leaf-blade extending down the stalk

delavayi After the Abbé Delavay

deltoides Shaped like the Greek D, delta

-dendron Tree-like

dentatus Toothed

denudatus Naked

digitate A compound leaf in which all the leaflets spring from one point, e.g. horse chestnut

discolor Of two colours

distichus Arranged in two rows

dolabratus Hatchet-shaped

douglasii After David Douglas, famous plant explorer

double Of flowers, those having more than one circlet of petals

drupaceus Having a fruit that consists of a hard kernel enclosed within a fleshy envelope, as in the plum.

elatus Tall

erythro- Red

Eugenei After Prince Eugene of Savoy

excelsior Tall

excelsus Very tall

fastigiate Slim-built, having the branches erect and pressed close to the trunk

ferrugineus Rust-coloured

-ferus Bearing, as in *pisifera*, bearing pea-like fruits

fibrous Composed of dense, thread-like tissues

flavus Pale yellow

floribundus Free-flowering

floridus Flowering

-florus Flowered, as in *multiflorus*, many-flowered

-folius Leaved, as in *longifolius*, long-leaved

formosanus Of Formosa (Taiwan)

formosus Beautiful

f.p. Short for *flore pleno*, double-flowered

fruticosus Shrubby

genus See "Botanical Jungle"

ginnala Native oriental name

glabrous Smooth, hairless

glaucous (and *glaucus*) With a sea-green or blue-grey waxy bloom

glutinosus Sticky

griseus Grey

gymn- Naked, as in *gymnocarpus*, naked fruited

gyn- Relating to the pistil (the female member in a flower), as in *monogyna*, having only one style in the pistil (though there may be several carpels)

henryana and *henryi* After Dr Augustus Henry

hetero- Mixed, as in *heterophylla*, having mixed foliage

hirsutus Hairy

hispanicus Spanish

holo- Complete, as in *hololeucus*, all white

homo- Similar, as in *homolepis*, having scales of one kind only

humilis Dwarf

hupehensis From Hupeh, China

ilex Latin for holly; *ilicifolia*, with holly-like leaves

imbricatus Overlapping

incanus Grey

indicus From India

inermis Thornless

insignis Remarkable

integri- Undivided, as in *integrifolia*

involucre See Bract

jacquemontii After Victor Jacquemont, French naturalist

kaki Abbreviation of Japanese name for the persimmon

kobus Corruption of Japanese name

kousa Japanese name for *Cornus kousa*

laciniatus Cut into strips, lacerated

laevis and *laevigatus* Smooth

lanceolatus Shaped like head of a lance

laricinus Larch-like

lateral A sub-branch, growing from a leader or other main branch

lasio- Having woolly flowers, as in *lasianthus*

lati- Broad, as in *latiloba*, broad-lobed

lavallei After M. Lavalle, French nurseryman

lawsoniana After Charles Lawson, Edinburgh nurseryman

-lepis Scaly. See next

lepto- Thin or weak, as in *leptolepis*, with thin scales

leylandii See under *Chamaecyparis*, conifer section

leuco- White or pale grey, as in *leucocarpus*, with pale fruits

linear Long and narrow, with nearly parallel sides

longi- Long

lusitanicus From Portugal

luteus Yellow

macro- Large, as in *macrocarpus*, large-fruited

maculatus Spotted

mandshuricus From Manchuria

maritima Maritime

maximowicziana After Carl Maximowicz, Russian botanist

medius Middle, intermediate

menziesii After Archibald Menzies, British naval surgeon and botanist

micro- Small, as in *microphyllus*, small-leaved

mollis Soft; *mollissimus*, very soft

mono- Single, as in *monogynus*, having but one pistil in the flower

monspessulanus From Montpellier, France

monticolus Of the hills

muricatus Rough and prickly

niger, nigra, nigrum Black

niphophilus Snow-loving

nitidus Shining

node A joint on a stem, often slightly swollen, from which a lateral branch will sprout, or will have sprouted

nuttallii After Thomas Nuttall, English collector of American plants

obovate (and *obovatus*) Egg-shaped, with the "big end" uppermost, applied to the shape of a leaf or to the whole tree

obtusus Blunt

occidentalis Western

officinalis Of commercial or medicinal use

-oides Similar to, as in *platanoides*, like the plane tree

omorika Serbian name for the native spruce

opposite Of leaves and stalks, deployed in opposite pairs on both sides of the stem

orientalis Eastern

ovate (and *ovatus*) Egg-shaped, with the big end lowermost

pachy- Thick, as in *pachydermis*, thick-skinned

padus Greek name for a wild cherry

palmate A compound leaf lobed or divided in the fashion of a hand *palustris* Of swamps

panicle (and *paniculatus*) With many branched flowers, clustered as in a bunch of grapes or truss of lilac

papyriferus Paper-bearing

parkmanii After Francis Parkman, American horticulturist

parvi- Small, as in *parvifolius*, small-leaved

pauci- Few, as in *pauciflorus*, few-flowered

pectinate Formed like a comb

pendulus Drooping

persicus From Persia

petiolaris and *petiolatus* Having a petiole, or leaf-stalk. See *sessile*

petraeus Of rocks

peuce Old Greek name for *Pinus peuce*

phaenopyrus Resembling a pear

phellos Corky

phyllode See in Acacia in the Register

-phyllos Relating to a leaf, as in *platyphyllos*, broad-leaved

pinnate A compound leaf having several leaflets arranged on both sides of a central midrib. From Latin *pinna* or *penna*, a feather

pisiferus Bearing pea-like fruits

platy- Broad, as in *platypetalus*, broad-petalled

plenus Short for *flore plenus*, double-flowered

plicatus Folded

poly- Many, as in *polyanthus*, many-flowered

procerus Very tall

pruinatus or *pruinosus* Having a glistening surface, as though waxed or frosted

pubescens Covered in downy hairs

pumilus Dwarf

raceme (and so *racemosus*) A floral arrangement in which the individual florets are disposed on short stalks springing from a central stem or rib, as in lupins and wisterias

regius Royal

riparius, *rivalis* and *rivularis* Of river banks

ruber, *rubra*, *rubrum* Red

saccharinus Sugary

saccharum The sugar-cane

salicifolia With leaves like a willow (*Salix*)

samara Seed equipped with membranous wings for dispersion by the wind; they may be double, as in maples, or single as in ashes

sanguineus Blood-coloured

sargentii and *sargentianus* After Professor Sargent

sativus Arising from cultivation, not spontaneous

scion A cultivated plant budded or grafted on to another, usually wild, rootstock

scoparius and *scopellatus* Broom-like

scopulinus Twiggy

scopulorus Of rocks

sempervirens Evergreen

serotinus Occurring late in the season

serratus Saw-edged

serrulatus Finely saw-edged

sessilis Stalkless

sieboldii After Philipp von Siebold

siliqua, *siliquastrum* and *siliquosus* Of seed-pods having a partition between the seeds

simple A single, undivided leaf "all in one piece". See Compound and Pinnate

sinensis and *sino-* Chinese

single Of flowers, having only one circlet of petals

spaethii After the German nursery of Späth

species See "The Botanical Jungle"

speciosus Showy

spectabilis Worthy to be admired

spike Of flowers, having a number of florets attached without any stalks to a central stem, as in catkins

spicatus Spike-like

squarrosus Having overlapping leaf-scales, with pointed, recurved tips

stamen The male member of a flower, composed of a filament topped by an anther

standard A tree with a clear trunk for several feet from the ground

stellatus Star-like

steno- Narrow, as in *stenophyllus*, narrow-leaved

stock The root-stock upon which a bud of a desired variety may be grafted or budded

strictus Erect and narrow

strobilus See introduction to Conifer Section

strobus Roman name for an aromatic tree

subhirtellus Very slightly hairy

sucker A shoot arising from the root-stock of a tree, either from below ground level or, in a standard tree that has been grafted high, from the main stem below the point of grafting. All such suckers must be removed at the point of origin. If the tree is "on its own roots" (not grafted) the suckers will be true to type but should similarly be removed, unless wanted for propagation by planting out a rooted sucker or unless a thicket is desired

sylvestris Of woodlands

tap root One that goes straight and deep down into the earth, like those of the carrot and the lupin

tetra- Four, as in *tetraptera*, four-winged

thunbergii After Dr Thunberg

tomentosus Thickly hairy

torminalis Curing (or causing) stomach ache

trachy- Rough

tricho- Hair-like

tschonoskii After the Japanese collector Tschonoski

umbel and *umbellatus* Having all the flower stalks coming from the same point on the stem, like the spokes of an umbrella, as in the polyanthus

variegatus Of leaves, having more than one colour

variety See "The Botanical Jungle"

veitchii and *veitchianus* After the historic English nursery of the Veitch family

velutinus Velvety

vernalis and *vernus* Appearing in spring

versicolor Many-coloured

vilmorinii After de Vilmorin, celebrated French nurseryman

viridis Green

vitellinus Of egg-yolk colour

vossii After Andreas Voss, German nurseryman

vulgaris Common

wilsonae After Mrs E. H. Wilson

wilsonii After E. H. Wilson

Some pinnate leaves: (a) rowan or mountain ash; (b) Cladrastis lutea; (c) Koelreuteria *(fastigiate form)*; (d) Robinia pseudoacacia; (e) Sophora japonica; (f) Albizia julibrissin.

Full-page Illustrations

Italic numbers indicate colour plates

Index

The numerals in **bold** type show the pages in the Register in which each genus is described under its botanical name. The species within each genus are not separately listed under these entries since they are easily picked out in their **bold** type within the text, usually in alphabetical order.

Vernacular names (when there are any) are given separately for both the genus and the species; this is done for the benefit of readers not familiar with botanical names and because the vernacular names are less easily picked out in the text. Thus *Acer* will have but one general entry but the entry for Maples will include the Norway maple, the silver maple, etc. In many instances there are double entries, as in Sycamore.

The drawings and photographs in the text are shown by the letter P and are included in both types of entry.